HIKING FIRE LOOKOUTS NEW ENGLAND

A GUIDE TO THE REGION'S BEST LOOKOUT TOWER HIKES

MARK AIKEN

FALCON GUIDES

GUILFORD, CONNECTICUT

Dedication

To my dad, who would be too scared to climb to the top of a fire lookout
but who expressed interest and support throughout this project.

FALCONGUIDES®

An imprint of The Rowman & Littlefield Publishing Group, Inc.
4501 Forbes Blvd., Ste. 200
Lanham, MD 20706
www.rowman.com

Falcon and FalconGuides are registered trademarks and Make Adventure Your Story is a trademark of The Rowman & Littlefield Publishing Group, Inc.

Distributed by NATIONAL BOOK NETWORK

Copyright © 2023 The Rowman & Littlefield Publishing Group, Inc.
Photos by Mark Aiken unless otherwise noted
Maps by Melissa Baker and The Rowman & Littlefield Publishing Group, Inc.

British Library Cataloguing in Publication Information available

Library of Congress Cataloging-in-Publication Data available

ISBN 978-1-4930-6544-8 (paper: alk. paper)
ISBN 978-1-4930-6545-5 (electronic)

∞™ The paper used in this publication meets the minimum requirements of American National Standard for Information Sciences—Permanence of Paper for Printed Library Materials, ANSI/NISO Z39.48-1992.

Printed in the United States of America

The author and The Rowman & Littlefield Publishing Group, Inc., assume no liability for accidents happening to, or injuries sustained by, readers who engage in the activities described in this book.

CONTENTS

THE HIKES

ACKNOWLEDGMENTS

It's hard to express how much one learns when one writes a book. With this book I not only learned about a lot of new places to hike, I learned about fire towers, firewatchers, wildfires, fire history, equipment, and lifestyles. How did I learn? I asked questions—lots of them. Thank you to Bill Cobb, Brad Eels, Peter Hayes, Ron Kemnow, and Mark Haughwout of the Forest Fire Lookout Association; Hugh and Jeanne Joudry, long-time firewatchers and Green Mountain Club caretakers at the Stratton Mountain look-out; Carolann Ouellette of the Maine Office of Outdoor Recreation; Allison Arbo, Executive Director of Destination Moosehead Lake; Walter Opuszynski of the Vermont Department of Forest, Parks, and Recreation; Kylie Bruce of Weeks State Park; Nelson O'Bryan of the Tamworth Conservation Commission; Bruce Farnham, longtime manager of Mount Blue State Park; Stephany Dauzat of Talcott Mountain State Park for her information on all the Connecticut hikes; Jay Willerup from Friends of Heublein Tower; Jim Perry of the Shelburne, Massachusetts, Open Space Committee; Nick Krembs of the Norwich Trails Committee; Colleen Kracik of Mass Audubon Moose Hill Wildlife Sanctuary; Jean-Luc Theriault of the Kennebec Land Trust; Colleen Mainville of the White Mountain National Forest; Adam Andrews of the West Greenwich Fire Department; Matt Krebs, operations manager of the Green Mountain Club; Hal Graham of the Belknap Range Trail Tenders (and longtime firewatcher on Belknap Mountain); Alicia Daniel of the University of Vermont and the Vermont Master Naturalist program; and Doug Miner of the New Hampshire Forest Protection Bureau. I asked the above people a *lot* of questions, and they gave me all the answers.

Thank you to Skip Knox, who was the only on-duty firewatcher I ever encountered despite hiking to every tower in this book. You were fun, inviting, hardworking, and I enjoyed our time.

A special thanks to Shelly Angers, public information officer in the New Hampshire Department of Natural and Cultural Resources, the agency responsible for many of the hikes in this book. Shelly answered a zillion and one questions, often first finding the right person in order to get the right answer.

Also, thank you to Katie O'Dell and Mason Gadd, my editors at Globe Pequot. They are amazing, talented, and supportive, and without a great editor, there is no book.

To my hiking partners Neil Preston, Liz Yasewicz, Chris Gallagher, Bob Gallagher, Emily Gallagher, Lisa Aiken, Ryan McKain, Michelle McKain, Abbie McKain, Ben McKain, Gunnar Aiken, and Ingrid Aiken: Thanks for providing your company and cheer and for putting up with my picture taking and note taking along the way. Also, to my number-one hiking partner (and life partner) Alison, thanks for all the times you came with me . . . and for all the times you held down the fort while I was away.

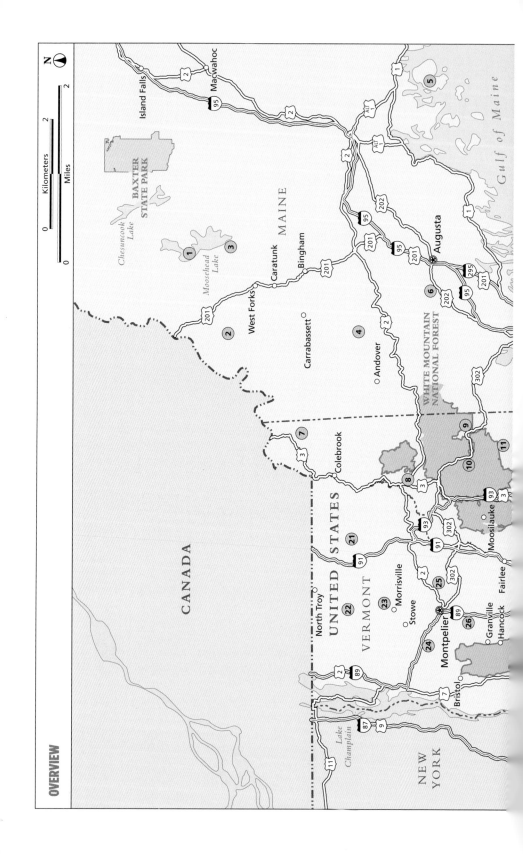

N

Kilometers
0   2

Miles
0   2

CANADA

Island Falls

Macwahoc

2

95

2

BAXTER
STATE PARK

Chesuncook
Lake

Moosehead
Lake

1

3

MAINE

Caratunk

Bingham

201

202

95

201

95

201

Augusta

6

202

95

201

295

201

Gulf of Maine

5

ALT
1

ALT
1

2

West Forks

201

2

Carrabassett

Andover

2

4

WHITE MOUNTAIN
NATIONAL FOREST

302

9

10

11

93

93

3

Mooslauke

302

91

91

302

8

3

Colebrook

7

3

302

93

25

2

21

UNITED STATES

91

North Troy

22

VERMONT

23

Morrisville

Stowe

24

Montpelier

26

89

Granville

Hancock

Fairlee

2

89

Bristol

7

Lake
Champlain

87

9

111

NEW
YORK

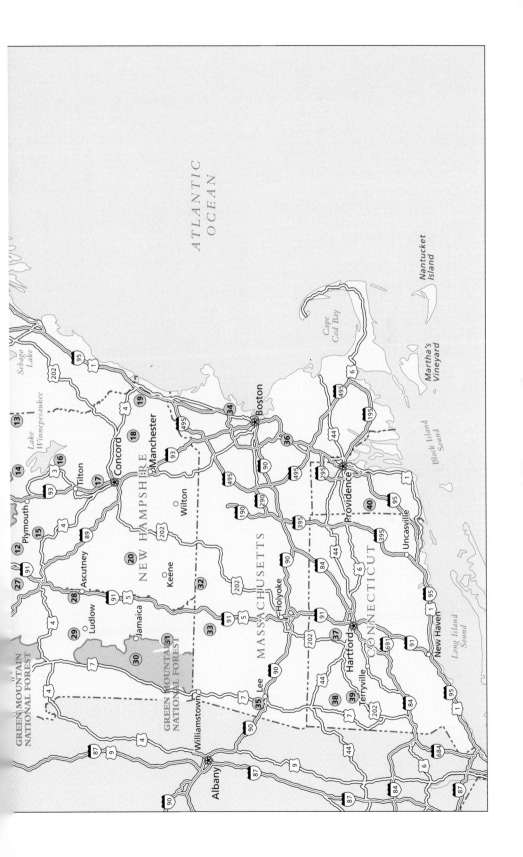

MEET YOUR GUIDE

Mark Aiken is an award-winning freelance writer and photographer and a professional ski instructor. He has spent most of his life in Vermont, except for the decade he spent exploring the Southwest and the Rocky Mountains. To say he is active and an outdoor enthusiast is putting it mildly. He is a trail runner, hiker, and backcountry skier. (Together with his wife, also a distance runner and cross-country skier, he's involved in the ultimate endurance sport: parenting.)

A book endeavor requiring him to hike and explore mountains in his home region and write about them is a dream project. Besides living that dream, he writes articles about the outdoors for local, regional, and national publications including *Ski*, *Backpacker*, and the *New York Times*. He has written scores of instructional articles for the Professional Ski Instructors of America, and he co-wrote their instructional manual *Teaching Children Snowsports*. When he's not skiing or writing, he is teaming up with his wife and kids on outdoor adventures. When he's not on an outdoor adventure, he's *thinking* about and planning the next one.

INTRODUCTION

This book is about two things: hiking and fire towers. A panoramic view always makes a hike more worthwhile. In New England, where many of the mountaintops are tree-covered, a tower rises above those trees. Most of these towers were put there in order to protect against fire.

Hiking to the fire lookouts of New England is to walk through a period of history (the last 150 years) and to get up close and personal with a diverse landscape. Fire towers were constructed to give fire observers a view of the surroundings in states where the landscape is over three-quarters forested, where one cannot always *get* above tree line, and where there's not always an expansive and unobstructed vista. As a lifelong Vermont hiker, I can vouch for the fact that many New England hikes are viewless (but we still value them for the sake of hiking, of breathing fresh air, and just getting out-of-doors!).

This book, however, takes advantage of the region's fire history to get readers above those trees to where there is a view. In the era of climate change, one need only tune into the national news from spring until fall: Discouragingly often, devastating wildfires

The vista from Signal Ridge on New Hampshire's Mount Carrigain

1

dominate headlines—usually in the American West. In the twenty-first century, we seldom hear of wildfires in the East.

But New England has seen fires—in some cases, large fires. The more than 400 fire towers, most constructed in the 1900s, that once dotted the New England landscape serve as evidence of the region's fire history. Logging companies built many of the towers to protect their investments; others were put up by state and federal agencies. The Civilian Conservation Corps put up hundreds of towers nationwide. Of the New England towers, fewer than half remain.

Information on fire lookouts exists online. There are plenty of hiking guides. New England, however, doesn't have a guide for hiking to fire towers that *also* contains information about said towers. This book changes that.

While there are plenty of open mountaintops and views in New England, there are also plenty of summits that are overgrown or blocked by trees. The fire towers of New England stand above the trees. There you'll get a view that was previously reserved for butterflies and birds.

LAND ACKNOWLEDGEMENT

The author recognizes and acknowledges that all of the places and lands covered in this volume are ancestral lands of indigenous people who did not necessarily cede these lands willingly or knowingly. As a white male, I also acknowledge the privilege I have experienced throughout my lifetime. This book is for everyone, and it is intended to support your exploration of these places, to come away with a deeper knowledge, and to connect more closely and experience more fully the wonders these lands offer.

All of the towers referenced in this book were constructed in the last 150 years, but human history in this area predates fire lookouts by 10,000 years. When possible, I have researched indigenous and native place names and their meanings. This can be challenging work as sometimes different groups and bloodlines claim different names and definitions. Discussing groups, languages, cultures, and traditions of those who didn't necessarily have written histories and whose lineage dates back over centuries and millennia is difficult. We respectfully acknowledge that this book covers the traditional land of Native peoples.

CONDENSED HISTORY OF FIRE TOWERS IN NEW ENGLAND

The most common question I hear in regard to fire towers in New England is "Are there wildfires in New England?" Western wildfires, often devastating, make annual headlines in these times of drought and climate change that are the twenty-first century. But what about New England? Do New England forests burn? In recent years the short answer is that the Northeast does not have fires anywhere near the scale of the fires we're seeing out west.

However, the Northeast does have a fire history, and five of the six New England states still staff fire towers.

Most of the 400 fire towers that have dotted New England mountains and forests were originally built in the early twentieth century. The need for lookouts was, in part, self-inflicted: Agricultural pursuits (like the merino sheep craze of the 1800s, at the height of which Vermont alone had a population of 4 million sheep) led to deforestation, and

The Mount Croydon lookout in 1909 PHOTO COURTESY OF NEW HAMPSHIRE FOREST PROTECTION BUREAU

the downed, dry timber made highly effective fire fuel. Also, a policy of fire suppression slowed the natural purging of fuel in the nation's forestlands. These factors, combined with a period of hot summers and dry winters, made for a wildfire-filled early twentieth century in New England.

New Hampshire's Mount Croydon was the location of New England's first tower, built by a sporting club and a logging company in 1903. (The tower on Croydon is still an active tower, although it is located on private land and not open to visitors.) Logging companies and forest landowners began to put up towers in order to protect their investments. Landowners banded together in organizations to pool funds and influence agencies for towers. The federal government officially established the United States Forest Service in 1905 to manage the nation's forests.

Early towers were made of wood, and steel models followed. With the formation of depression-era Civilian Conservation Corps crews, the 1920s and 1930s became a heyday for the building of fire towers nationwide.

In 1938 a hurricane ravaged much of New England, devastating thousands of acres of forestlands and knocking down or damaging many of the region's fire towers. The hurricane of 1938 must have been a sight to behold. Many of the towers were rebuilt, repaired, or replaced. A rash of fires followed—the result of the fuel created by the downed timber and several dry summers and winters with low snowpacks.

During World War II many towers had a dual purpose: They became sentries looking for enemy aircraft. During the war women staffed many of the towers, although women were not strangers to New England's fire towers prior. Alice Bailey Henderson, Maine's first female firewatcher, served as the lookout at Mount Kineo during the summers of 1918 and 1919. When Henderson told her mother she was applying for a job to spend the entire summer on a mountaintop, her mother called her crazy. "I was twenty-one at the time and had listened to her advice until then," Henderson wrote in *Lookout Network* magazine, the journal of the Forest Fire Lookout Association. "But the urge within me was too great. . . . I think my love of forests was the main reason I chose that work." Often, spouses would accompany firewatchers for the summer, effectively giving timber companies and government agencies two employees for the price of one.

After World War II, aircraft surveillance began to replace fire towers for fire detection. Many towers were abandoned, fell into disrepair, or were removed. Today, several of the New England states have renewed interest in the preservation of fire lookouts—as do advocacy groups and other nonprofits. In some cases the preservation is for safety: "Technology has not caught up with human eyeballs," says Brad Eels, FFLA president, the nonprofit committed to the preservation of towers (and, sometimes, staffing them). Even aircraft surveillance can't compare with eyes on the ground—firewatchers in a tower become intimately connected to and familiar with their surroundings.

FFLA and others have another reason behind their interest in preservation: paying homage to a chapter of public safety—and to the men and women who staffed the towers.

Maine, New Hampshire, Massachusetts, Connecticut, and Rhode Island still maintain active fire towers, and it is an added treat to visit a tower staffed with an active lookout. Often they are volunteers. Sometimes they are government employees. Vermont, Maine, New Hampshire, Massachusetts, and Connecticut have towers to hike to and, in many cases, safely climb. It is these towers and their histories that inspired the writing of this book.

GEOLOGY

The New England region is wedged between two coasts: the Atlantic Ocean to the east and Lake Champlain and the Hudson River to the west. Looking back hundreds of millions of years, New England was once part of the supercontinent Gondwana along with Europe and Africa, while the Adirondack range made up the eastern coast of the smaller continent Laurasia, which contained what became North America. New England broke away from Africa 200 million years ago (taking the granite that forms much of the north Atlantic coast with it). The west coast of New England—that is Lake Champlain and eastern New York's Hudson River—is a suture line where New England finally joined North America.

"That suture zone is real," says Alicia Daniels, lecturer at the University of Vermont and executive director of Vermont's Master Naturalist program. "The mountains of the Adirondacks are 1.3 billion years old; the Green Mountains and east are 500 million years old." In other words, the lands of New England joined the rest of the North American continent relatively recently, geologically speaking.

Lake Champlain, the west coast of New England

Many of the landscape features visible today as we hike in Maine's mountains and forests, New Hampshire's Whites, Vermont's Greens, the Berkshires, and the Taconics of southern New England are much newer. The Laurentide glacier that covered much of northeastern Canada and the United States 18,000 to 12,000 years ago removed layers of soils and formed cirques, notches, gaps, kettle ponds, and land protrusions along the coast. The glacier also left rocks, stones, and boulders of all sizes. Many of the hikes detailed in this volume parallel or cross the stone walls that farmers made as they cleared their fields. A Vermont adage has a visitor asking a New England farmer where the rocks came from. "Glacier brought 'em," he answers. Truer words were never spoken.

FLORA AND FAUNA

New England is a vastly diverse region from its northern mountaintops to its southern coastlines. The region boasts several different life zones, from the boreal forests below 2,000 feet in elevation to the alpine zones on a few of the highest peaks. Wildflowers are plentiful in spring and summer, and fall foliage explodes in brilliant yellows, oranges, and reds.

Wildlife is plentiful in New England forests, although it often stays out of sight. You are likely to pass through the habitat of black bear, moose, and deer in northern Maine, Vermont, and New Hampshire, but you'll likely see more scat, tracks, and tree scrapings than actual animals. If you do encounter large game, be respectful and keep your distance. Bears and moose will most likely be more afraid of you than you are of them. If you meet a bear on the trail, remain calm, talk calmly (which tells the bear you are human),

White trillium is a springtime delight across the forests of New England.

make yourself as big as possible by holding your arms or jacket out to the sides, avoid eye contact, and move slowly. If attacked (which would be extremely rare), fight back by kicking and punching.

If you encounter a moose on the trail, talk or shout loudly to try to shoo it away. If it doesn't move or if it seems agitated, take a detour yourself. These herbivores can weigh 1,800 pounds and can move surprisingly quickly. Most often, they amble away and don't want much to do with people.

You are much more likely to encounter chipmunks, red and gray squirrels, hares, beavers, porcupines, garter snakes, toads, newts, and a wide variety of birds on your hikes to fire lookouts. It's possible you could glimpse a bobcat, coyote, or fox, and if you do, you should consider yourself lucky. Common birds will be chickadees, woodpeckers, ruffed grouse, red-winged blackbirds, and swallows. Peregrine falcons—once on the endangered species list—may inhabit cliff areas, and there are often bulletins at trailheads informing hikers to steer clear of areas that are home to nesting peregrines. Ponds and lakes may be home to mallards, geese, herons, and loons.

Regardless of the wildlife you encounter, be respectful and keep your distance. You're a visitor in their home, and their survival—even at home—becomes increasingly precarious.

A red squirrel prepares a winter store.

WEATHER

New England has quaint towns and villages, but make no mistake: The region has a rugged landscape and wildly fluctuating weather conditions. New Englanders are strangely proud of the fickleness of the weather ("Don't like the weather here? Well, wait 5 minutes!"), and conditions truly can change in minutes.

While a storm can sneak up, all weather comes from somewhere, and it pays to be informed. Even your smartphone weather—while providing rudimentary information—is worth checking before heading out. Weather.com and noaa.gov both provide hourly forecasts. Keep in mind that on many of the hikes outlined in this book, you may not have cell service. Know your forecast before you leave civilization.

New England temperatures in the summer reach the 90s Fahrenheit with 90 percent humidity—and unannounced thunderstorms sweep in. Likewise, winter temperatures regularly dip below zero, and blizzards and snow squalls—sometimes forecast but not always—can come seemingly out of nowhere. The single-biggest danger to hikers heading out in New England is bad weather. However, a prepared hiker who takes proper precautions should have nothing but enjoyable and memorable experiences.

- **Lightning.** If you hear thunder, assume there's lightning even if you don't see it. Some of the hikes in this book outline places above the tree line or on bare mountaintops. Do not climb a fire tower if a storm is imminent. At the slightest inkling of a storm, descend to lower ground. If this is impossible, find a low spot in which to hunker down. Even if you are at low ground, don't seek shelter under the tallest tree. Also, have your group spread out so that if the worst happens, the entire group doesn't get singed or struck.

- **Humidity.** High humidity is a fact of life in New England—the only defense against it is to hydrate. Carry plenty of water (and drink it!). Also, carry a water filter or water-treatment tablets in case you run out.

- **Wind and cold.** Winter hiking is rewarding, beautiful, and typically less crowded. Keep in mind that hiking is physical activity and your body will sweat. A change of clothes—particularly your base layer—can help to prevent hyperthermia when you reach your destination. Also, the wind does blow year-round, and temperatures are cooler on the mountaintops of New England. Even on a warm summer day, you will be surprised how chilly it can get on top of a fire tower in the wind. Always carry extra layers and dry layers to change into.

The weather will change based on season and elevation. Prepared hikers are fun and successful hikers.

ACCESS

In the twenty-first century, beautiful places in which to hike, camp, explore, and recreate don't just happen. Behind every open space is an agency, organization, or group protecting, preserving, conserving, or stewarding that space. Great trails (whether a backcountry wilderness hiking trail, a trail in a town forest, or a walking path in a park) aren't mistakes; they too are the results of groups and individuals who have in all cases worked on their behalf (and, in many cases, *fought* to protect them). All of the hikes listed in this book are on public land (or, in a number of cases, they are on private lands to which agencies and landowners have cooperated to provide public access). All of the agencies and organizations responsible for these spaces need support. All those responsible for these spaces—and those who use them—require respect.

HIKING SAFETY

One interesting aspect of a book about hiking the fire lookouts of New England is the great variety in the types of hikes you might find yourself undertaking. Some are pleasant walks in parks for less than a mile or two (like Stratham Tower, Bear Hill, Lynn Tower). Some (like Oak Hill, Pitcher Mountain) are in town forests but remain close to civilization and, more importantly, emergency services. Still others are backcountry undertakings requiring commitment, preparation, and experience (Number Five Mountain, Mount Carrigan, Smarts Mountain). In the latter case, help could be many hours away.

Therefore, an understanding of route-finding and basic hiking safety is important.

- **Tell someone where you are going.** Also let them know when you plan to return. If something goes awry, this person can notify the appropriate authorities. Also, do sign in at trailhead registers. Not only is this a record of when you left, it also provides information to the agency stewarding the trail.

- **Getting lost.** Many of the trails in this guidebook are marked with blazes, signs, or rock cairns. GPS units or apps are helpful until batteries die or signals fade. If you get lost, don't panic. It is often likely that you didn't stray far from the trail. Cell service is sporadic in many areas covered in this book, so rather than rely on it, carry a map and compass and practice your map-reading and orientation skills.

- **Drinking water.** Many of the hikes in this guidebook cross the clearest, most beautiful streams, brooks, lakes, and ponds. Assume they all contain the waterborne parasite *Giardia lamblia*. Symptoms from this parasite include vomiting, diarrhea, and severe nausea. Prevent this by filtering, boiling, or treating any drinking water from a backcountry source.

- **Ticks.** Lyme disease has long been a problem in southern New England, and it has inched its way northward so that hikers in all of the areas covered in this book need to be tick-aware. There are several types of ticks; deer ticks, which tend to be smaller (often barely visible), carry Lyme and other diseases. The bite from a deer tick is often characterized by a bulls-eye-shaped rash around the bite. All tick bites are unpleasant. Insect repellents are moderately effective; long pants tucked into socks can help keep ticks off. After hiking—especially in hardwood forests or through tall grass—it is prudent to do careful checks for ticks.

HIKING ESSENTIALS

What you wear and what you carry will affect your hiking outcome. Many agencies promote different approaches to safety (the state of New Hampshire, Vermont Public Safety, and others subscribe to HikeSafe.com). The Appalachian Mountain Club, steward of the 2,190-mile Appalachian Trail (on which some of the hikes in this book travel), supports the Ten Essentials for Hiking. These essentials are as follows:

- Hydration
- Nutrition
- Navigation
- Emergency shelter
- Layers
- Illumination
- Fire starter
- First-aid kit
- Gear repair kit
- Sun protection

Of course, all of the equipment in the world will mean nothing without experience and good sense. A short 0.7-mile morning trip to Stratham Tower probably doesn't require a backpack full of fire starter and emergency supplies; likewise, you don't want to overpack for a trek to the summit of Mount Carrigain in the Pemigewasset Wilderness. Regardless of the specific items on the particular list you subscribe to, bring what's necessary for the task at hand and to deal with unforeseen curveballs. Then make good decisions and use common sense.

What you bring on your hike will impact your enjoyment and success on the trail.

When it comes to hiking to fire towers, a few of the essentials stand out in my mind: hydration, nutrition, and layers. Food and water are important to keep you going. And it never ceases to amaze me, even on hot summer days, how chilled one can get in the wind on a summit in a fire lookout. A lightweight winter hat, gloves or mittens, a dry base layer, and insulated top may make your time at the top so much more enjoyable. You worked so hard to get to the lookout; you don't want to come down at once because you're cold.

One final, unofficial essential that I predict will one day be included on this list: a trash bag (a quart-size ziplock bag may be plenty) to help pack out everything.

MINIMIZE YOUR IMPACT

Leave No Trace ethics will preserve the beautiful spaces listed in this book and beyond. Here are seven tenets of Leave No Trace:

- Plan and prepare.
- Travel and camp on durable surfaces.
- Dispose of waste properly.
- Leave what you find (but take plenty of photos!).
- Minimize campfire impact (in fact, use small camp stoves when possible).
- Respect wildlife.
- Be considerate of other visitors.

Human impact poses the greatest threat to the trails and spaces we love and treasure. Leave No Trace principles should govern your behavior on the trail—and, in many ways, the way you approach life in general.

Packing rain gear can make the difference if the weather changes.

HOW TO USE THIS GUIDE

The 80,000 square miles that make up New England represent a diversity of places to hike. There are nearly 200 fire lookouts still standing in the region, many of them behind fire departments or along roadways. Others, however, stand in harder-to-reach places on trails, on distant mountaintops, or in quiet forests. This book selects forty of the best hikes to fire towers, dispersed among four regions: Maine, New Hampshire, Vermont, and a southern region encompassing Massachusetts, Connecticut, and Rhode Island.

Maine's towers are some of the most remote—hike to these and you'll never doubt that there are plenty of wildlands in New England. New Hampshire's towers offer a diversity of short hikes, long hikes, and everything in between. Vermont no longer has active towers, but the state and other nonprofits have prioritized the preservation of its remaining towers. Massachusetts, Connecticut, and Rhode Island are grouped together. More highly populated than their northern neighbors, they have a number of active roadside towers. This book lists some of the remaining hike-to towers in Massachusetts and Connecticut. Rhode Island has no remaining hike-to towers, but hikers at Wickaboxet Management Area can discover evidence of where a fire tower once stood.

Within the three northern regions, you will find hikes of varying lengths and difficulties. The hikes in Massachusetts, Connecticut, and Rhode Island are easy to moderate. Each hike is described as "out-and-back," "loop," or "lollipop." A lollipop hike is a loop hike that retraces at some point along the route before returning to the trailhead. For each hike, the following specifications are given:

General location. This is the town in which a majority of the hike is located or the nearest town to the trailhead.

Highest point. This is the highest point reached on the hike, generally the location of the fire tower. Altitude can affect a hike's level of difficulty, the lower atmospheric pressure creating "thin air" that makes breathing harder and causes increased respiration and heart rates. None of the mountains in New England reach elevations with decreased oxygen levels, but some New England peaks are as rugged, steep, and exposed as mountains anywhere.

Elevation gain. This is the total elevation change from the lowest point of the hike to the highest. Elevation gain is one factor in weighing a hike's difficulty.

Distance. The total distance of the hike. For example, if an out-and-back hike is 2 miles one-way, the distance will be noted as 4 miles.

Hiking mileages—regardless of how painstakingly and with which equipment they are measured—will vary. Matt Krebs, operations manager of the Green Mountain Club, which stewards over 400 miles of trails (including some of the hikes listed in this book), told me that GMC crews use state-of-the-art equipment to measure distances. "If two different people go out on the same trail on two different days using the same equipment, they are likely to come back with two different mileage numbers," says Matt. The author has cross-referenced other available resources including topographic maps, government measurements, trail signs and markers, other guidebooks, and his own (usually multiple) GPS measurements. Different resources often disagree, so the number noted here is the author's best estimate; your GPS watch may give you a different number too. Therefore, pay attention to physical landmarks in addition to mileages in this book and on trail signs.

Regarding trail signs, in this book I have referred mostly to natural features and trail intersections (both of which could change as easily as trail signs!) instead of signs. Signs simply aren't permanent.

Trail signs are helpful, but they aren't permanent.

Difficulty. Assessing a hike's difficulty is subjective; what is easy for you may be strenuously difficult for me. Maximum elevation, vertical gain, and distance are all factors, as are trail conditions, weather, and the physical condition and fitness of the hiker. To make this rating as objective as possible, I used the following criteria:

- Easy: under 4 miles and under 1,000 vertical feet
- Moderate: 4 to 7 miles and/or 1,000 to 1,500 feet vertical gain
- Strenuous: 7 to 10 miles and/or 1,500 to 2,500 feet vertical gain
- Expert only: 10 miles or more and/or more than 2,500 feet vertical gain

These ratings are a general guideline. In some cases, a hike may be rated above or below these criteria based on my observations of the terrain. Also, take note: A heavy backpack can make even an easy hike strenuous.

Hiking time. This is another subjective measurement. You may be faster or slower than me. Very fit, fast-moving hikers will be able to complete hikes in less time than the time listed here. In general, super-fit hikers can cover 2 miles per hour on relatively smooth, flat terrain. Trail runners may cover 3 or 4 mph or more. Most hikers are slower; they generally travel 1 mph.

To make this measurement completely objective, I used the following formula to note hiking time: half the distance plus 1 hour for each 1,000 vertical feet. In other words, if a hike is 4 miles and gains 1,000 feet, its hiking time is 3 hours.

Ultimately, hiking time is an educated guess. The best way to estimate hiking time is to do a few hikes and then compare your hiking time to that listed in the book.

Some speedy hikers will cover about 2 miles per hour.

When to go. Most of the trails listed in this book are open year-round. Keep in mind that New England winters are extreme. Some areas receive 300 inches of snow or more annually, and a mid-February hike in an area listed in this book will look different from the same hike in May. Temperatures vary—more now than ever before—and more concerning than the extreme cold are the thaw-freeze cycles (that is, warm temperatures that cause melting followed by below-freezing temperatures that cause wet areas to turn to ice), which make trails treacherous. From the time of the first frost—usually mid-October but often earlier—traction aids like crampons, micro-spikes, and trekking poles become necessary equipment, as does skill at winter hiking. An experienced winter hiking partner isn't just a welcome companion but also important for safety.

Another consideration in the winter is the care required to actually climb a fire tower. Rime ice and frost can make steps and railings slippery. You may decide to keep your micro-spikes on to climb the tower.

Finally, be aware of an infamous "fifth season" in parts of New England: mud season. At the end of a long winter, melting snow turns some New England trails to muddy soup. In these conditions, widespread human use can cause profound damage. Therefore, some trail managers (like Vermont Department of Forests, Parks, and Recreation, the Green Mountain Club, New Hampshire State Parks, and the Appalachian Mountain Club) will post restrictions or advisories during this time on the higher peaks. Mud season usually runs from late April until Memorial Day weekend. Check websites or make phone calls for the latest information on trail status.

Fees and permits. Any trail-use fees, parking fees, tolls, or entrance fees are indicated here. If no fees or permits are required, that is also indicated.

Trail contact. Many agencies and organizations manage the trails of New England. Here you will find the name of the organization and relevant contact information including address, phone number, and website. In some cases, more than one organization is listed. Call or check websites for the latest trail information.

Canine compatibility. This describes whether dogs are allowed, whether it's advisable to bring dogs, or whether there are rules regarding leashes or packing out poop. It is a great gift to be able to share these special places with our furry friends. Keep in mind, however, that not all trail users are as enthusiastic about your family's pet as you are. Keep your dog under voice or leash control at all times, and give dogless hikers the right of way.

Always pick up after your dog.

Also, the hikes described in this volume end at fire towers. Do not bring your dog up a fire tower. Dogs find the geometry and scaffolding confusing. Going up is often easier than coming down. For the safety of you, your dog, and others, leave your dog below on a lead. Dogs don't care about the view, but they may want to follow you up the steps.

Some state parks require that dogs remain on leashes. Also, dogs should be on leashes and on the trail in the alpine zone found on some peaks in Vermont, New Hampshire, and Maine.

Trail surface. Simply, this describes the surface you'll be hiking on. Many hikes start on dirt paths and become rockier as they gain elevation. Also, some trails are better maintained or better signed than others.

Land status. All of the trails in this book, even those on private land, are managed by a government agency, trail organization, or other group.

Other trail users. This lists other users you may encounter. Some trails only allow hikers, snowshoers, and skiers. In other cases, you may encounter mountain bikers, equestrians, all-terrain vehicles, or snow machines.

Happy trail dogs have happy and responsible dog owners.

Water availability. Reliable water sources are listed here. Remember to boil, treat, or filter all water obtained on the trail.

Special considerations. You do not need a permit for any of the hikes listed in this book (at the time of printing). I list any landowner requests or special circumstances here.

Amenities. Many of the hikes detailed in this book are rugged backcountry adventures, and their trailheads are equally remote and rustic. Others, however, are more civilized. Any amenities like restrooms or other facilities are listed here.

Maps. The maps in this book are as accurate as possible. Additional maps—usually US Geological Survey quadrangle maps—are listed here to supplement your route-finding. Sometimes, the USGS Quads note the area where you are hiking but not the trails. USGS Quads are available for purchase at mytopo.com or store.usgs.gov.

Maximum grade. This lists the steepest ascent or descent of the hike. This number doesn't necessarily reflect the difficulty of an entire hike.

Trail conditions. Trail conditions change constantly based on weather, season, and use. I have tried to generally comment on each trail's condition here.

Finding the trailhead. This provides detailed directions to the trailhead, generally from the nearest town or intersection. The mileages were taken from a car odometer with reference to mapping applications and will vary. Bear in mind as you navigate to trailheads that GPS units in your car may not account for road conditions of little-traveled forest roads. Also, remember that cell signals don't reach many of the trailheads in this book. I included GPS coordinates for each trailhead.

I traveled to all of these trailheads in a passenger car. Any rough roads are indicated here.

Remember not to leave valuables in your vehicle at the trailhead, or lock them away out of sight. The emptier your vehicle appears, the less interested vandals and thieves will be.

A passenger car can get you to the trailheads in this book.

About the Lookout. One thing that sets this book apart from other hiking guidebooks is, of course, the fire towers at the end of each hike! This section lists the height of the tower, the dimensions of the cab or observation deck, what the frame is made of, and what the steps are made of. Some of the towers are actively used as fire lookouts; that is also indicated. If a firewatcher is on duty, lucky you—they are generally welcoming and enthusiastic about inviting you into the cabin to answer questions.

This section also lists basic history: when the current tower was built and when an original tower, if there was a predecessor, was built. Finally, it details what you can expect to see on a clear day.

The Hike: All of the hikes in this book are detailed as day hikes, although, for the longer hikes, I have indicated campsites for those wanting to turn their hike into an overnight. Any hiker in good physical condition can do the hikes in this book.

Most of the hikes are marked with blazes, signs, or rock cairns. Blazes are generally rectangular squares painted on rocks and trees (remember to look up *and* down for blazes). Cairns are piles of rocks placed by trail crews, most often above the tree line. Don't add your own rock piles—you could be inadvertently adding confusion to the route. *Do* volunteer to help your local nonprofit trail organization. Many of these markers (and the trails themselves) are the result of efforts of enthusiasts exactly like you who volunteered on organized work days.

As this is a book about hiking and fire towers, I have included information about the hikes and the lookouts. History, stories, and any relevant information will give you a thorough understanding of the route and the tower.

Read the hike descriptions and choose one that seems like a good fit for you. Keep an eye on the time and go as far as your ability and desire allow. It's always OK to turn back; remember that getting to the tower is only half the trip. There is no obligation to complete any hike, and the trail will always be there on another day.

Miles and Directions. This is a shorthand description with just the facts. It lists the major landmarks and the mileages.

The maps in this book are as accurate as possible, including landmarks, trails, and land features of importance. You may decide to make a copy of the map and description or just slip the entire book into your pack. Have no fear: This book is OK with getting dirty and used. The goal is to give you the information on the front end to choose the right hike and tower and then guide you through it step-by-step and mile-by-mile. By all means, beat it up! Be safe and enjoy your trip. The rest is up to you.

Over the weekend, I climd a fire Towr for my firste time!

You'll always remember your first tower.

TRAIL FINDER

	TOWER	CAN CLIMB TOWER	ENCLOSED CABIN AT TOP OF TOWER	OPEN OBSER-VATION DECK ON TOWER	ACTIVE FIRE TOWER	BACK-COUNTRY HIKE	WOODSY FRONT-COUNTRY HIKE
MAINE							
1. Mount Kineo	●	●		●			●
2. Number Five Mountain	●					●	
3. Big Moose Mountain						●	
4. Mount Blue	●	●	●	●		●	
5. Beech Mountain	●	●	●	●			●
6. Mount Pisgah	●	●	●				●
NEW HAMPSHIRE							
7. Magalloway Mountain	●	●	●	●	●	●	
8. Mount Prospect	●	●	●		●		●
9. Kearsarge North	●	●	●	●		●	
10. Mount Carrigain	●	●		●		●	
11. Great Hill	●	●	●		●		●
12. Smarts Mountain	●	●	●	●		●	
13. Green Mountain	●	●	●	●	●		●
14. Red Hill	●	●	●	●	●		●
15. Mount Cardigan	●	●	●		●	●	
16. Belknap Mountain	●	●	●	●	●		●
17. Oak Hill	●	●	●				●
18. Pawtuckaway Tower	●	●	●	●	●	●	
19. Stratham Tower	●	●	●				●
20. Pitcher Mountain	●	●	●	●	●		●

	TOWER	CAN CLIMB TOWER	ENCLOSED CABIN AT TOP OF TOWER	OPEN OBSER-VATION DECK ON TOWER	ACTIVE FIRE TOWER	BACK-COUNTRY HIKE	WOODSY FRONT-COUNTRY HIKE
VERMONT							
21. Bald Mountain	•	•	•				•
22. Belvidere Mountain	•	•		•		•	
23. Mount Elmore Loop	•	•	•			•	
24. Camel's Hump						•	
25. Spruce Mountain	•	•	•			•	
26. Bear Hill	•	•	•				•
27. Gile Mountain	•	•		•			•
28. Mount Ascutney Tower	•	•		•		•	
29. Okemo Mountain	•	•	•			•	
30. Stratton Mountain	•	•	•			•	
31. Mount Olga	•	•	•				•
MASSACHUSETTS							
32. Warwick Tower on Mount Grace	•	•	•		•		•
33. Shelburne Tower on Massaemett Mountain	•	•	•		•		•
34. Lynn Tower	•	*	•				•
35. Laura's Tower	•	•		•			•
36. Sharon Tower	•		•				•
CONNECTICUT							
37. Heublein Tower	•	•	•				•
38. Mohawk Mountain	•		•				•
39. Mount Tom	•	•		•			•
RHODE ISLAND							
40. Wickaboxet Hill						•	

* Sometimes

MAP LEGEND

Municipal

91	Interstate Highway
302	US Highway
201	State Road
341	Local/Forest Road
= = = =	Unpaved Road
—•—	Railroad
•—•—•	Utility Line
--·---·--	State Boundary

Trails

------	Featured Trail
- - - -	Trail

Water Features

⬭	Body of Water
∿	River/Creek
⌇	Intermittent Stream
⋙	Waterfall
⌐	Spring

Symbols

⌣	Bridge
‖‖‖	Boardwalk/Steps
⬤	Boat Launch
⌣	Bridge
▪	Building/Point of Interest
▲	Campground
((A))	Communication Tower/Antenna
⬛	Fire Tower
🅿	Parking
▲	Peak
🚻	Restroom
◀	Scenic View/Overlook
▲	Tent Site
○	Town
①	Trailhead
❓	Visitor/Information Center

Land Management

▭	National Park
▭	Wilderness Area
▭	State Park/Forest, County Park
▭	Management Area

The view over Moosehead Lake of Katahdin (left) and the Hundred Mile Wilderness from Big Moose Mountain, the site of the state's first fire tower

MAINE

Maine proudly holds the flag as having the wildest, most remote, and most diverse landscape in New England. Before he ever headed into the American frontier or on African safaris (or even contemplated running for president), Theodore Roosevelt fell in love with the forests of Maine and the possibility of losing himself in them.

The six towers here include differing designs and landscapes. Beech Mountain is on the seacoast, Kineo and Big Moose in the northern lakes, Mount Blue and Number Five Mountain lose themselves in vast forestlands, and Mount Pisgah is miles from the capital city of Augusta.

With its logging history, so too does Maine have a storied fire detection history. According to the Forest Fire Lookout Association, there were 144 known fire towers in Maine. Of these, 55 still stand in varying condition with two towers remaining active.

The hikes in this book just scratch the surface of Maine's fire lookouts. They are a great starter kit and will give you a taste of the diversity New England's largest state offers.

The lonely lookout on the summit of Number Five Mountain

1 MOUNT KINEO

A lollipop hike with breathtaking views through sheer cliffs to an island tower surrounded by Moosehead Lake and the northern forests of Maine

General location: Rockwood, Maine
Highest point: 1,789 feet
Elevation gain: 762 feet
Distance: 3.6 miles
Difficulty: Moderate
Hiking time: 2.5 hours
When to go: Year-round
Fees and permits: Kineo State Park charges a fee for hikers over 5 years old, collected at a self-serve cannister at the trailhead.
Trail contact: Maine State Parks, Bureau of Parks and Lands, Northern Region Office, 106 Hogan Rd., Suite 7, Bangor, ME; (207) 941-4041; maine.gov/dacf/parks/
Canine compatibility: Pets must be on leash, and owners must clean up pets' waste.
Trail surface: Packed dirt and rocky scrambles
Land status: Public
Other trail users: Hikers
Water availability: None
Special considerations: Mount Kineo State Park is located in the middle of Moosehead Lake and not accessible by car, so hikers will need a plan to get there. The trailhead is 0.8 mile over water from the Rockwood public boat landing. Mount Kineo Golf Course offers ferry service from Memorial Day through Columbus Day for a fee

(don't forget to tip the shuttle pilot!). Hikers taking the responsibility for their own lake crossing should be aware of potential lake and weather conditions (spring, summer, and fall) and the thickness of the ice (winter). Also, back on dry land, hikers should be aware that the Indian Trail includes low-level scrambles and lookouts at the top of high cliffs; a hiker uncomfortable with heights should stick to the Bridal Trail.
Amenities: The Mount Kineo Golf Course clubhouse is located about 0.5 mile from the trailhead and operates a restaurant from Memorial Day until Columbus Day (mooseheadlakegolf.com).
Maps: USGS Mount Kineo, ME Quad and mainetrailfinder.com/trails/trail/mount-kineo-state-park
Maximum grade: There are a few rocky scrambles on the Indian Trail where the pitch gets as steep as 39 percent. Confident hikers will have little issue.
Trail conditions: The trails are well maintained. Again, hikers should be aware that the route up the Indian Trail leads along the top of sheer cliffs. There aren't fences, and a fall would be fatal.

FINDING THE TRAILHEAD

From the junction of ME 15/ME 6 and Village Road in Rockwood, Maine, turn east onto Village Road, which leads down a hill toward Moosehead Lake. In 0.1 mile turn left onto Lake Street. The boat landing, which includes a pier where the ferry shuttle picks up passengers and a boat launch, is on the right. Note that these are directions to the boat landing in Rockwood, not the trailhead, which is across the lake. GPS: N45° 40' 37" / W69° 44' 17"

(Coordinates for the actual trailhead are N45° 41' 27.132" / W69° 44' 23.171".)

ABOUT THE LOOKOUT

Height: 64 feet
Open deck dimensions: 11 x 11 feet
Frame construction: Steel
Steps: Steel
No longer active
Current tower: 1917

Original tower: 1910
What you'll see: Mainly, Moosehead Lake. Also, Big Moose Mountain, Little Kineo, Big and Little Spencer Mountains.

THE HIKE

Mount Kineo is one of New England's most stunning and exciting hiking routes. Its location on a peninsula in the middle of Moosehead Lake (many refer to it as an island) adds a layer to your trip planning and the need to watch the time and weather. This additional layer, however, only increases the experience of a hike that has everything—adventure, amazing scenery, a wonderful tower, and lake and mountain views all around. In addition to the novelty of the lake crossing, kids will love the rocky scrambles (although parents will want to impress upon them the seriousness of the cliff edges on the ascent up the Indian Trail), and hikers of all ages will appreciate the variety of this route.

Mount Kineo has the appearance of a mountain that's been sliced in half—600-foot sheer cliffs tower over Moosehead Lake. The cliffs have historical significance: Indigenous people came to the mountain for its rhyolite—hard, flintlike rock that they used to make stone tools like arrowheads and hatchets. Later, Henry David Thoreau camped here and famously wrote his impressions.

Hikers need to cross Moosehead Lake in order to access Mount Kineo.

Although there is a road to the northeastern end of the peninsula, driving isn't a reliable way to approach Kineo as the roads are unpredictable, and private landowners restrict motor vehicle access. All the more reason to take the ferry shuttle, a canoe, or a paddleboard in the spring, summer, and fall, or snow machine, snowshoe, or Nordic ski across as the ice gets thick enough in the winter.

The Mount Kineo peninsula has both private and public land. From the beach at the trailhead, everything to the right (east) belongs to the Mount Kineo Golf Course, which operates the ferry shuttle service, although, to be clear, they welcome hikers on the boat. Everything to the north and west is Mount Kineo State Park. Follow the trail west toward the self-serve kiosk to pay the park entry fee.

A smooth, wide trail—the Carriage Road—follows the shoreline. The cliffs, which tower overhead, come down to the edge of the trail at 0.4 mile. Two-tenths of a mile beyond, come to the intersection with the Indian Trail. The Carriage Road continues straight; this will be your return route. For now, follow the Indian Trail (blue blazes) to the right (northeast) through a break in the sheer cliffs. Note: For hikers who do not appreciate heights or who prefer a pleasant "walk" instead of rocky scrambles, be aware that the Indian Trail has both heights and scrambles. For those seeking a less adventurous route, go straight on the Carriage Road and, at the next intersection, follow the Bridal Trail to the summit.

The scrambling begins immediately on the Indian Trail as you attain the top of the first cliff band. From here, the trail bends into the cedars, hemlocks, and towering pines before popping back out at a rocky lookout (0.9 mile). It's your first of many viewpoints south across the lake looking directly at Big Moose Mountain—the site of Maine's first fire lookout.

The shuttle is an inexpensive and easy way to get across Moosehead Lake to Mount Kineo.

Just beyond, the trail ducks back into the woods, climbs a steep pitch, pops out at another airy perch, and then begins a series of switchbacks that feel as though you are ascending the cliff face itself. At 1.3 miles the trail comes to a clearing (with more views, and—have no fear—they don't get redundant!). The top of the Bridal Trail comes in on the left (northwest), which will be the route down. Continue straight (northeast) on the Indian Trail, which descends through maples, oaks, and birches in a small depression and then begins a final ascent through balsam fir and red spruce. Summit Mount Kineo at 1.7 miles.

The summit is not open and the spruce and fir block any views unless you scale the tower, which feels a bit more open than many towers in this book. It lacks protective chain-link fencing and other reassuring safety features. The reward at the top is substantial, however. All around are mountains and forests. Immediately surrounding you is the 117-square-mile Moosehead Lake. Big Moose dominates the southern view past

At 64 feet tall, the Mount Kineo tower is high and airy.

the lake, while Little Kineo rises straight from the northeastern shoreline in the same shape as Kineo, only smaller. Behind Little Kineo loom Little and Big Spencer Mountains. West and northwest are Coburn and Boundary Bald Mountains. Take your time on the tower—there's plenty to look at.

The North Trail departs the summit clearing on the northwestern side of the summit, leading to Hardscrabble Point and the longest route down, a trail that picks up the Carriage Road. The Carriage Road circumnavigates most of the shoreline and passes a primitive Bureau of Parks and Lands campground consisting of three first-come, first-served sites (available for no charge).

For this route, however, leave the way you came on the Indian Trail until you come to the intersection with the Bridal Trail at 2.1 miles. Even thrill seekers are advised to take the Bridal Trail down; it's a smoother, easier descent that avoids the scrambles, which are fun going up but more precarious going down. The Bridal Trail drops elevation in a hurry but eventually levels out at 2.3 miles. Cross puncheon at 2.7 miles before returning to the Carriage Road and the shoreline at 2.8 miles. Turn left (south) on the Carriage Road and return to the trailhead at 3.6 miles.

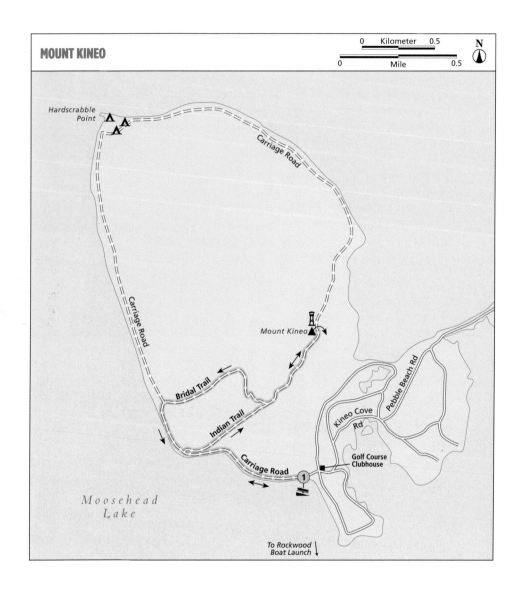

MOUNT KINEO

0   Kilometer   0.5

0   Mile   0.5

N

Hardscrabble
Point

Carriage Road

Carriage Road

Mount Kineo

Bridal Trail

Indian Trail

Carriage Road

Kineo Cove
Rd

Pebble Beach Rd

Golf Course
Clubhouse

1

Moosehead
Lake

To Rockwood
Boat Launch

However you return to the mainland (whether on the ferry, on your paddleboard, or across the ice on skis), you are likely to find yourself reflective. Mount Kineo isn't especially taxing physically, but it is a one-of-a-kind place and deserving of a quiet moment to ponder what you just experienced.

MILES AND DIRECTIONS

0.0   From the trailhead at Mount Kineo Golf Course boat launch, head west on Carriage Road along the shoreline.

0.6   Intersection with Indian Trail. Follow Indian Trail right (northeast).

0.9   Viewpoint.

1.3   Intersection with Bridal Trail. Stay straight (northeast) on Indian Trail.

1.7   Summit and tower. Return the way you came on Indian Trail.

2.1   Intersection with Bridal Trail. Turn right (northwest) on Bridal Trail.

2.8   Intersection with Carriage Road. Turn left (south) on Carriage Road.

3.6   Trailhead at the boat launch.

The Mount Kineo Golf Course shares the peninsula with Mount Kineo State Park. Big Moose Mountain looks over Moosehead Lake at upper right.

2 NUMBER FIVE MOUNTAIN

A remote backcountry out-and-back hike through wild bear and moose habitat to a bald summit and rustic tower.

General location: Jackman, Maine
Highest point: 3,168 feet
Elevation gain: 1,151 feet
Distance: 5.2 miles
Difficulty: Moderate
Hiking time: 3.5 hours
When to go: Year-round
Fees and permits: None
Trail contact: The Nature Conservancy, 14 Maine St., Suite 401, Brunswick, ME; (207) 729-5182; naturemaine@tnc.org
Canine compatibility: Pets are allowed.
Trail surface: Packed dirt, rocks
Land status: Privately owned
Other trail users: Hikers, snowshoers
Water availability: None
Special considerations: As the access road is 16.9 miles long and Number Five is located in a remote area, be sure to have a full tank

of gas and provisions just in case. Also, a note about the drive to the trailhead: The final half-mile track before the trailhead is narrow, steep, and a little loose. Most cars will make it up the half mile; all high-clearance, 4x4 vehicles will make it. If you don't feel comfortable attempting the last push on a remote backroad, there is space to pull off at the end of the trailhead access road and for the first 100 feet before the gravel starts getting loose. The walk to the trailhead adds just a half mile (one-way) to the hike.
Amenities: None
Maps: USGS Tumbledown Mountain Quad, USGS Spencer Lake Quad
Maximum grade: 21 percent
Trail conditions: Dirt and slabby rock at summit

FINDING THE TRAILHEAD

Approaching from the north, follow ME 201 south from the intersection of ME 6/15 and ME 201 in Jackman, Maine, for 11.5 miles. Turn right (west) onto Spencer Road. *Approaching from the south,* follow ME 201 north from the intersection of ME 16 and ME 201 in Bingham for 36.6 miles. Turn left (west) onto Spencer Road. Follow the wide, dirt Spencer Road for 16.9 miles. The smaller dirt road to the trailhead is on the right (north) side. Follow for 0.5 mile to the trailhead. GPS: N45° 28' 30.684" / W70° 22' 25.824"

ABOUT THE LOOKOUT

Height: 47 feet
Cabin dimensions: 7 x 7 feet
Frame construction: Steel
Steps: Steel
No longer active
Current tower: 1933

Original tower: 1933
What you'll see: Big Moose Mountain, Number Four Mountain, Sugarloaf Mountain, Saddleback Mountain, and many more

THE HIKE

If you prefer bear, moose, and deer to people, Number Five Mountain is for you. This remote and beautiful hike is as far from civilization as you are likely to get in the East. The rocky summit deserves a much more descriptive moniker than simply a number.

It's no matter that the tower on Number Five Mountain is unsafe to climb, because the views are amazing from the treeless summit.

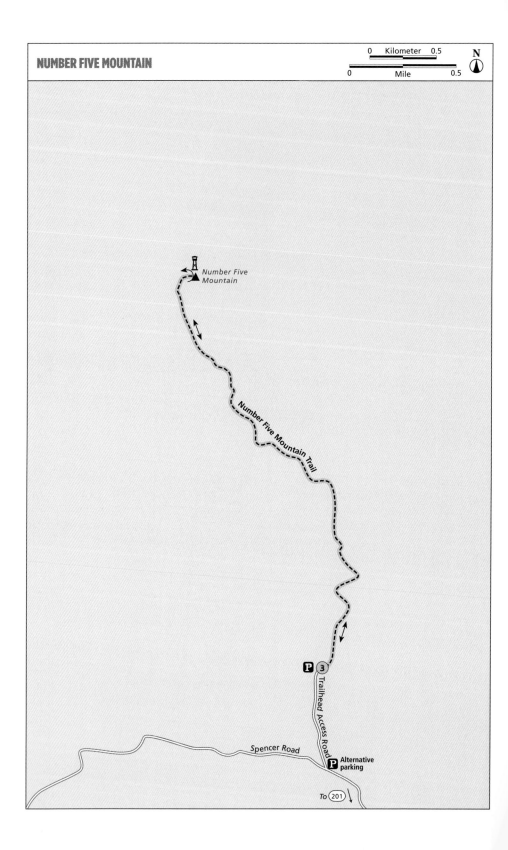

NUMBER FIVE MOUNTAIN

0   Kilometer   0.5

0   Mile   0.5

N

Number Five
Mountain

Number Five Mountain Trail

P 3

Trailhead Access Road

Spencer Road

P Alternative
parking

To 201

The least we can do is attach a few adjectives: The stunningly magnificent Number Five Mountain makes a wonderful and worthwhile hike.

The hike comes courtesy of two worthwhile organizations. The entire hike falls within the Nature Conservancy's 16,394-acre Leuthold Forest Preserve, a tract of conserved land that comprises Maine's fourth-largest contiguous spruce-fir/northern hardwood forest. Weyerhaeuser, the giant forest-products company that owns millions of acres of North American forestlands and has operated under a premise of stewardship and sustainability since long before such ideals were mainstream, built and maintains the 17-mile dirt road to the trailhead access road. This access road, as mentioned above, is maintained by the Nature Conservancy, not Weyerhaeuser, and is much less traveled. The gravel is loose and the pitch is steeper on this last half mile before the trailhead. You may opt to park by the main road, which adds a half mile (one-way) to your hike. All mileages are from the actual trailhead.

The trailhead is a field teeming with wild raspberries. The trail leaves by an informational sign at the northwestern corner of the parking area. At first the trail follows a wide, grassy, potentially overgrown track. At 0.2 mile the doubletrack comes to a Y; the left (northwest) fork is significantly more overgrown, and the actual trail leads due north on the right fork. This part of the trail is marked at intersections with green and yellow Nature Conservancy–logoed arrows. The next marker comes at another Y intersection at 0.4 mile; follow the left fork, still north.

At 0.6 mile come to a barrier of rocks. The green and yellow arrow points right, and the trail veers into the trees on a more traditional singletrack hiking trail, marked from here forward with blue blazes. The forest is, as advertised, a mix of maple, beech, birch, and spruce and follows a gentle contour slightly uphill. At 0.8 mile the pitch increases as the trail climbs a series of switchbacks. At the top of this ascent, an older trail comes in from the left; the way forward is obvious as the trail continues northeast and uphill and is clearly blazed.

For the next 0.75 mile, the path is mostly flat as it traverses a shelf on the side of Number Five. Fallen spruce needles make the going quiet, and there are moose droppings everywhere. It's shocking every time you round a turn and *don't* encounter one of these towering mammals. The trail ducks through a marshy area and crosses several sets of puncheon before passing through a Tolkienesque notch with moss-covered embankments (2.3 miles).

After more puncheon the trail ascends a rocky scramble and the tree cover fades away. After 2.5 miles of Maine forest, you burst onto a treeless summit at 2.6 miles with 360-degree views of Maine's vast northern forestlands. The tower stands in the middle of the summit. It has fallen into disrepair—the stairs don't reach the ground, there is no flooring in the top observation deck, and the Nature Conservancy has posted signs prohibiting climbing on it.

There is no need to climb the stairs though as the views from the ground are breathtaking. To the northeast is Big Moose Mountain, the site of Maine's first fire lookout. Straight west is Number Six Mountain with the province of Quebec behind it in the distance, while Sugarloaf and Saddleback Mountains rise in the distant south. It's hard to describe the enormity of the expanse around Number Five Mountain. Rather than describe it, you continue looking in all directions before finally returning the way you came.

I'm not just a number! Number Six Mountain (right) stands in front of Kibby, Tumbledown, and Snow Mountains in Maine.

MILES AND DIRECTIONS

0.0 From the trailhead (whether you parked here or down the road), pick up grassy trail by sign at northwestern corner of parking area.

0.2 Come to Y intersection. Take right (north) fork.

0.4 Come to another Y. Take left (north) fork.

0.5 Trail leaves grassy track and enters forest. Look for blue blazes.

0.8 Switchbacks.

1.1 Older trail comes in from left. Continue uphill.

1.3 Continue over a flat stretch through spruces.

2.3 Mossy notch.

2.5 Ascend rocky scramble.

2.6 Summit and tower. Return the same way you came.

5.2 Arrive back at the trailhead.

3 BIG MOOSE MOUNTAIN

An awesome out-and-back hike to the site of the first fire tower in Maine and amazing ridgeline views including Mount Katahdin.

General location: Greenville, Maine
Highest point: 3,078 feet
Elevation gain: 1,716 feet
Distance: 4.4 miles
Difficulty: Strenuous
Hiking time: 4 hours
When to go: Year-round
Fees and permits: None
Trail contact: Maine Bureau of Parks and Lands, Western Lands Office, PO Box 327, Farmington, ME 04938; (207) 778-823; maine.gov/dacf/parks/
Canine compatibility: Dogs are allowed.

Trail surface: Dirt, gravel, rocky slab
Land status: Public
Other trail users: Hikers, snowshoers
Water availability: None
Special considerations: None
Amenities: None
Maps: USGS Big Moose Pond Quad, mainetrailfinder.com/trails/trail/big-moose-mountain
Maximum grade: 47 percent (a brief steep scramble)
Trail conditions: It's a well-traveled and well-marked route.

FINDING THE TRAILHEAD

From the Destination Moosehead Lake Visitor Center (and the home of the fire tower that was formerly located on the summit of Big Moose Mountain), head north on ME 6/ME 15. In 2.4 miles ME 6/ME 15 turns 90 degrees to the left (west) in the center of the town of Greenville onto Pritham Avenue, which follows the edge of Moosehead Lake. At 3.9 miles the road again turns 90 degrees to the right (north) and passes the Greenville Junction Boat Launch on the right side. At 7.4 miles turn left onto North Road (dirt). At 8.8 miles the trailhead is on the right (north) side of North Road. GPS: N45° 28' 32.484" / W69° 41' 14.748"

ABOUT THE LOOKOUT

Height: 12 feet
Cabin dimensions: 7 x 7 feet
Frame construction: Steel
Steps: Steel
No longer active
Current tower: 1919. Located 2.4 miles south of Greenville, Maine, on ME 6/ME 15. This tower was removed from the summit of Big Moose

Mountain in 2011 and reconstructed at the current site in 2015.
Original tower: 1905
What you'll see: Moosehead Lake and the peaks beyond its eastern shore. To the north, Big and Little Kineo Mountains, Big and Little Spencer Mountains, and Katahdin, Maine's highest peak.

THE HIKE

Standing on the ledgy summit ridge of Big Moose Mountain, it is hard to imagine what it must have been like to stand alone atop the original 22-foot-tall wooden structure that the earliest firewatchers used. The fire lookout is no longer located on the summit of Big Moose—it was removed in 2011 and only the tower footings remain. Big Moose is included in this list because it is the site of one of North America's earliest lookouts and because its tower was rebuilt at the Moosehead Lake Visitor Center (a regional chamber of commerce of sorts for the area) a few miles away.

View of Mount Katahdin, the highest peak in Maine, from the Big Moose ridge

Big Moose is Maine's first lookout site, and only New Hampshire's Croydon Mountain tower (which is located on private property and isn't open for public visitation) precedes Big Moose in the East. Its selection as the site of a lookout is no mystery: The views of Maine forestlands are vast and stunning. And the hike to the summit is interesting, diverse, and totally worth it.

The Big Moose Trail (blue blazes) departs from the parking area heading northwest. At 0.2 mile the trail bends left at a sort of T; the left branch is wide and blazed; the right is rough and unmarked. Gain altitude pleasantly, ignoring a crossing work road (0.4 mile) and another unmarked trail crossing (0.7 mile). Cross some muddy puncheon at 0.7 mile and veer slightly north.

At 1.3 miles the trail zigs and zags before crossing a small bridge over a stream. After the stream the pitch increases significantly as the trail surface changes from dirt to rocks. The surrounding trees are balsam firs and white pines and the ground cover consists of herbaceous bunchberry dogwood displaying its clusters of red berries. The berries are edible but not tasty (native peoples preserved them with bear fat for consumption in the winter), but birds love them. As the trail climbs the steep grade, the left side drops off sharply to the stream below.

At 1.5 miles a short spur goes down to the stream. At this junction with the spur trail, a small plaque remembers firewatcher John Hutchinson, who lost control of his forestry jeep here in 1959. It toppled over the embankment and rolled twice, killing him at the age of 47. The plaque prompts a moment of pause to consider the difficult lives of the men and women who worked as firewatchers. It also begs the question: Someone drove a jeep at this spot? The trail no longer resembles anything like a doubletrack road, and

The footings from the former Big Moose fire tower. Moosehead Lake is in the background.

even if it did, it's a 30 percent grade and the surface is covered with large rocks. John Hutchinson and his colleagues were clearly extraordinary and courageous people.

A tenth of a mile farther, the remains of the firewatcher's cabin stand on the right side of the trail. No longer used, it is a cute little cabin that was probably quite cozy (and an exact replica stands next to the reconstructed tower at the visitor center south of Greenville). The trail twists several times before settling on a northerly course, running parallel to the stream. At 1.7 miles two large red spruce trees frame the trail as it crosses the stream and then ascends stone steps. The steps end at 1.9 miles, but the going continues steeply before relenting at a Y intersection in the trail. The left fork is a spur to a breathtaking lookout (it's about 0.2 mile and totally worth the effort for western views of miles and miles of Maine forestlands into Canada). The Big Moose Trail continues on the right fork past views of Moosehead Lake to the northeast. From this slabby ridge, make a final summit push over ledges and rocks. At 2.0 miles you reach the narrow summit ridge. Follow the ridge to the summit at 2.1 miles.

The view at the summit is spectacular. Trees obstruct the northern and western views, but the view to the east includes the magnificently blue Moosehead Lake and, beyond it, Maine's Hundred Mile Wilderness and Elephant, Indian, Lily Bay, and Baker Mountains. Somewhere in the vast forests that comprise this wilderness is the final stretch of the 2,190-mile Appalachian Trail, which begins at Springer Mountain in Georgia and terminates at the summit of Mount Katahdin in Maine. Speaking of Katahdin, on a clear day it is visible to the northeast, but there's a better view of Maine's highest peak in a moment.

At the summit of Big Moose, you'll find the footings of the former fire tower. Again, you'll most likely experience a moment of reflection as you take account of the narrow

MAINE'S FIRST FIRE LOOKOUT TOWER

The steel tower that graced the summit of Big Moose Mountain from 1919 until 2011 still exists in pristine condition at the Moosehead Lake Visitor Center (run by Destination Moosehead Lake, the area's regional chamber of commerce organization) on ME 6/ME 15, 2.4 miles south of Greenville. Many organizations (private, government, and nonprofits) contributed to the restoration project. Next to the restored tower is a replica of the firewatcher's cabin, which was located down the trail from the tower, down to the kitchen supplies and bed clothes with which the cabin was equipped. The Maine Firetower Association maintains the tower and cabin; Destination Moosehead Lake maintains the visitor center. Both make worthwhile visits on your way to or from hiking Big Moose Mountain.

The original Big Moose Mountain fire tower located at the Moosehead Lake Visitor Center

ridgeline and the steep descents on either side. Standing atop that tower must have been an exhilarating experience, to be sure. Standing on the exposed ridge with no tower certainly is.

The trail continues for another 0.1 mile—and it's worth your time. The ridge passes a small shed with a solar array and some communications equipment. Pass this area and descend slightly to the very edge of the Big Moose summit ridge. Here, the view in three directions opens up. Directly below you on the northern slopes are the trails of a currently defunct ski resort that the state of Maine (and winter sports enthusiasts) hopes to reopen in the future. To the northwest and west are miles of Maine forestlands that stretch to the Canadian border. Peaks include Boundary Bald Mountain (which also has an abandoned fire tower) and not-so-creatively named Number Five Mountain (abandoned tower) and Number Six Mountain.

Directly north is Mount Kineo, which rises directly out of the waters of Moosehead Lake with its distinctive sheer rhyolite cliff faces, Mount Shaw, Little Kineo, Big and Little Spencer Mountains, and—50 miles beyond—the hulking Katahdin. Anyone who thinks

BIG MOOSE MOUNTAIN

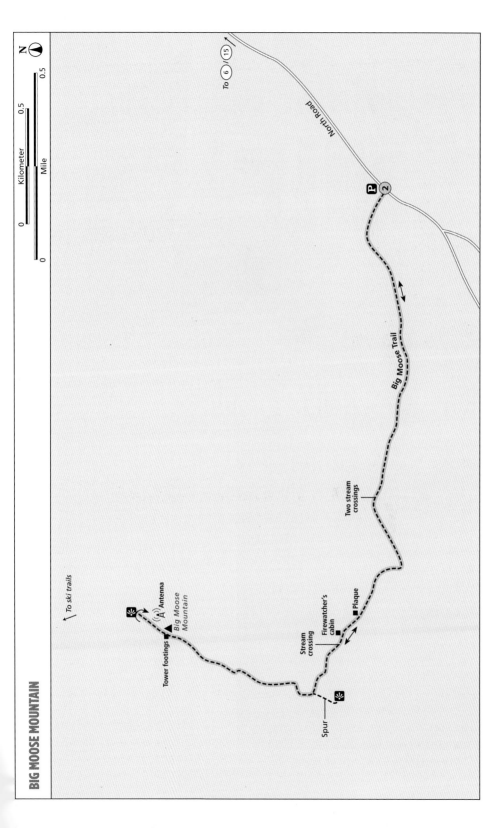

Kilometer

Mile

N

To ski trails

Tower footings

Antenna

Big Moose Mountain

Spur

Stream crossing

Firewatcher's cabin

Plaque

Two stream crossings

Big Moose Trail

North Road

To 6 / 15

P

2

The original firewatcher's cabin below the summit of Big Moose Mountain

of New England as "cute" or "quaint" has never looked across the largely uninhabited and wild northern forests of Maine. It's as untamed a region as anywhere in the United States.

After adequately contemplating the wilderness of Maine and the history of fire detection, return to the parking area by the same route.

MILES AND DIRECTIONS

0.0 The Big Moose Trail (blue blazes) departs northwest side of parking area.

0.2 Following blazes, turn left at T intersection.

0.4 Work road crosses trail (stay straight on trail).

0.7 Unmarked trail crosses (stay straight on blue-blazed Big Moose Trail).

1.3 Cross stream. Trail becomes steeper.

1.5 Spur down to stream. Plaque memorializing John Hutchinson, firewatcher who perished in a jeep accident in 1959.

1.7 Two large red spruces frame a stream crossing. Ascend stone steps.

1.9 Come to a Y in the trail. Spur trail goes left (southwest) to lookout to west. Big Moose Trail continues right (north).

2.0 Reach summit ridge.

2.1 Summit and tower footings.

2.2 End of summit ridge and amazing views. Return the way you came.

4.4 Arrive back at the trailhead.

4 MOUNT BLUE

A steep out-and-back climb to a tower with an observation deck with beautiful views.

General location: Weld, Maine
Highest point: 3,187 feet
Elevation gain: 1,783 feet
Distance: 3.2 miles
Difficulty: Moderate
Hiking time: 3.5 hours
When to go: Year-round (although be aware the road to the trailhead is not plowed in the winter).
Fees and permits: None. *Note:* There is a fee to enter Mount Blue State Park, but there is no charge just to hike Mount Blue.
Trail contact: Mount Blue State Park, 299 Center Hill Rd., Weld, ME; (207) 585-2347; maine.gov/dacf/parks
Canine compatibility: Dogs must be on a leash, and owners must clean up their waste.

Trail surface: Dirt, roots, rocks
Land status: Public
Other trail users: Hikers, snowshoers, skiers
Water availability: Limited
Special considerations: The road to the trailhead is maintained from May 15 until the snow falls. It then becomes a snowmobile track and ski and snowshoe trail. Parking at the gate will add 2.4 miles each way to your trip.
Amenities: None
Maps: USGS Mount Blue Quad, mainetrailfinder.com/trails/trail/mount-blue-state-park-mount-blue-trail
Maximum grade: 38 percent
Trail conditions: Steep, dirt, rocks

FINDING THE TRAILHEAD

At the intersection of ME 142 and ME 156 in Weld, drive east on Center Hill Road, which veers slightly left at 0.5 mile. Center Hill Road passes the state park headquarters at 1.6 miles and turns to dirt. At 2.7 miles the road splits in a Y. Take Mount Blue Road, the right fork. Come to another fork at 3.5 miles. Although the main road (Dickey Mills Road) seems to go left, follow Mount Blue Road straight. This road is narrow and rough, but it's usually passable for passenger cars. It is not plowed in the winter. The Mount Blue Trailhead is at 5.9 miles. GPS: N44° 43' 22.872" / W70° 21' 42.948"

ABOUT THE LOOKOUT

Height: 40 feet
Cabin dimensions: 10 x 10 feet
Frame construction: Steel
Steps: Steel
No longer active
Current tower: 2011
Original tower: 1932

What you'll see: Tons of northern mountains. Mountains surrounding Webb Lake like Little Jackson, Jackson, Mount Tumbledown, and on a clear day New Hampshire's Mount Washington.

THE HIKE

Together with the Tumbledown Public Lands tract, Mount Blue State Park—the largest state park in Maine—comprises 19,000 acres. It contains lakes, streams, mountains, and forests, and it is a shining example of the state of Maine's commitment to conservation and keeping wildlands wild. The hike to the fire lookout atop Mount Blue is a no-frills, no-nonsense hike; you'll find neither amenities at the trailhead nor turns on the hike.

The Mount Blue replica tower is a joint venture between Maine State Parks and Maine State Communications Network.

This hike is listed as "moderate" based on distance and elevation gain, but it is about the shortest possible distance one can cover and still gain 1,783 vertical feet! On the one hand, it's a short distance to hike to a beautiful lookout. On the other, Mount Blue makes you earn it!

If you come in the summer or fall, you'll park at the trailhead. In winter the road will likely not be plowed so you'll have to park at the beginning of Mount Blue Road, which adds about 2 miles to your trip each way. From the trailhead, pick up the Mount Blue Trail at the northeastern corner of the parking area. The trail isn't blazed, but it's fairly obvious.

The trail gets rocky and steep immediately, and red trillium decorates the trail sides in early summer. At 0.5 mile the trail levels out and a side trail runs down to a stream. Onward (and upward), the trail comes to another side trail (0.6 mile) to the former fire-watcher's cabin. The tower on Mount Blue is no longer used for fire detection, and the cabin has fallen on hard times—huge trees have fallen and crushed it. It's quite dilapidated and therefore no place to play, but its historical significance is interesting.

After another 0.1 mile, cross a dry streambed, and beyond that get your first glimpse of the summit through the trees to your right (west). The trail nears Mount Blue's summit ridge at 1.1 miles and bends southeast as you enter the balsam firs, tall white pines, and Norway spruce. The trail circles behind the pinnacle and, at 1.4 miles, begins a demanding summit push. Just before the summit, the going suddenly mellows (finally!) and you reach the summit clearing at 1.6 miles.

L–R, Little Jackson, Jackson, and Blueberry Mountains from Mount Blue

The tower isn't a fire lookout—it's a replica of the old abandoned tower that formerly served as the fire lookout. This structure's primary purpose is to hold radio antennae and public safety communications equipment. The cabin is locked (it houses much of the aforementioned apparatus), but there is an observation deck below the top landing. Although there are views from the summit clearing, it is partially wooded and doesn't give you the 360-degree views that you get on this perch.

Mount Blue tower this way!

Straight west over the roof of the cabin (also owned by the state) are Webb Lake, the town of Weld, and the group of Blueberry, Jackson, and Little Jackson Mountains. Far in the distance is Mount Washington, keeping watch over the New Hampshire–Maine state line. Back on solid ground, there are various rocky perches, all worthy of the view seeker. Take it all in, and then return by the same route.

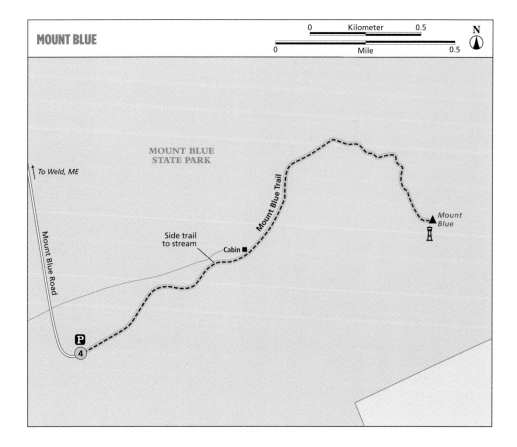

MILES AND DIRECTIONS

0.0 Start on Mount Blue Trail from northeastern corner of parking lot.

0.5 Side trail to a stream.

0.6 Dilapidated firewatcher's cabin.

1.6 Summit and tower. Return the way you came.

3.2 Arrive back at your car at the trailhead.

5 BEECH MOUNTAIN

An easy loop hike to a granite mountaintop tower with views of Acadia National Park and the Atlantic coast of Maine.

General location: Southwest Harbor, Maine
Highest point: 807 feet
Elevation gain: 351 feet
Distance: 1.3 miles
Difficulty: Easy
Hiking time: 1 hour
When to go: Year-round
Fees and permits: There is a fee to enter Acadia National Park. The trailhead for Beech Mountain is located outside of the fee area; however, the park asks that you purchase a pass at Hulls Cove Visitor Center, at Sand Beach Entrance Station, or at recreation.gov and display it in your vehicle.
Trail contact: Acadia National Park, PO Box 177, Bar Harbor, ME 04609-0177; (207) 288-3338; nps.gov/acad

Canine compatibility: Dogs must be on leash at all times in the park.
Trail surface: Packed dirt, rocks, granite slab
Land status: Public
Other trail users: Hikers
Water availability: None
Special considerations: Beech Mountain Trail is inside Acadia National Park but outside the park gates. Hikers can pay the park entrance fee at Hulls Cove Visitor Center, at Sand Beach Entrance Station, or online at recreation.gov.
Amenities: Restrooms at trailhead
Maps: USGS Southwest Harbor Quad
Maximum grade: 24 percent
Trail conditions: This is a wide, well-maintained trail.

FINDING THE TRAILHEAD

From the junction of ME 102/ME 198 and ME 3 on Mount Desert Island just after the Trenton Bridge, follow ME 102/ME 198 south. In 4.3 miles stay straight on ME 102 as ME 198 veers left. At 4.9 miles, when ME 102 splits, take the left (west) fork. At 5.2 miles turn left on Beech Hill Road. Follow to the end of Beech Hill Road; the parking lot is at mile 8.3. GPS: N44° 18' 55.188" / W68° 20' 37.572"

ABOUT THE LOOKOUT

Height: 20 feet
Cabin dimensions: Approximately 15 x 15 feet
Frame construction: Steel
Steps: Steel
Active lookout

Current tower: 1962
Original tower: 1937 (wooden tower)
What you'll see: The Maine coast, Long Pond, Southwest Harbor, Acadia Mountain

THE HIKE

The original tower on Beech Mountain, constructed by Civilian Conservation Corps (CCC) crews, was made of wood in 1937. By the 1950s the structure had deteriorated so, as Beech Mountain is within Acadia National Park, the National Park Service flew parts by helicopter to the site in 1960. The tower's spacious cabin was built with the intention of accommodating a live-in firewatcher, but with its proximity of about a half mile from the trailhead, no lookout ever lived at Beech Mountain. It can be assumed that the firewatchers-by-day that staffed the Beech Mountain tower prior to its deactivation as

The Beech Mountain tower stands on a perch of solid granite.

an active lookout in 1976 enjoyed their daily hikes up the Beech Mountain Trail—and you will too.

What makes Beech Mountain—and many of the mountains in Acadia—distinctive is hard granite. In fact, you get your first glimpse at the parking lot, which is built around a gigantic—almost a perfect cube—20-foot-tall granite block that stands in the middle of the lot. If you come for an evening hike, you'll most likely see climbers laying thick pads at the foot of the block as they boulder on it.

The Beech Mountain Trail (blue blazes) starts at the northwestern corner of the parking lot. Almost immediately, come to an intersection. Both directions are valid; this route goes up on the steeper pitches and down the mellower trail. Take the left (south) fork. At 0.1 mile ascend stone steps; at 0.4 mile, rather than steps, ascend natural steplike slabby granite. The rock is grippy and solid. Reach the summit and tower at 0.5 mile.

The summit of Beech Mountain is a granite dome. You don't need to climb the tower for great views; of course, they do give you a slightly higher perspective. The park generally staffs the tower during the day in the summertime, and the cabin is open. Otherwise, there is a small observation deck halfway up the tower. Wherever you stand, you get the idea that you are on the edge of a continent, because, well, you are.

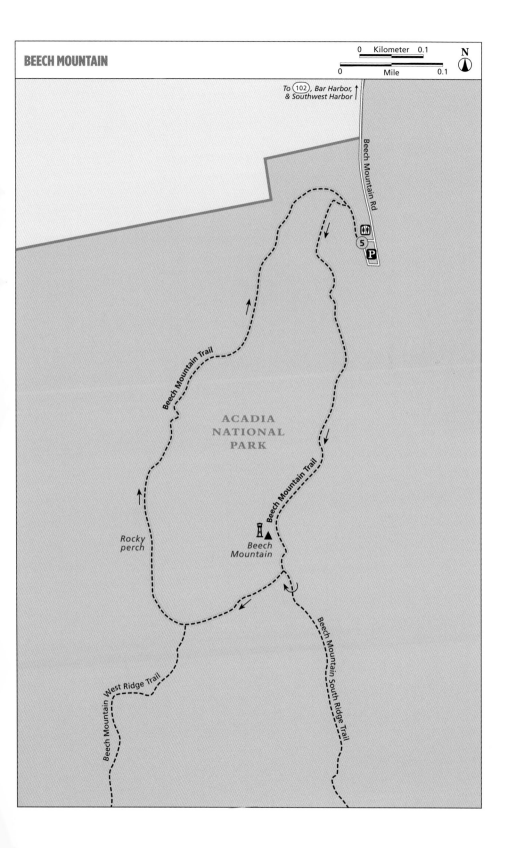

BEECH MOUNTAIN

0   Kilometer   0.1

0   Mile   0.1

N

To (102), Bar Harbor, & Southwest Harbor

Beech Mountain Rd

5

P

Beech Mountain Trail

ACADIA NATIONAL PARK

Beech Mountain Trail

Rocky perch

Beech Mountain

Beech Mountain South Ridge Trail

West Ridge Trail

Beech Mountain

The trail to the Beech Mountain tower is easy, much of it ascending grippy granite.

To the east of Beech Mountain is Acadia Mountain and behind it Sargent Mountain. To the west is Bernard Mountain and southeast is the hamlet of Southwest Harbor and beyond it the Atlantic.

The Beech Mountain South Ridge Trail departs from the southern end of the summit (a beautiful 2.1-mile loop hike that ends back at the same trailhead). The Beech Mountain Trail, however, leaves the summit just below the tower heading west. The trail descends granite steps and passes a maintenance shed and another intersection with Beech Mountain West Ridge Trail, which heads left (southwest). Stay right on Beech Mountain Trail, which turns north and leads past another rocky perch, this one offering a beautiful view of Long Pond and Bernard Mountain.

The trail descends into red spruce and northern white cedar and at 1.2 miles passes the original trail junction. Return to the parking area at 1.3 miles.

MILES AND DIRECTIONS

0.0 Pick up the Beech Mountain Trail (blue blazes) at northwestern corner of parking lot. Turn left (south) 200 feet later at junction.

0.1 Ascend stone steps.

0.4 Ascend slabby granite.

0.5 Summit and tower! To descend, continue on Beech Mountain Trail, which heads west from directly below the tower.

0.6 Intersection with Beech Mountain West Ridge Trail. Stay on the right (north) fork, which is the Beech Mountain Trail.

0.7 Rocky perch with views to the west.

0.8 Trail descends into spruce and cedar.

1.2 Junction with Beech Mountain Trail. Stay straight.

1.3 Arrive back at the parking lot.

6 MOUNT PISGAH VIA TOWER TRAIL–BLUEBERRY TRAIL LOOP

A moderate loop through a beautiful mixed forest to a classic Maine fire tower.

General location: Winthrop, Maine
Highest point: 810 feet
Elevation gain: 329 feet
Distance: 2.4 miles
Difficulty: Easy
Hiking time: 1.5 hours
When to go: Year-round
Fees and permits: None
Trail contact: Kennebec Land Trust, PO Box 261, 331 Main St., Winthrop, ME 04364; (207) 377-2848; tklt.org
Canine compatibility: Dogs are welcome and should be either leashed or under strict voice control.
Trail surface: Packed dirt with some roots and rocks

Land status: Public
Other trail users: Hikers, skiers, snowshoers
Water availability: None
Special considerations: None
Amenities: None
Maps: USGS Wayne, Maine Quad (*Note:* These trails aren't depicted on the Quad), mainetrailfinder.com/trails/trail/mount-pisgah-conservation-area-trails
Maximum grade: 12 percent
Trail conditions: These are mostly smooth, well-maintained trails.

FINDING THE TRAILHEAD

Approaching from the south: At the junction of ME 202 and North Main Street southwest of Winthrop, Maine, turn north on North Main Street. Turn right on New Street in 0.7 mile. New Street becomes Mount Pisgah Road when it crosses Wilson Pond Road at 1.0 mile. The trailhead is on the right (east) at 2.6 miles. *Approaching from the north:* At the junction of ME 133 and Fairbanks Road east of Wayne, Maine, turn south on Fairbanks Road. Fairbanks Road ends at a T at mile 1.2. Turn left (east) onto Mount Pisgah Road, which immediately bends right. The trailhead is on the left (east) at mile 3.1. GPS: N44° 18′ 4.788″ / W70° 2′ 12.911″

ABOUT THE LOOKOUT

Height: 60 feet
Cabin dimensions: 7 x 7 feet
Frame construction: Steel
Steps: Wood
No longer active

Current tower: 1949
Original tower: 1949
What you'll see: Mount Washington, Androscoggin Lake, Mount Megunticook, Camden Hills

THE HIKE

The fire lookout on Mount Pisgah has been inactive since 1991, but the town of Winthrop, Maine, and the Kennebec Land Trust have maintained the tower and have created a nice trail network around it on a 94-acre property. The town owns the land and holds a conservation easement on the parcel through the Land Trust, and it is a cherished landmark for locals.

The trails begin on the eastern side of the parking area at a wooden kiosk on the side of Tower Road—the gated gravel auto road to the summit. Just past the kiosk, Blueberry

Mount Pisgah is a viewless summit . . . until you
climb the tower.

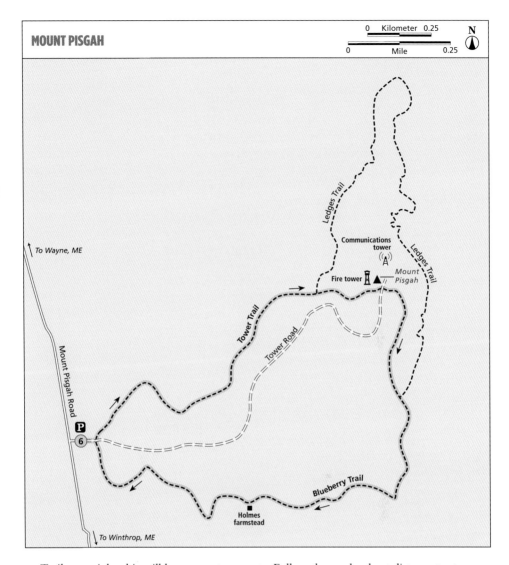

0   Kilometer   0.25

N

0   Mile   0.25

Ledges Trail

↑ To Wayne, ME

Communications tower

Ledges Trail

Fire tower

Mount Pisgah

Tower Trail

Tower Road

Mount Pisgah Road

P

6

Blueberry Trail

Holmes farmstead

↘ To Winthrop, ME

Trail goes right; this will be your return route. Follow the road a short distance to stone steps on the left (north) side of Tower Road to find the start of the Tower Trail, which was formerly called the Warden's Trail. Follow Tower Trail into the woods, where towering maples greet you. The trail follows a smooth surface and occasional puncheon to a junction at 0.9 mile. Ledges Trail comes in from the left. Continue straight (east) on Tower Trail, which comes to a rocky climb—the steepest section of the trail. Arrive at the summit at 1 mile.

The summit is a grassy clearing with no view as it is surrounded by large trees. The tower, however, dwarfs the trees, so all you need to do for a view is ascend the 60-foot Aermotor-design lookout. The tower is in great shape. The inside of the windowless cabin is painted brilliant green, which may catch you off-guard when you first crest the stairs. The outlets for the fire lookout's communications equipment are still there, spray-painted gold.

On a clear day, you can see fast to Mount Megunticook and the surrounding Camden Hills nearly at the Atlantic coast. To the west is Norris Island in the middle of Androscoggin Lake, and 60 miles beyond, New England's highest peak, Mount Washington, and the Presidential range.

At the summit, a communications tower stands a hundred feet north of the Mount Pisgah tower; the gravel Tower Road goes through the summit clearing to it. Across the road on the eastern side of the clearing is the Blueberry Trail. The first 0.1 mile of this trail (like the Tower Trail) descends quickly then levels off. At mile 1.3 come to another junction with the other end of the Ledges Trail (your other option for descending). Both the Ledges and the Blueberry Trails are rolling, traverse beautiful mixed forests, and cross many old stone walls. The Ledges Trail is a bit more meandering (making your total trip 3.9 miles) and eventually reconnects with the Tower Trail.

The Blueberry Trail continues its descent to a small bridge across a small stream and puncheon at 1.5 miles before ascending for another 0.4 mile to a small wild blueberry–filled clearing—the site of the farmstead of Ezekiel Holmes, a nineteenth-century farmer who helped to establish the University of Maine at Orono as an agricultural college. The many stone walls on this hike are reminders of the area's agricultural history and cause hikers to ponder the farmers who picked the thousands of stones out of farm fields and added them to these walls. Today, much of the former farmland of New England has returned to forestland, with the walls the only evidence of a bygone time.

After the clearing, the Blueberry Trail continues its descent through hemlock, spruce, maple, and red oak until it comes to more puncheon at 2.3 miles. It empties onto Tower Road and the parking area at 2.4 miles.

MILES AND DIRECTIONS

0.0 From the parking lot and the kiosk at the beginning of the trail, pass Blueberry Trail on the right. Take Tower Trail 50 feet farther on the left (north).

0.9 Ledges Trail comes in on the left (north) side. Continue straight (east) on Tower Trail.

1.0 Summit and tower! Cross gravel Tower Road at summit and descend on Blueberry Trail.

1.3 Ledges Trail goes left. Stay straight (south) on Blueberry Trail.

1.5 Cross small stream.

1.9 Clearing. Wild blueberries!

2.4 Tower Road and parking area.

NEW HAMPSHIRE

Home to the highest mountains in New England, New Hampshire also has more active fire towers than any New England state. Many of the towers fall under state jurisdiction, and part of the job description of a firewatcher in the employ of the Department of Cultural and Natural Resources is "outreach." Firewatchers are usually cordial, prone to inviting visitors into their upper cab, and open to answering questions and pointing out landmark sights.

New Hampshire's pride in its towers shows in the state's Tower Quest program—also run through the DCNR. Climb any five of the fifteen state-owned active fire towers and get a Tower Quest patch. You're in luck: Nine of the towers in this book are part of the Tower Quest program.

The Granite State's pride in its towers—and its commitment to protecting its 4.8 million acres of forestland (that is, 83 percent of the state)— are the reasons why there are more New Hampshire towers in this book than any other state. These hikes range from walks in town parks to serious backcountry commitments. All of them offer towers to climb with great views.

Above tree line on the trail to the Mount Cardigan tower

The Whites looking south from the top of Mount Cardigan

7 MAGALLOWAY MOUNTAIN

A steep but short loop hike to a remote backcountry tower with views into three states (and Canada) at the northernmost tip of New Hampshire.

General location: Pittsburg, New Hampshire
Highest point: 3,383 feet
Elevation gain: 800 feet
Distance: 1.75-mile loop
Difficulty: Moderate
Hiking time: 1.5 hours
When to go: Spring, summer, and fall. The Forest Service roads that access this hike are not maintained in wintertime. This is certainly a worthy winter trek—if you are up for an 8-plus-mile snowshoe or cross-country ski over the forest roads in order to access the trailhead.
Fees and permits: None
Trail contact: New Hampshire Forest Protection Bureau, Division of Forests and Lands, Department of Natural and Cultural Resources, 172 Pembroke Rd., Concord, NH; (603) 271-2214; dncr.nh.gov
Canine compatibility: Dogs allowed.
Trail surface: Varied. Gravel, rocks, dirt, and grass.
Land status: Public
Other trail users: Hikers, skiers, snowshoers

Water availability: None
Special considerations: Note that the trailhead is at the end of over 8 miles of forest roads—a pretty big commitment. Low-clearance vehicles can make the drive, but it requires focus as there may be ruts, dips, rocks, or other obstacles that could damage the underside of your vehicle. Drivers must be vigilant as you don't want to become stranded in this area.
Amenities: Despite the remote nature of this trailhead, there is a surprisingly clean and new pit toilet restroom at the trailhead.
Maps: USGS Mount Magalloway Quad
Maximum grade: 29 percent
Trail conditions: Much of the Coot Trail going up follows what was an old jeep road and is mostly loose gravel. The summit area is grassy. A loop to a viewpoint near the summit is dirt as is the down-route on Bobcat Trail.

FINDING THE TRAILHEAD

From the intersection of NH 3 and Magalloway, follow the dirt Magalloway Road south. Ignore any sideroads. Cross the Connecticut River at mile 1.3 and a parking area used mostly by anglers. At mile 4.8 the road, which has been as wide as a highway thus far, narrows. Turn right on Tower Road at mile 5.3. Tower Road descends for the first third of a mile, and the first mile tends to be rutted and rocky. Pay attention! Tower Road ends at the trailhead at mile 8.3. GPS: N45° 4' 9.84" / W71° 10' 18.551"

ABOUT THE LOOKOUT

Height: 37 feet
Cabin dimensions: 10 x 10 feet
Frame construction: Steel
Steps: Wood
Active lookout
Current tower: 1935

Original tower: 1910
What you'll see: Canada, First Connecticut Lake, the Great North Woods in Maine, the distant Whites to the south

Not all days are sunshine daydreams. Fog and mist encompass Magalloway Tower.

THE HIKE

You don't just stumble into Pittsburg, New Hampshire. Those who come to the northernmost community in New Hampshire likely came on purpose. A popular hunting and fishing destination, it is also an out-of-the-way vacation spot known to New Hampshirites and New Englanders but not many others.

Similarly, if you show up at Magalloway Mountain and its fire lookout, it wasn't by mistake. Several miles out of Pittsburg and over 8 miles on dirt forest service roads, anyone making this hike has done their research and is here on purpose. That said, because of the remote nature of the trailhead and the many miles traveled on not-heavily-traveled (but surprisingly well-maintained) dirt roads, be sure you have plenty of gas in your vehicle's tank, plenty of food, water, clothes, and a comfort level for being far from the nearest town and help of any kind.

It's hard to miss the people-sized rock cairns on the Coot Trail.

The Coot Trail begins at the western end of the parking area beside a restroom building. Immediately pass a private camp labeled "Camp Magalloway." The trail, formerly the firewatcher's jeep road, is a doubletrack, which at mile 0.1 crosses a wide bridge with signs outlawing ATV traffic. (The trail most certainly gets use as a snowmobile track in the winter, however.)

Although this is a pretty short hike, you have to earn it; a steep pitch starts immediately and continues relentlessly for over a half mile. Over this stretch you begin to notice a theme on the Coot: oversized rock cairns. They don't just make little rock stacks to show the way, they use giant stones, or they pile smaller stones 6 or 7 feet high. At mile 0.6 ignore an unmarked trail to the right. Shortly thereafter, the Bobcat Trail enters from the right. Continue following the Coot, keeping in mind that Bobcat is your route down.

Shortly after the intersection, the going flattens (and even descends in a spot or two) and the trail surface shifts from loose gravel to grass and dirt. Minutes later at mile 0.8, you encounter picnic tables in a grassy clearing and the Magalloway Tower dominating the far (southern) end. On the western side of the clearing are some maintenance cabins amid widely dispersed trees. A short quarter-mile loop spur trail leads to a breathtaking lookout point over sheer cliffs with northeasterly views of Maine and Quebec.

For the same view minus the additional hike, climb the 37-foot tower. With its 360-degree views of vast woodlands, it's easy to see why it was one of the original fire lookout sites in New Hampshire. In their book *A Field Guide to New Hampshire Firetowers*, Baird and Haartz report that an early firewatcher complained that the tower was placed poorly; it is hard to agree with him. He also complained of rotting wood in the original

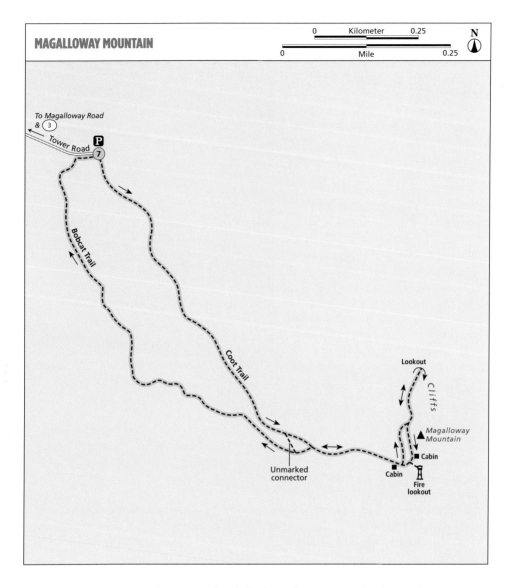

tower. The current steel tower replaced the last of New Hampshire's wooden towers. The original tower was built by the New Hampshire Timberland Owners Association. It remains in active service, operated by the New Hampshire Forest Protection Bureau. The northern view stretches into Canada (you're situated about 12 miles from the border). To the northeast stretch the Great North Woods of Maine, and south are the peaks of the White Mountains. To the southeast is First Connecticut Lake, which feeds the headwaters of the Connecticut River, which forms the border of Vermont and New Hampshire and flows 410 miles southward, where it empties into Long Island Sound.

To descend, initially retrace your steps down the Coot Trail until mile 1.0, where you'll come to a Y intersection. Follow Bobcat Trail, the left (west) trail. Ignore a track to the right, which just hooks back up with the Coot. Bobcat is a pleasant and soft dirt-covered singletrack. At mile 1.1 take a moment to admirl another northern viewpoint at a break in the fir trees. Although the way down has a better trail surface, there is no avoiding the steep grade. By mile 1.4 birch trees begin to take precedence over the firs. At mile 1.6 puncheon leads through a muddy patch, and you arrive at the parking area at mile 1.75.

Magalloway Mountain is New England's answer to the larger and more remote states of the West. Although short, you earned this hike because of its steep pitches. Get a drink and some food and prepare for the long drive back to civilization.

MILES AND DIRECTIONS

0.0 From the parking lot, ascend on Coot Trail.

0.1 Cross bridge.

0.6 Pass an unmarked trail on the right side. Then pass a marked spur trail to Bobcat Trail.

0.8 Summit. Return on the Coot Trail . . . at first.

1.0 Turn left on Bobcat Trail.

1.6 Puncheon leads over muddy section.

1.75 Arrive back at the parking lot.

8 MOUNT PROSPECT

A moderate loop hike to a fire lookout that is still active and, built of stone, unique in the region.

General location: Lancaster, New Hampshire
Highest point: 2,058 feet
Elevation gain: 576 feet
Distance: 3.4-mile loop
Difficulty: Moderate
Hiking time: 2.75 hours
When to go: Year-round (see "Special Considerations" below)
Fees and permits: Admission to Weeks State Park is free. There are, however, donation cannisters placed at the summit area. Admission to the museum inside the John Wingate Weeks summer home is $5 at the time of this writing.
Trail contact: Weeks State Park, 304 Prospect St., Lancaster, NH; (603) 788-4004; nhstateparks.org, trailfinder.info/trails/trail/weeks-state-park
Canine compatibility: Dogs should be on leash at all times.
Trail surface: Varied. Paved road, packed dirt, grass, rocks.
Land status: Public and private
Other trail users: Hikers, skiers, snowshoers
Water availability: There are public restrooms and running water at the summit from May until October. Otherwise, there is no water.
Special considerations: This summit is accessible by car and part of this hiking route is along the paved road. The auto road—and access to the tower—closes from Columbus Day in October until Memorial Day. Hikers are still welcome and, in fact, many snowshoe hikers enjoy the hike more in the winter; however, be advised that the tower, museum, and restrooms are closed during those dates. If climbing tower is important to you, do this hike between Memorial Day and Columbus Day.
Amenities: At the trailhead, none. There are free restrooms with running water at the museum inside the John Wingate Weeks summer home when the state park is open (Memorial Day to Columbus Day) at the summit. There are also picnic tables at the summit.
Maps: USGS Lancaster Quad
Maximum grade: 20 percent
Trail conditions: This year-round route has pros and cons depending on the season. A portion of the route follows the auto road to the summit. The auto road is a narrow, winding, scenic road with slow-moving traffic. In the summer and early fall when the auto road is open, there are, obviously, cars. In the winter the snow-covered road is a snowshoeing highlight; the problem then is that you cannot access the tower as Weeks State Park doesn't operate in winter and the tower is therefore locked.

FINDING THE TRAILHEAD
From the junction of US 2 and US 3 at the rotary in Lancaster, follow the two routes together south on Main Street. At 0.8 mile veer right on US 3 South. Turn left on Weeks State Park Road at 2.9 miles. From the junction of US 3 and NH 116 in Whitefield, follow US 3 North. At 6.3 miles turn right on Weeks State Park Road. The parking area is on the right. GPS: N44° 27′ 10.8″ / W71° 34′ 40.8″

Prospect Tower is unique in that it is New Hampshire's lone stone fire lookout.

ABOUT THE LOOKOUT

Height: 56 feet
Cabin dimensions: 15 feet diameter
Frame construction: Stone
Steps: Concrete
Active tower

Current tower: 1912
Original tower: 1912
What you'll see: Mount Washington, Mount Jefferson, Mount Lafayette, Vermont countryside

THE HIKE

The hike to the Mount Prospect Observation Tower forces you to make some decisions—mostly about when to go. Stretches of this hike, which is located almost entirely inside Weeks State Park, run along the park's auto road; yes, this tower is also accessible by car. It's no superhighway (far from it), rather, the road, while paved, is extremely narrow and twisting. For those who would prefer not to walk on an auto road, note that the road, which remains open to pedestrians year-round, closes to cars from Columbus Day in October until Memorial Day. Snowshoeing on the road in winter is, no doubt, a highlight of the hike and a popular pastime among locals. But here's where you have to make your decision: When the park closes the road, they also close the stone observation tower at the summit. So hikers must decide whether they want to walk alongside cars on part of the route and have access to the top of the tower, or hike car-free, but no climbing inside the tower. There are strong arguments to be made both ways.

Either way, the hike is pleasant and the tower unique. The tower was built by, and the state park named for, the conservationist John Wingate Weeks, a congressman and senator

Topograph with place names inside the Mount Prospect Tower

in the early twentieth century and secretary of war under two presidents. As a senator, he sponsored legislation that resulted in the establishment of national forests in the East—something that has obvious benefits for readers of this guidebook. The summit of Mount Prospect was Weeks's summer home. In addition to the observation tower, he built two stucco-finished buildings (the main house, which now features a museum, and a carriage house) and the access road—his driveway. From the observation tower, a short (0.2-mile-long) interpretive path points out features like wildflowers, towering white pines, and the clearing on which the family tennis courts formerly stood.

From the parking area, walk through (or, if you're coming in late fall or winter, around) the gate and find the New Hampshire Heritage Trail twenty steps beyond. The loop trail departs in both directions; this route goes north (left). The Heritage Trail was a project that had its roots in the late 1980s: The plan was to connect New Hampshire from Canada to Massachusetts, similar to the Long Trail in Vermont. Unfortunately, the model depended on individual communities to obtain and protect land with no other centralized support outside of advice on where to route the path. The result is a patchwork of trails throughout New Hampshire, some in better condition than others. The Lancaster section, however, is intact and in fairly good shape. From Weeks State Park Road, the Heritage Trail descends 0.4 mile and crosses ski trails maintained by the Mount Prospect Ski Club, a volunteer group that operates a 1957-Chevrolet-powered rope-tow ski lift in the winter months just east of this spot.

Cross the ski trail and continue along the narrow Heritage Trail, which traverses sideways around Mount Prospect. At mile 0.8 come to a trail intersection. Left leads

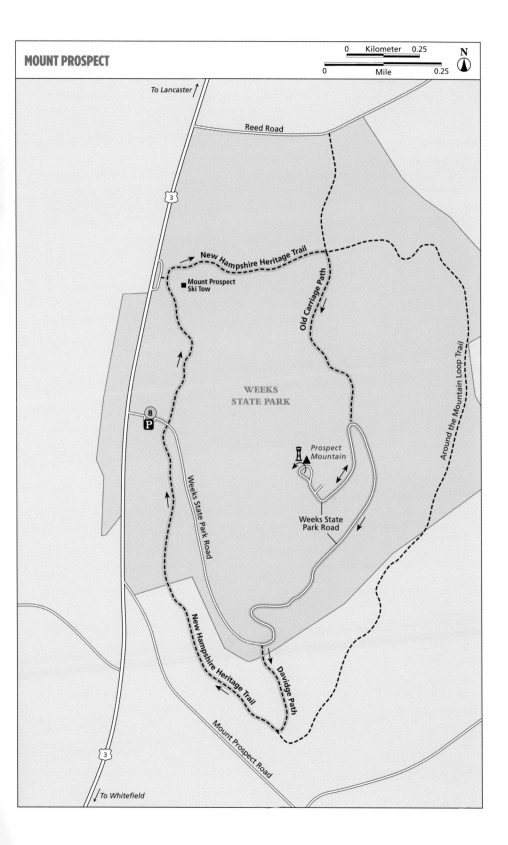

MOUNT PROSPECT

0   Kilometer   0.25

0   Mile   0.25

N

To Lancaster

Reed Road

3

New Hampshire Heritage Trail

Mount Prospect
Ski Tow

Old Carriage Path

WEEKS
STATE PARK

Around the Mountain Loop Trail

8
P

Prospect
Mountain

Weeks State Park Road

Weeks State
Park Road

New Hampshire Heritage Trail

Davidge Path

Mount Prospect Road

3

To Whitefield

to another trailhead on Reed Road (the use of which is discouraged by the state park due to the lack of adequate parking; therefore, the trail to the left is not well maintained). Straight ahead (east), the Heritage Trail becomes the aptly named Around the Mountain Loop Trail. Our route, however, takes a right (south) on the Old Carriage Path, which follows a route constructed in 1859 over which horses and buggies used to drive to a summit hotel (no longer in existence). The way gets rocky and steep, which leads one to wonder how sketchy it must have been to ride over this stretch in a horse-drawn carriage.

At 1.3 miles the trail spills onto the auto road at a hairpin turn. Turn right (south) and follow the road the remaining 0.3 mile to the tower and Weeks estate at the summit. The Mount Prospect Observation Tower was built in 1912 by John Wingate Weeks. When the Weeks family gifted the estate to the state in 1941, part of the deal was that the tower be made accessible to the public and that it be used for fire detection, which it still is. The New Hampshire Forestry Service added 15 feet to the tower as a firewatcher's cabin. When the observer is present, the public is welcome to visit the observer's cabin; otherwise it remains locked. There is still an observation deck equipped with a topograph that points out notable peaks including Mounts Washington and Jefferson to the east and Mount Lafayette to the southwest. Cherry Mountain is the closest peak standing due south.

When your explorations of the summit area (including the nature path, the museum, and the other buildings) are complete, follow the single-lane auto road down. Pass the Old Carriage Path (1.9 miles) that you ascended and continue until you come to the Davidge Path at 2.4 miles. Most of the Davidge Path is actually outside the park boundaries as it crosses the property of a Christmas tree farm owned by the trail's namesake family. The path bisects stands of red spruce and white pine. At 2.8 miles the Davidge Path reunites with the Around the Mountain Loop Trail (left) and the New Hampshire Heritage Trail. To complete the loop, turn right (west) to take the Heritage Trail. For a longer hike, you could go left on the Around the Mountain Loop Trail, which would return you to the junction with the Heritage Trail and the Old Carriage Path.

The Heritage Trail meanwhile traverses the remainder of Mount Prospect, terminating at the auto road at 3.4 miles, just uphill from your car.

MILES AND DIRECTIONS

0.0   From the parking lot, ascend on the paved road through (or, if the road is closed, around) the gate. The trail crosses the road about twenty steps uphill. Turn left (north) on the New Hampshire Heritage Trail.

0.4   Cross the Mount Prospect ski-tow trails.

0.8   Turn right (south) onto the Old Carriage Path.

1.3   Turn right onto the paved auto road.

1.6   Summit. To return, descend on the auto road.

1.9   At the hairpin turn, pass by (but don't take) the turn onto the Old Carriage Path.

2.4   Turn left (south) to descend on the Davidge Path.

2.8   Follow the New Hampshire Heritage Trail right (north).

3.4   Arrive back at the paved auto road and the parking area twenty steps downhill.

9 KEARSARGE NORTH (MOUNT PEQUAWKET) VIA KEARSARGE NORTH TRAIL

A beautiful White Mountain out-and-back hike through a diverse forest to a unique tower with amazing views of the Presidentials including Mount Washington.

General location: Intervale, New Hampshire
Highest point: 3,268 feet
Elevation gain: 2,533 feet
Distance: 6.2 miles
Difficulty: Strenuous (due to elevation gain)
Hiking time: 5.5 hours
When to go: Year-round
Fees and permits: None
Trail contact: White Mountain National Forest, 71 White Mountain Dr., Campton, NH; (603) 536-6100; fs.usda.gov/whitemountain
Canine compatibility: Dog friendly
Trail surface: Dirt and granite
Land status: Public

Other trail users: Hikers, skiers, snowshoers
Water availability: None
Special considerations: None
Amenities: None. There are just a few parking spaces at the trailhead. On summer weekends and in foliage season, it pays to arrive early as all of the spaces will fill, and cars will park up and down Hurricane Mountain Road.
Maps: USGS North Conway Quad
Maximum grade: 28 percent
Trail conditions: The route has a variety of trail conditions from dirt footpath to rocky trail and from smooth granite above the tree line to fir-lined craggy scrambles.

FINDING THE TRAILHEAD

From the junction of US 302 and Hurricane Mountain Road, turn east on Hurricane Mountain Road. The trailhead is 1.4 miles on the left (north) side of the road. Additional parking along Hurricane Mountain Road. GPS: N44° 4' 31.368" / W71° 6' 32.472"

ABOUT THE LOOKOUT

Height: 20 feet
Cabin dimensions: 12 x 12 with an outside catwalk
Frame construction: Wood
Steps: Wood
Active lookout

Current tower: 1951
Original tower: 1918. In 1909 the site went into service using scraps from a summit hotel building.
What you'll see: Mount Washington, the Moats, Maine

THE HIKE

What's in a name? Kearsarge North is one of two New Hampshire mountains called Kearsarge—this one near North Conway and the other located near Concord in the south-central part of the state. You can't even refer to this Kearsarge as "the one with a fire tower" because the southern Mount Kearsarge also has a tower. This Kearsarge is also commonly known as Mount Pequawket ("land of hollows") for the local group

Not necessarily the tallest tower, but the cabin atop Kearsarge North is most definitely one of the largest.

of Abenakis that lived in the North Conway area. The hike to the tower on Kearsarge North is exciting and varied, and the tower is one of the best options for those who want to overnight in a fire lookout.

There are several routes to this tower: Bartlett Mountain Trail approaches from the southwest and the little-used Weeks Brook Trail goes from South Chatham near the Maine border. This route highlights the Kearsarge North Trail (yellow blazes), which departs from the parking area on the north side of Hurricane Mountain Road. All three routes are within the White Mountain National Forest. From the trailhead, the trail passes a residence on the left (west) side of the trail. Once past that house the trail climbs gently through a forest of beech, hemlock, and white pine. At 0.6 mile notice an unmarked side trail to Kearsarge Brook on the left (west) side of the trail. On the return trip this is a nice place to cool off on a warm day.

At 0.7 mile the pitch steepens and the trail winds around giant pine trees and shanty-sized boulders. Listen for songbirds, the chatter of red squirrels, and the occasional distant whistle from the Conway Scenic Railroad.

The trail parallels Kearsarge Brook as it climbs doggedly until turning in an easterly direction and away from the brook at 1.4 miles. It follows this contour for 0.1 mile before turning back to the north as it continues a relatively relentless ascent.

At 1.9 miles the canopy opens as the trail turns to bedrock. Here, the trail winds from opening to opening and past a rainbow of chokeberry, Canadian serviceberry, and blueberry bushes. Pause as often as possible for delicious blueberry snacks. As the trail

A White Mountain picnic atop Kearsarge North

ascends, from openings to spruce groves, be sure to turn back for views of climbers' mecca Cathedral Ledge and the Moats ridge along the western side of North Conway.

At 2.2 miles a trail that comes in from the left (west) follows the ridge between Kearsarge North and Bartlett Mountain to the summit of Bartlett, which is really more like an outcrop on Kearsarge's shoulder. Stay straight on Kearsarge North Trail.

The trail zigs and zags across the shoulder of Kearsarge until you reach a ditch, through which runoff tumbles in the spring, and a scrambly ledge at 2.9 miles. From here, you'll break out of the birches and balsams at 3.1 miles as you approach the summit and the tower. You'll see the terminus of the Weeks Brook Trail at the summit.

The tower is shorter and wider than many—just 10 feet high (and a very reasonable dozen steps on the stairway to the wraparound deck) with a 10-foot cabin on top. There are views in all directions: Mount Washington to the west, the Moats to the southwest, and rural Maine to the east. The tower itself, with its glass windows and spacious cabin, makes a perfect camping shelter. There is an open-air toilet a short distance from the tower. The summit is above the tree line and makes the perfect viewing platform on a clear day. Sources vary regarding when this lookout went into service: the FFLA website offers two dates, 1901 and 1909. The National Register of Historic Places says 1913, and Baird and Haartz's *Field Guide to New Hampshire Firetowers* doesn't specify a year other than to mention that the firewatcher began identifying plumes of smoke almost from his first day on the job.

After checking out the tower and sampling wild blueberries at the summit, return to your car by the same route.

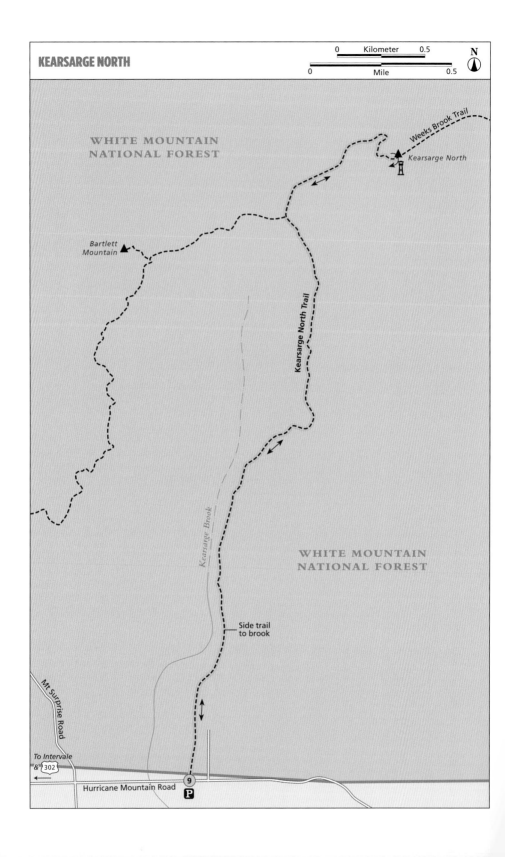

KEARSARGE NORTH

0   Kilometer   0.5

0   Mile   0.5

N

Weeks Brook Trail

Kearsarge North

WHITE MOUNTAIN
NATIONAL FOREST

Bartlett
Mountain

Kearsarge North Trail

Kearsarge Brook

WHITE MOUNTAIN
NATIONAL FOREST

Side trail
to brook

Mt Surprise Road

To Intervale
& 302

9

P

Hurricane Mountain Road

MILES AND DIRECTIONS

0.0   From the parking lot, head north on the Kearsarge North Trail.

0.1   Pass a residence on the left (west) side of trail.

0.6   Side trail to Kearsarge Brook.

0.7   Trail begins to wind around giant pine trees.

1.4   Trail turns away from Kearsarge Brook as it flattens briefly and heads in an easterly direction.

1.9   Trail breaks out of the trees as it begins to lead through open, rocky clearings.

2.2   Junction with trail to Bartlett Mountain.

2.9   Pass a ditch and hike up a scrambly ledge.

3.1   Summit and tower. Return by the same route.

6.2   Arrive back at your car at the trailhead.

10 MOUNT CARRIGAIN VIA SIGNAL RIDGE AND DESOLATION TRAIL

A steady backcountry climb to a 4,000-foot mountain tower with one of the best views in the Presidentials, and a return lollipop hike through the Pemigewasset Wilderness.

General location: Bartlett, New Hampshire
Highest point: 4,700 feet
Elevation gain: 3,360 feet
Distance: 13.2 miles
Difficulty: Expert only
Hiking time: 9 hours
When to go: Year-round
Fees and permits: None
Trail contact: White Mountain National Forest, 71 White Mountain Dr., Campton, NH; (603) 536-6100; fs.usda.gov/whitemountain
Canine compatibility: The National Forest requires that dogs be on leash in trailhead parking areas.
Trail surface: Dirt, rock, loose rock
Land status: Public

Other trail users: Hikers, snowshoers
Water availability: There are several streams along the trail.
Special considerations: Sawyer River Road is not maintained in the winter, which will add about 2 miles to your trip.
Amenities: None
Maps: USGS Mount Carrigain, NH Quad
Maximum grade: 50 percent
Trail conditions: The trail is well maintained but has been rerouted due to damage over the years. Older route descriptions may differ slightly; also, although the trail is marked with yellow blazes, they can be sporadic.

FINDING THE TRAILHEAD

From US 302 between Crawford Notch and Bartlett, turn west on Sawyer River Road (which is a narrow dirt road). At 2 miles cross a bridge. Immediately after the bridge, the trailhead is on the right side of the road. Trailhead parking is on the left. GPS: N44° 4' 12.432" / W71° 23' 0.672"

ABOUT THE LOOKOUT

Height: 30 feet
Observation deck dimensions: 14 x 16 feet
Frame construction: Steel
Steps: Wood
No longer active
Current tower: 1940
Original tower: 1910

What you'll see: Forty-three 4,000-foot peaks are visible from Mount Carrigain—one of the most amazing views in the Whites. Highlights include Mount Washington, Mount Lafayette, Mount Chocorua, and Crawford Notch.

THE HIKE

There are forty-eight 4,000-foot peaks in New Hampshire. Often, members of the "48 Club" save Mount Carrigain for last, because only Mount Washington surpasses the number of 4,000ers you can see from its summit (forty-three). Some would argue that the view from Carrigain is more impressive since Carrigain's includes the view of the mighty Washington, New England's tallest peak.

The hike to Mount Carrigain is simply awesome. It is long and difficult (you'll be tired), the views are incredible (try to save it for a clear day), and it is located on the

The observation deck on Mount Carrigain from Signal Ridge

edge of the Pemigewasset Wilderness area. Mount Carrigain is named for an early-nine-teenth-century New Hampshire secretary of state; the Pemigewasset River comes from an Abenaki word meaning "swift current and where the side (entering) current is."

Most hikers tackle Mount Carrigain as an out-and-back up the Signal Ridge Trail (a 10.4-mile round-trip), and you could too. However, the loop that returns on the Desolation Trail to the Carrigain Notch Trail, while it adds almost 3 miles to the trip, is a wonderful—and flatter—return trip, and is most definitely worth the extra miles. The description details both options. Note that the trail has undergone reroutes, and there are a number of side trails, therefore mileages may vary from earlier guidebooks and online postings. Generally, the approach and return lead through Carrigain Notch; the ascent and descent (both strenuous) go up Signal Ridge and down the Desolation Trail.

From the parking area, cross Sawyer River Road to the trailhead for Signal Ridge Trail, just to the left of the bridge. The trail is sporadically blazed with yellow and follows Whiteface Brook on a gentle but steady incline. At 0.6 mile pass a small waterfall and pool, and then the trail switches back away from the brook, eventually rejoining it at 0.8 mile. At 1.0 mile the trail is perpetually muddy with strategically placed stones to help hikers through. Shortly afterwards the trail turns away from Whiteface Brook. Here the trail flattens and the going is easy walking.

At 1.8 miles the trail crosses Carrigain Brook. There is no bridge, so you'll either hop from rock to rock or wade through. In the springtime or in times of high water, this can be a challenging crossing. At 2.0 miles cross puncheon and then come to the junction with the Carrigain Notch Trail. If you do the whole loop, this is your return route. For now, stay on Signal Ridge Trail, the left (west) branch of the Y intersection.

Foreground: Mount Lowell makes the far wall of Carrigain Notch. Background: the more famous Crawford Notch and Mount Washington.

The Signal Ridge Trail starts with two long switchbacks, then crosses a bridge over a small stream leading you through balsam fir and red spruce. At 2.5 miles there's a conspicuous seat-sized boulder. In the woods behind the boulder are remnants of an old iron cookstove lying in pieces.

At 2.8 miles the trail becomes significantly steeper and rockier. The increased pitch is your new reality for the next couple miles as you ascend Signal Ridge; in places the rocky trail is loose rubble, in others there are stone steps, and there are a few switchbacks too. Mostly, though, it's one foot in front of the other as you climb diagonally across Mount Carrigain to Signal Ridge. At 4 miles there are some sharp switchbacks, then at 4.4 miles the trail begins to break out of the forest as you gain Signal Ridge.

The going is easier on the ridgeline, although you are subject to whatever White Mountain weather elements may be thrown at you. At 4.6 miles you reach a clearing and the view northeast across the valley to Mount Washington opens up. It's a big reward, and you've earned it.

You're not finished, however. The trail follows the exposed Signal Ridge before dipping back into the stunted forest. You pass a couple of tent sites and a spring (complete with a bucket chained to a tree) at 5.1 miles. Reach the summit of Mount Carrigain at 5.2 miles.

The tower itself is no longer an active fire lookout. It was originally funded in 1910 by the New Hampshire Timberland Owners Association, an organization established in the same year to assist the state in fighting forest fires and that exists still today. The original towers were rickety wooden structures—archival photos are cringe-worthy considering

There are many dry stream crossings on the Carrigain Notch Trail, but the chaos and debris in the streambeds hints at intense spring runoff.

the winds that routinely blow through the Whites. The US Forest Service built the current steel structure in 1940 with a cab, which was removed in lieu of the current observation deck in 1979.

Trees on the summit are as tall as the tower; without the tower, there would be no view. But climb up, and the views are 360 degrees. There's a lot to look at on the north-eastern side of the large wooden observation deck: directly below the tower is the entire Pemi and Carrigain Notch, Mount Lowell forming its far wall. Farther north is the sheer northeastern wall of Crawford Notch and the towering Mount Washington overseeing Mount Adams, Mount Monroe, and the rest of the Presidentials. West is Mount Lafayette and the impressive saddle to Mount Lincoln. On a clear day Vermont's Camel's Hump peeks around Lincoln from 80 miles away. Look west to see 4,000ers Mount Hancock and the more distant Mount Moosilauke. Back east is Signal Ridge, the route of your ascent, and Mount Chocorua dominates the south. And in between are hundreds of miles of wild, mountainous forestlands.

When you tear yourself away from the tower, it's decision time. For the shortest route back to the car—but not necessarily the easiest, due to the sustained steep descent—like many hikers, you could retrace your steps down the Signal Ridge Trail.

Your other, longer option—which boasts a descent that is equally difficult but steeper and shorter—goes through the heart of the Pemi via the Desolation Trail to the valley floor, returning on the mostly flat and leisurely Carrigain Notch Trail. The Desolation Trail begins its descent between the northern tower legs under the observation deck. For the first quarter mile, the going is as steep as the trail you

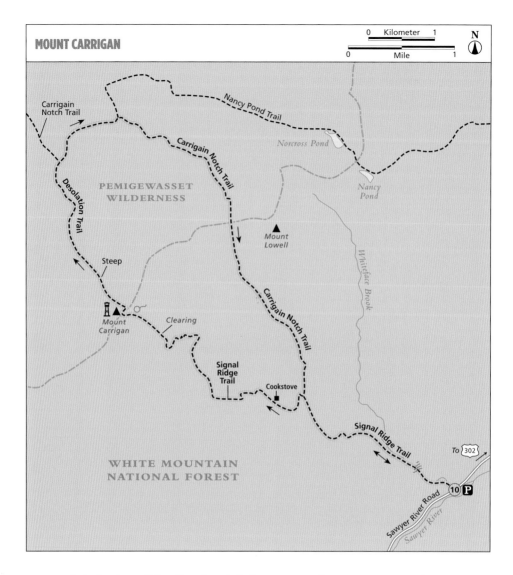

ascended. At about 5.5 miles the pitch increases to sit-on-your-rear-end steepness until about 5.7 miles.

The trail begins to level out, and by mile 6.2 the trail is flat. At mile 6.8 the ground turns muddy and you cross puncheon before arriving at a T intersection with the Carrigain Notch Trail. Turn right (northeast) on Carrigain Notch Trail and follow the flat and narrow singletrack through the spruce until 7.7 miles, when you come to the intersection with Nancy Pond Trail, which leads to popular dispersed camping sites. Stay right (east) on the Carrigain Notch Trail. Here you begin to gain elevation as you approach the pass between Vose Spur and Mount Lowell, the two sides of the actual notch. This is rugged country, and the trail passes many streambeds created by raging spring runoff. At 8.8 miles cross aging puncheon and continue ascending (although nothing like the earlier ascent up Carrigain!).

At 9.5 miles the trail leaves the Pemigewasset Wilderness area and finally begins to descend again. Cross several streambeds—some dry and some running, depending on the time of year and on how much snow fell the previous winter—until the intersection with the Signal Ridge Trail at 11.2 miles. Turn left (southeast) on Signal Ridge and retrace your steps to the trailhead at 13.2 miles, where you'll know you completed an epic White Mountain classic.

MILES AND DIRECTIONS

0.0 From the parking lot, cross Sawyer River Road to the Signal Ridge Trailhead.

0.6 Waterfall in the Sawyer River.

2.0 Intersection with Carrigain Notch Trail (your return route). Stay left (west) on Signal Ridge.

2.5 Old camp stove pieces behind a boulder.

4.4 Trail opens up as you find clearings along the ridgeline. Great view!

5.2 Summit and tower! (And some of the most stunning views in the Whites.) Return on Desolation Trail, which starts beneath northeastern side of tower.

5.5 Descent gets very steep.

6.8 Intersection with Carrigain Notch Trail. Turn right (northeast) on Carrigain Notch.

7.7 Follow Carrigain Notch Trail to intersection with Nancy Pond Trail. Stay right (east) on Carrigain Notch, which ascends gently for a mile.

9.5 Leave Pemigewasset Wilderness and begin a gentle descent.

11.2 Intersection eft (southeast) on Signal Ridge.

13.2 Arrive back at the trailhead and parking area.

11 GREAT HILL VIA BIG PINES NATURAL AREA

An easy reverse lollipop hike through a conserved forest of giant pines to a tower with White Mountain views.

General location: Tamworth, New Hampshire
Highest point: 1,277 feet
Elevation gain: 548 feet
Distance: 2.3 miles
Difficulty: Easy
Hiking time: 1.5 hours
When to go: Year-round
Fees and permits: None
Trail contacts: New Hampshire Forest Protection Bureau, Division of Forests and Lands, Department of Natural and Cultural Resources, 172 Pembroke Rd., Concord, NH; (603) 271-2214; dncr.nh.gov. Tamworth Conservation Commission, 84 Main St., Tamworth, NH; tamworth conservationcommission.org.
Canine compatibility: Dog friendly
Trail surface: Varied. Packed dirt, rocks, roots, and pine needle duff.
Land status: Public

Other trail users: Hikers, skiers, snowshoers
Water availability: None
Special considerations: None
Amenities: None
Maps: USGS Mount Chocorua Quad (note that these trails aren't depicted on the USGS Quad), Big Pines Natural Area & Great Hill Trails & Tower Map (tamworthconservationcommission .org/managed-lands-trails)
Maximum grade: 26 percent, but this is fleeting
Trail conditions: This short reverse lollipop (that is, the loop part is at the beginning of the hike, not the end) is a pleasant walk on packed dirt and pine needle duff. The fallen pine foliage ensures peaceful quietude and the dirt makes for a very-low-impact walk. The main hazard: lots of tree roots.

FINDING THE TRAILHEAD

From the junction of Routes 113 and 113A in Tamworth village, turn north on Route 113A. The trailhead is on the western side of the road at 2.6 miles. GPS: N43° 53' 12.516" / W71° 17' 38.687"

ABOUT THE LOOKOUT

Height: 35 feet
Cabin dimensions: 7 x 7 feet
Frame construction: Steel
Steps: Wood
Active lookout
Current tower: 1934

Original tower: 1934
What you'll see: Mount Chocorua, Mount Passaconaway, Mount Whiteface, rooftops of Tamworth village

THE HIKE

The hike to the tower on Great Hill is an example of the positive results that can come from teamwork and cooperation between public organizations. These hiking trails fall inside the boundaries of the Hemenway State Forest (named for Augustus Hemenway, who deeded the land to the state in 1932), which, like all state forests in the Granite State, is owned and managed by the New Hampshire Department of Natural and Cultural

Some of the trees on Great Hill have caught up to the tower's height, although the views from the cabin are unobstructed.

The Great Hill trail has a low-impact surface . . . except for some big tree roots!

Resources. The town of Tamworth owns the Great Hill fire lookout, and the Tamworth Conservation Commission, a municipal committee, maintains the tower and the trails to the tower. The tower is not active, although part of the town's ownership stipulates that it be made available for fire detection if necessary.

The trailhead is more a pull-off on the side of New Hampshire State Route 113A than a parking area. This hike leads you through a coniferous forest that aptly reflects the name of the municipal forest: "Big Pines." These majestic trees tower over you. Meanwhile, the fallen pine needles make for a soft and quiet trail surface underfoot. This hike truly removes you from the rat race of the populated world.

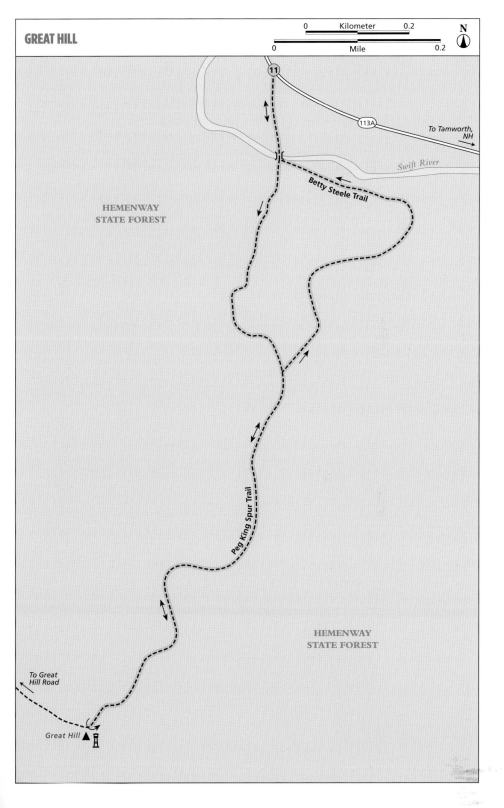

GREAT HILL

0   Kilometer   0.2
0   Mile   0.2

N

To Tamworth, NH

Swift River

Betty Steele Trail

HEMENWAY STATE FOREST

Peg King Spur Trail

HEMENWAY STATE FOREST

To Great Hill Road

Great Hill

At 0.1 mile you come to your first landmark: a well-made bridge across the Swift River. At the far side of the bridge is a trail intersection. The Betty Steele Trail comes in from the west (left); you'll return on the Betty Steele. For now, however, follow the Peg King Spur Trail (yellow blazes) straight ahead. The trail ascends and descends to cross a small stream that trickles along on its way to the Swift. The trail continues over twisting tree roots, soft soil, and pine needle duff; no matter how hard you slam your feet, there are no loud footfalls on this surface.

The path snakes its way past gigantic pines to the other trail junction with Betty Steele at 0.5 mile. Stay on the Peg King Spur Trail, which begins to ascend more steeply at 0.8 mile. Your efforts are rewarded 0.3 mile later when you come to a clearing and the Great Hill fire lookout at 1.1 miles.

Trees encroach the clearing, but the lookout tower, which was constructed in 1934, still rises above them to give you clear views. The unmistakable pyramid-shaped peak of Mount Chocorua dominates the northern view, Mounts Passaconaway and Whiteface are northwest, and the rooftops of the village of Tamworth are visible to the south. Trails and roads—not passable by motor vehicles—come into the clearing from other directions. The tower was in active operation from 1934 until 1973; it was part of the Aircraft Warning Service system during World War II.

After taking in the sights, you'll descend the way you came on the Peg King Spur Trail. Come to a Y at 1.7 miles and follow the Betty Steele Trail to the right, passing more giant white pines. Wooden puncheon keeps you out of the mud at 1.9 miles until the trail meets the Swift at 2.1 miles. Walk along the river until you return to the Peg King Spur Trail and the bridge. Cross the bridge and return to your car at 2.3 miles.

MILES AND DIRECTIONS

0.0 Leave trailhead.

0.1 Cross Swift River over well-engineered bridge. Ignore trail to the right. Instead follow Peg King Spur Trail straight ahead.

0.5 Come to intersection with Betty Steele Trail. Stay straight (right) on Peg King Spur Trail.

1.1 Clearing and fire lookout. Retrace your steps to return.

1.7 Intersection with Betty Steele Trail. Take right fork (Betty Steele Trail).

2.1 Come to Swift River.

2.2 Return to Peg King Spur Trail. Go north (right) and cross bridge.

2.3 Arrive back at the trailhead and your car.

12 SMARTS MOUNTAIN VIA LAMBERT RIDGE AND RANGER TRAILS

An exciting reverse lollipop hike with a "big mountain" feel. Smarts Mountain has a bit of everything: elevation gain, breathtaking views, forested trails, and scenic streams. The exposed ledges on Lambert Ridge with their views of Smarts Mountain and some sustained steep pitches make you feel more like you're on one of the taller Whites in northern New Hampshire.

General location: Lyme, New Hampshire
Highest point: 3,225 feet
Elevation gain: 2,122 feet
Distance: 7.4 miles
Difficulty: Strenuous
Hiking time: 4.75 hours
When to go: Year-round
Fees and permits: None
Trail contact: White Mountain National Forest, 71 White Mountain Dr., Campton, NH; (603) 536-6100; fs.usda.gov/whitemountain. Dartmouth Outdoors, Robinson Hall, Dartmouth College, PO Box 9, Hanover, NH 03755; (603) 646-2428; outdoors.dartmouth.edu.

Canine compatibility: Dogs are allowed and should be under voice command.
Trail surface: Packed dirt, rocks, and much exposed quartzite and granite
Land status: Public
Other trail users: Hikers, snowshoers
Water availability: There are several stream crossings.
Special considerations: None
Amenities: None
Maps: USGS Smarts Mountain, NH Quad
Maximum grade: 20 percent
Trail conditions: The trail conditions vary from dirt to rocky to sheer rock. For a low-elevation mountain, the Lambert Ridge Trail has a distinct "big mountain" feel to it.

FINDING THE TRAILHEAD

From the town green in Lyme, turn east onto the Dorchester Road from SR 10. Follow the Dorchester Road through Lyme Center to a Y at 3.1 miles. Follow the left fork to stay on the Dorchester Road. The trailhead is on the left at 4.7 miles just before an iron bridge. GPS: N43° 47' 49.596" / W72° 4' 16.067"

ABOUT THE LOOKOUT

Height: 41 feet
Cabin dimensions: 7 x 7
Frame construction: Steel
Steps: Wood
No longer active

Current tower: 1939
Original tower: 1915
What you'll see: Vermont's Green Mountains, the Presidentials, Franconia Notch

THE HIKE

Compared to the high peaks of the Presidential Range to the north, Smarts Mountain is smaller and lesser known. With a 3,238-foot elevation, it doesn't even enjoy status as one of New Hampshire's forty-eight must-climb 4,000-footers. Do not, however, let any of

One of several ledgy outcrops on Lambert Ridge

this cloud your perception of this hike up the dome that is Smarts Mountain—the loop includes a significant elevation gain, varying trail surfaces, numerous ledgy lookouts with beautiful views, and, of course, a memorable fire lookout at the summit.

Pick up the Lambert Ridge Trail (white blazes), also known as the Appalachian Trail, on the northwestern end of the parking area (you'll return via the Ranger Trail, which comes in at the northeastern back end of the lot). The route begins with a strenuous climb immediately for the first half mile as you pass giant boulders and large hardwoods. After crossing a stone wall at 0.6 mile, the going finally levels out thanks to some switch-backs before descending slightly. At 0.7 mile the going steepens yet again until you ascend a stone staircase, which puts you onto a lookout facing east, where you can see Reservoir Pond and Cummins Pond, two backcountry fishing spots, and the slopes of the Dartmouth Skiway.

The trail ducks back into the woods and pops out on another couple of ledges until scaling an almost-vertical ascent at 1.2 miles. At 1.5 miles the character of the forest shifts as spruce and hemlock gain prevalence, and their needles cover a softer, packed-dirt trail surface that rolls over several tenths of a mile.

At 1.8 miles, toward the northern end of Lambert Ridge, the trail bursts onto a large ledge where you'll notice bands of pinkish, grayish quartzite, a rock type that dates back 400 million years to when New Hampshire stood along the edge of a volcanic island chain. You also get your first view of the Smarts Mountain dome—none too close

The fire lookout on Smarts Mountain was restored in 2016.

(indeed it's still nearly 2 miles away)—to the northeast. Look closely and you can make out the fire lookout—a speck on the summit.

Following the white blazes painted on the rocky trail, the trail reenters the woods as you lose elevation in the gap between Lambert Ridge and the shoulder of Smarts. The rolling traverse through this col can be muddy as the path follows low wooden footbridges in places. At 3.0 miles your climb begins again, gently at first, then becoming steeper. At some pitches the trail is worn to the slabby bedrock and you are assisted in places by stone steps. At 3.3 miles the Ranger Trail (formerly the Appalachian Trail route) comes in from the southeast. This is your return route on the descent. For now, however, continue straight on the Lambert Ridge Trail over rock slab. You're assisted at 3.4 miles by wooden steps and metal rungs.

Your summit push is steep. You pass a tent site on the right side of the trail at 3.6 miles as the trail plateaus. At the tent site is a view of Mount Cardigan, home to another fire lookout, to the south. There are a number of side trails between here and the summit, including one to a privy, but if you stay on the AT, you arrive at the summit at 3.8 miles.

The tower occupies most of the summit clearing, and there is no view from below. The New Hampshire Forestry Commission originally erected a lookout on this site in 1915. The state built the current steel tower, an International Derrick model, after the hurricane of 1938. The tower was in and out of active service until 1973. Many of the years the lookout was out of service, maintenance and upkeep fell to the Dartmouth

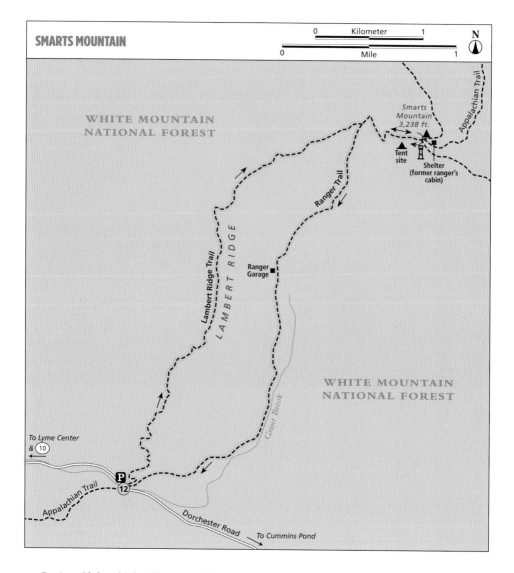

Outing Club, which still stewards the area and the trails. The state decided to take the tower down in 1951; poor weather scuttled these plans. The tower itself was restored in 2016 by the nonprofit HistoriCorps.

The views from the tower cabin are awesome, with the spine of the Green Mountains visible to the west and Franconia Ridge and the Presidentials to the northeast. Back on the ground, the Dartmouth Outing Club also maintains the original fire warden's cabin, which they transformed into an overnight shelter on a path about 100 feet east of the fire lookout. The shelter has space for about eight people and is available on a first-come, first-served basis.

After chatting with AT through-hikers who likely overnighted in the cabin, you (different than them) will retrace your steps back down the Lambert Ridge Trail over the slabby (and potentially slippery) rock that you climbed on the way up. At 4.3 miles you come to the intersection with the Ranger Trail, so named because it was the route fire rangers historically used en route to the tower. Many hikers opt to go up and down Lambert Ridge; the US Forest Service no longer recognizes the Ranger Trail as an officially "maintained" trail. However, the Dartmouth Outing Club does periodically steward the Ranger Trail, and although it doesn't boast the ledgy overlooks of Lambert Ridge, it offers different kinds of beautiful—a stream crossing, a walk along said stream—and the lower portion is much easier-going than Lambert Ridge (and slightly less distant).

At first the descent onl (marked with blue blazes) is more of the same—that is, a steep downhill pitch over sometimes exposed slab. After a third of a mile, the trail surface shifts to gravel streambed, and the pitch mellows. You cross and recross a small stream at 5.4 miles and later Grant Brook, a larger stream at 5.5 miles. On your right after the Grant Brook crossing is an old building known as the Ranger Garage. Fire rangers would park their vehicles here and use the Ranger Trail to ascend Smarts, which means that the rest of the way down follows what at one time was a jeep road, although you'd never guess it. The trail is mostly a path. Follow Grant Brook for the better part of a mile (to mile 6.4) until the trail breaks right. Arrive at the parking area at 7.4 miles.

MILES AND DIRECTIONS

0.0   From the Lambert Ridge Trailhead, climb an immediately steep ascent. No slow warmup here!

0.8   Atop a stone staircase, come to a ledgy lookout point. Continue over a couple more lookouts.

1.5   After an almost vertical ascent, the surrounding woods change to quiet hemlock and spruce softwoods.

1.8   Another craggy lookout point with a view of your destination and, for those with good eyesight or glasses, the tower.

3.3   Intersection with the Ranger Trail (your return route). Take the left (north) fork to continue ascending on the Lambert Ridge Trail.

3.6   Pass tent site on right.

3.8   Arrive at tower and summit. Retrace your steps back to the intersection with the Ranger Trail.

4.3   At the intersection take the left fork to follow the Ranger Trail.

5.5   Cross Grant Brook (Ranger Garage on right after crossing). Follow Ranger Trail as it parallels Grant Brook.

6.4   Stay on Ranger Trail as brook heads into woods.

7.4   Arrive back at the parking area.

13 GREEN MOUNTAIN VIA HIGH WATCH TRAIL

A challenging out-and-back climb to a beautiful tower with a new cab and rewarding views.

General location: Effingham, New Hampshire
Highest point: 1,907 feet
Elevation gain: 1,119 feet
Distance: 2.8 miles
Difficulty: Moderate
Hiking time: 2.5 hours
When to go: Year-round
Fees and permits: None
Trail contact: New Hampshire Forest Protection Bureau, Division of Forests and Lands, Department of Natural and Cultural Resources, 172

Pembroke Rd., Concord, NH; (603) 271-2214; dncr.nh.gov
Canine compatibility: Dogs are allowed under voice or leash control.
Trail surface: Dirt, rocks
Land status: Public
Other trail users: Hikers, snowshoers
Water availability: None
Special considerations: None
Amenities: None
Maps: USGS Freedom, NH Quad
Maximum grade: 30 percent
Trail conditions: Wide, fairly steep ascent

FINDING THE TRAILHEAD

At the intersection of NH 153 North and NH 25, turn south onto Green Mountain Road. At 1.2 miles turn left (southeast) onto Winter Road. At 1.4 miles turn left (east) onto High Watch Road. At 1.1 miles pass a rehabilitation and treatment center on the right (south) side of the road. Just past this large gated facility, the road turns to dirt. There is a parking place or two at this point, but if you continue to mile 1.2, there are several parking spots at the trailhead. GPS: N43° 47' 1.788" / W71° 2' 46.716"

ABOUT THE LOOKOUT

Height: 57 feet
Cabin dimensions: 7 x 7 feet
Frame construction: Steel
Steps: Wood
Active lookout
Current tower: This tower was moved from Cedar Mountain in 1922 and lowered 8 feet in 1977.

Original tower: 1922. This is the original!
What you'll see: Ossipee Range, Ossipee Lake, Maine, a sliver of Lake Winnipesaukee, Mount Washington

THE HIKE

There are three routes to the summit of Green Mountain (the Dearborn Trail, the Libby Trail, and the High Watch Trail), and they are all steep. This hike earns a "moderate" rating due to its short distance and modest vertical gain. However, make no mistake: Every step of the 1.4 miles on the way up the High Watch Trail is uphill.

Pick up the High Watch Trail (orange blazes) on the south side of the small parking area. For the first 0.1 mile, the trail runs alongside the back parking lot of the fenced rehabilitation center next door. A stone wall starts opposite the parking lot and briefly runs parallel

The lookout on Green Mountain is an active fire tower with a cabin renovated in 2015.

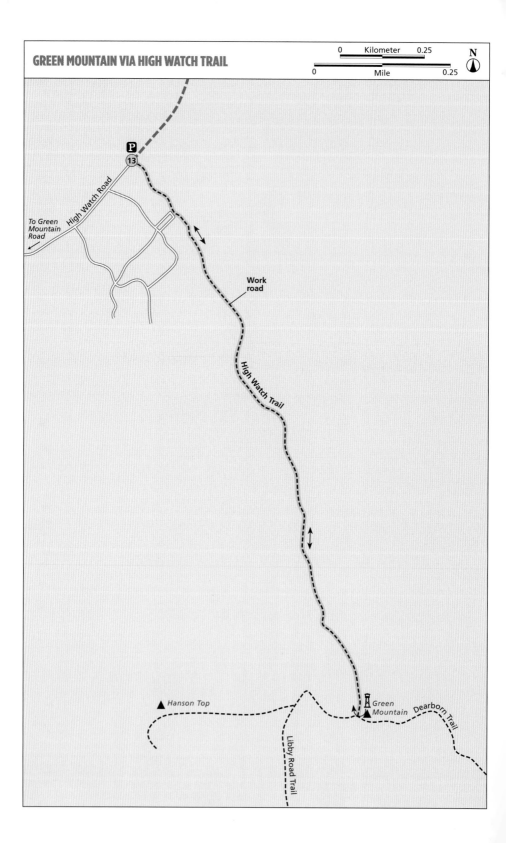

GREEN MOUNTAIN VIA HIGH WATCH TRAIL

0   Kilometer   0.25

0   Mile   0.25

N

P
13

High Watch Road

To Green
Mountain
Road

Work
road

High Watch Trail

Hanson Top

Green
Mountain

Dearborn Trail

Libby Road Trail

to the trail until the trail veers right. At 0.4 mile the trail crosses a work road. After the work road, another stone wall runs away from the trail to the right. Inexplicably, a lone random telephone pole without a cable (but with a white electrical box) stands watch over the wall.

The trail continues along a steep uphill through a diverse forest of beech, red spruce, eastern white pine, and hemlock. From here, the trail doesn't turn much, and it continues steeply uphill until it enters a stand of Engelmann spruce trees and a couple of picnic tables. You're at the summit.

Hopefully you came on a day when there is a firewatcher in the tower (most weekends and in times of high fire danger), because the aforementioned spruces stand higher than the observation deck constructed about two-thirds of the way up the tower. If there is a firewatcher, knock politely and ask if you can come in. From the

Firewatcher Skip Knox observes his Osborne Fire Finder in the 100-year-old Green Mountain tower.

cab, which was renovated in 2015 (making it one of New Hampshire's nicest towers), the views are awesome. Ossipee Lake and the Ossipee range stand through the windows on the west side. Beyond Province Lake to the south, you can see as far as Massachusetts. You can see Maine to the east, and Mount Washington dominates the northern view.

The cabin is equipped with radio equipment and an Osborne Fire Finder—an alidade that helps a firewatcher take a bearing on a plume of smoke. Firewatchers are in the towers every weekend to prevent fire but also to provide outreach to visitors. Generally, they welcome visits and will invite hikers into the cabin. If that happens at Green Mountain, you are in for a treat.

Back on the ground, the Dearborn Trail departs from the west side of the summit clearing and leads to a spur to Hanson Top, a subpeak of Green Mountain. It's also wooded and gives you similar views as the summit of Green (without the tower). On the right (eastern) side of the tower, the Libby Road Trail heads south. To return to your car, retrace the steps you took coming in. As it is downhill, the descent will be quicker—and easier—than the way up.

MILES AND DIRECTIONS

0.0   From the parking lot, parallel the rehab center's back parking lot.

0.4   Cross a work road. The trail continues uphill and mostly straight from here.

1.4   Summit and tower. Return the same way you climbed.

2.8   Arrive back at your car and the trailhead.

14 **RED HILL**

A beautiful lollipop hike through a locally conserved hardwood forest with plenty of diversions like cellar holes, a cabin, and signage that describes the area's history dating back to before the American Revolution. And, of course, there's a fire lookout with amazing views of New Hampshire mountains and lakes.

General location: Moultonborough, New Hampshire
Highest point: 2,030 feet
Elevation gain: 1,321 feet
Distance: 3.6-mile lollipop
Difficulty: Moderate
Hiking time: 3 hours
When to go: Year-round
Fees and permits: None
Trail contact: Lakes Region Conservation Trust, PO Box 766, 156 Dane Rd., Center Harbor, NH 03226; (603) 253-3301; lrct.org
Canine compatibility: Dogs are allowed and should be under leash or verbal control.
Trail surface: Packed dirt, gravel, rocks
Land status: Public
Other trail users: Hikers, skiers, snowshoers, and, on one stretch, snowmobiles
Water availability: The trail crosses a small stream and a natural spring.

Special considerations: None
Amenities: The neighbor next door to the trailhead has a small and quirky self-serve concession with snacks, drinks, artwork, and herbal remedies and insect repellent, set up from June until August and on weekends from September through November. They also have a sitting area surrounded by garden statues, New England lawn decorations, cartoonlike buildings, and whimsical artwork.
Maps: Castle in the Clouds and Red Hill Conservation Area Hiking Trails Map by Lakes Region Conservation Trust and USGS Center Harbor Quad (the USGS map doesn't show the trails)
Maximum grade: 20 percent
Trail conditions: This is a well-marked and well-maintained trail.

FINDING THE TRAILHEAD

From Route 25 East, immediately turn left onto Bean Road after the light at the junction of Routes 25 and 25B in Center Harbor, New Hampshire. At 1.4 miles turn right on Sibley Road, which turns to dirt at mile 2.3 before ending at a T. Turn left on Red Hill Road. The trailhead is on the right at mile 2.6. The parking area feels almost like a driveway to the homestead just before it. There are a few overflow parking spaces on the opposite side of the road. GPS: N43° 44' 21.732" / W71° 27' 47.52"

ABOUT THE LOOKOUT

Height: 37 feet
Cabin dimensions: 10 x 10 feet
Frame construction: Steel
Steps: Wood
Active lookout
Original tower: 1927

Current tower: 1927 (with a new cab added in 1972)
What you'll see: Mount Israel, Ossipee Mountains, Squam Lake, Lake Winnipesaukee

A hiker makes his way down from Red Hill tower.

THE HIKE

Red Hill is a gem of a hike and perfect for families and children because of the many diversions along the way. It starts with the quirky homestead sitting area and concession set up at the trailhead during the summer months by an artsy neighbor who sells snacks, drinks, herbal remedies, and homemade insect repellent.

Managed by the Lakes Region Conservation Trust, the 2,650-acre Red Hill Conservation Area is one of several locally conserved tracts. It's conserved with good reason: The Lakes Region is a beautiful and heavily visited corner of New Hampshire with close proximity to mountain hiking and scenic lakes, including Lake Winnipesaukee, New Hampshire's largest, and Squam Lake, where the movie *On Golden Pond*, starring Henry Fonda and Katherine Hepburn, was filmed.

From the trailhead, the trail is enthusiastically blazed with red diamond trail markers (every 50 feet for the first quarter mile). Cross a logging road at 0.2 mile and a bridge over a stream at 0.3 mile. At 0.5 mile you come to the opening of a fence designed to keep winter snowmobile traffic on track; the snowmobile trail comes in from the left and briefly shares the route with the hiking trail. Just past the fence is a Lakes Region Conservation Trust kiosk and a junction. The Cabin Trail goes straight; that will be your return route.

Turn left onto the Red Hill Trail, but not before exploring a well-preserved cellar hole on the left side of the trail. The cellar hole was the site of the pre–Revolutionary War homesteading Horne family, whose work (along with that of other homesteaders) is evidenced throughout this hike. The area's agricultural history is on display as you pass apple trees, blueberry bushes, and plenty of stone walls. (When farm fields were covered with rocks left by glaciers in the last ice age, New England homesteaders built stone walls). Although this recent history is on display, the area's history, of course, predates homesteaders, as the area was peopled by the Abenaki and the Ossipee.

The trail at this point is wide and gravelly, ascending gradually yet steadily until you pass a natural spring at 1.1 miles. Here the trail narrows, and you begin to encounter occasional natural granite steps.

At 1.7 miles the Eagle Cliff Trail comes in from the left. Several steps beyond this junction, you'll come to the summit clearing, a few locked maintenance buildings, and the Red Hill tower. Ernest Dane, a resident of Center Harbor, donated funds for the construction and maintenance of the tower, built in 1927. He also allowed the state of New Hampshire to occupy the summit, provided the tower be used for fire observation purposes. When the state ceased to use the tower for fire observation fifty-four years later, occupancy of the summit area reverted back to the Dane family, who leased the property and the tower to the town of Moultonborough. In 2000 the land was acquired by the Lakes Region Conservation Trust and conserved for perpetuity, and local fire departments still use the tower for observation purposes during times of high fire danger, working in concert with the NH Forest Protection Bureau and the other active towers in the area.

The views from the lookout are stunning in all directions. To the north is Mount Israel (where the tower responsible for the area's fire detection originally stood). South and west, respectively, are Lake Winnipesaukee and Squam Lake, and the Ossipee Mountains stretch to the east.

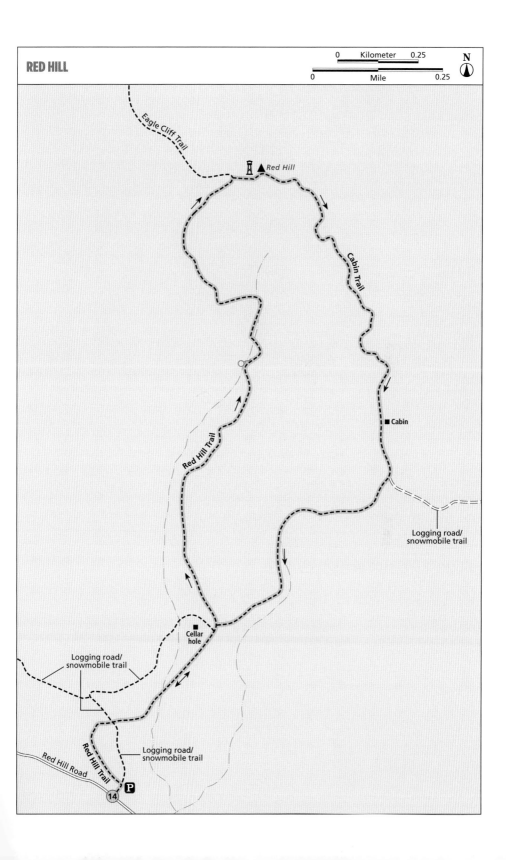

If you do the Red Hill hike in the summer, be sure to keep your eyes open for wild blueberries.

After exploring the views from the tower (and exploring the summit area for wild blueberries in the summer), descend via the Cabin Trail (blue diamond trail markers) on the northeastern side of the summit clearing. The packed-dirt trail passes through a meadow at 1.9 miles. At 2.4 miles come to a dilapidated homesteading cabin. Beyond the cabin the trail widens when the snowmobile trail comes in at 2.5 miles. At 3.1 miles the Cabin Trail reunites with the Red Hill Trail. Retrace your steps back to the trailhead at 3.6 miles.

MILES AND DIRECTIONS

0.0 Leave trailhead.

0.5 Junction with Cabin Trail at Horne cellar hole. Follow Red Hill Trail to the left.

1.1 Pass a spring on the left side of the trail.

1.7 Eagle Cliff Trail comes in from left. A few steps later, come to summit clearing and the fire tower. The Cabin Trail departs from the northeastern end of the clearing.

2.4 Pass a cabin on left side of trail.

2.5 Snowmobile trail comes in from left.

3.1 Junction with Red Hill Trail. Follow Red Hill Trail downhill (left).

3.6 Arrive back at the trailhead and your vehicle.

15 MOUNT CARDIGAN VIA WEST RIDGE–SOUTH RIDGE LOOP

A hike that takes you above the tree line to a unique tower on a bald summit with incredible 360-degree views.

General location: Orange, New Hampshire
Highest point: 3,121 feet
Elevation gain: 1,192 feet
Distance: 3.4-mile lollipop
Difficulty: Moderate
Hiking time: 2.75 hours
When to go: Year-round
Fees and permits: None
Trail contact: Cardigan Mountain State Park, 658 Cardigan Mountain Rd., Orange, NH; (603) 227-8745; nhstateparks.org
Canine compatibility: Pets must be on leash, and owners must clean up their waste.
Trail surface: Packed dirt, rocks, roots, rock slab
Land status: Public
Other trail users: Hikers, skiers, snowshoers

Water availability: Some small stream crossings, but not necessarily reliable as drinking water sources
Special considerations: The gate to Cardigan Mountain State Park is locked during the winter months, but there is parking nearby (but not blocking) the gate. This adds 0.75 mile to your hike.
Amenities: Picnic tables, a kiosk, rustic restrooms
Maps: USGS Mount Cardigan Quad
Maximum grade: On the ascent, 22 percent. Descending, 30 percent.
Trail conditions: This is a well-maintained yet rough trail. On the return trip South Ridge Trail includes a steep and rocky scramble beginning after the junction with the Skyline Trail.

FINDING THE TRAILHEAD

From the junction of US 4 and NH 118 in Canaan, New Hampshire, follow NH 118 east. After 0.5 mile turn right (east) on Cardigan Mountain Road. Follow this road past the Orange town line, several graveyards, and the Orange Town House (built in 1769) before it bends sharply right at an intersection and crosses a bridge over Orange Brook at 3.2 miles. New Colony Road and Peaslee Road both go left; stay on Cardigan Mountain Road, which turns to dirt after the bridge. Enter the Cardigan Mountain State Forest at 3.9 miles at a gate (which is locked in winter). Burnt Hill Road goes right at the gate; stay on Cardigan Mountain Road. Arrive at the Cardigan Mountain State Park parking area at 4.4 miles. GPS: N43° 38' 39.755" / W71° 56' 6.896"

ABOUT THE LOOKOUT

Height: 15 feet
Cabin dimensions: 10 x 10 feet
Frame construction: Steel
Steps: Wood
Active lookout
Current tower: 1924
Original tower: 1924

What you'll see: Franconia Ridge, Mount Washington, Mount Sunapee, Vermont's Mount Ascutney

Once above tree line, follow the cairns to the Mount Cardigan tower.

THE HIKE

Mount Cardigan is one of those hikes whose reward-to-effort ratio is very high. Although the cabin of the tower features a great big padlock, rendering it inaccessible to visitors unless a lookout is present and on the job, the top of Cardigan is not one of those viewless summits that needs a tower in order to see above the vegetation. Rather, the granite dome atop Mount Cardigan is well above tree line, and the views are stunning in all directions. Meanwhile, although much of the route leads you over granite slab above the trees, the hike is not overly taxing. Note that there is a myriad of trails surrounding Mount Cardigan and there are several worthy routes to the top. The route listed here is the easiest and most commonly traveled.

The West Ridge Trail (orange blazes) starts on the uphill side of the picnic area at the Mount Cardigan State Park parking area and ascends a few railroad-tie stairs and rough stone steps before several long and gradual switchbacks. At 0.3 mile the trail descends to cross a small stream before continuing its ascent. Shortly thereafter, the trail becomes granite and you pass through a stand of impressively large American beech and maple. At 0.5 mile you'll come to a rocky intersection with the South Ridge Trail, which will be your return trip. For now, stay left (north) on West Ridge Trail. The trail climbs steadily, sometimes paralleling a babbling brook.

In a stand of red spruce at 0.8 mile, the trail veers left (northeast). Pay attention to the orange trail blazes and beware of false side trails. Also, take advantage of strategically placed logs and stones as the going can be muddy here.

Mount Sunapee and Mount Kearsarge South from the shoulder of Mount Cardigan

At 1.0 mile the Skyland Trail comes in from the right (south), but you will continue on the West Ridge. Cross a bridge over a small stream and come to another intersection, this one a Y. The West Ridge Trail continues on the left fork (your route); the right fork is called the Ranger Cabin Trail.

At 1.3 miles you break out of the canopy of trees. The remainder of your ascent—and some of your subsequent descent—is above tree line. It is a unique and incredible feeling to be so exposed and out in the open. Enjoy your time up here—it is what makes this hike magical.

Follow orange blazes and large rock cairns to the summit of Mount Cardigan. Fifty feet below the summit, the Clark Trail comes in from the east (this will be the route of your descent—but not yet . . .). First, check out the tower perched atop this rocky knob (1.5 miles). One of the few towers built by state crews and not from a prefabricated kit, this is the original Mount Cardigan tower built in 1924, although the Forest Fire Lookout Association believes there was possibly an earlier wooden tower constructed in 1903. Mountain conditions have beaten this tower, but it is nonetheless impressive, mostly because of the immediate landscape around its perch. If the door to the cabin is padlocked, you can still climb the wooden stairs and get more or less the same views that you get standing on top of the slabby mountaintop itself. The New Hampshire Forest Protection Bureau will staff the tower on some weekends and in times of high fire danger, and firewatchers often allow visitors to enter the cabin. The views include Franconia

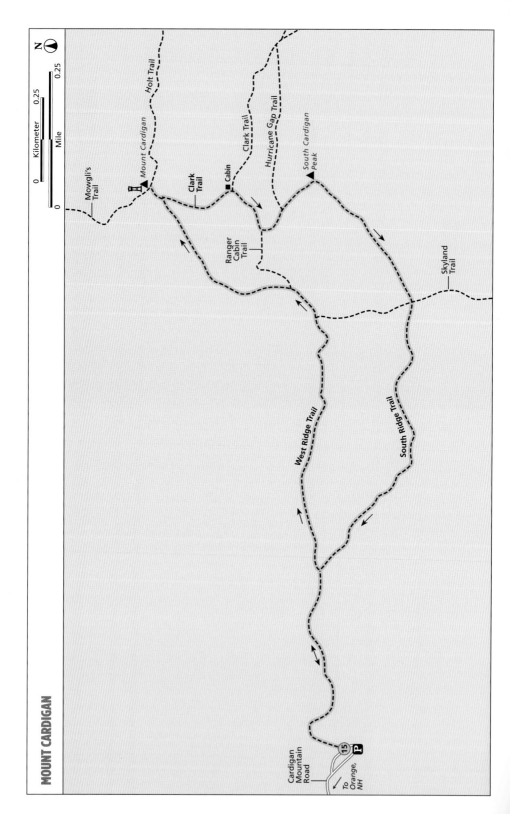

MOUNT CARDIGAN

N

0   Kilometer   0.25

0   Mile   0.25

Mowgli's Trail

Holt Trail

Mount Cardigan

Clark Trail

Clark Trail

Cabin

Hurricane Gap Trail

South Cardigan Peak

Ranger Cabin Trail

West Ridge Trail

South Ridge Trail

Skyland Trail

Cardigan Mountain Road

15

P

To Orange, NH

Ridge, with Mount Washington lurking in the distance to the northeast; Mount Sunapee and another fire tower–adorned peak, Mount Kearsarge, to the south; and Vermont's Mount Ascutney (yet another with a tower) to the west.

Mowgli's Trail (north) and the Holt Trail (east) also depart from the summit, but don't follow these. You could return by the same route, but the South Ridge Trail allows you more time above the tree line and follows a ridgeline from the summit to South Cardigan Peak. To get to the South Ridge Trail, descend the West Ridge Trail to the intersection with the Clark Trail, 50 feet below the summit. Turn left (south) onto the Clark Trail and follow the white blazes and rock piles as you descend along the southern shoulder of Cardigan.

At 1.8 miles you'll reenter some stunted spruce and lots of mountain holly bushes, which turn bright red in autumn, and you'll come to a ranger cabin and an intersection as the Clark Trail continues straight southeast. Turn right (southwest) onto the South Ridge Trail, which, like West Ridge, is marked with orange blazes. You'll come to another intersection at 2.0 miles. The Ranger Cabin Trail goes straight; stay left on South Ridge, which traverses a saddle. The trail remains slabby with bunches of short spruce trees along the way.

In less than a tenth of a mile, ignore another incoming trail (Hurricane Gap Trail) from the left before the saddle ends after a short ascent to South Cardigan Peak and its impressive rocky windbreak structure (2.1 miles). From here, the descent is gradual until you cross the Skyland Trail at 2.5 miles.

In another tenth of a mile, you realize these trails are serious about getting you off the mountain; a steep, scrambly descent brings you to a quiet stream crossing among the spruce, where the going mercifully levels somewhat as you descend a packed-dirt trail with nothing but the chatter of red squirrels interrupting the solitude.

At 2.9 miles hardwoods take back over before the South Ridge Trail terminates at the West Ridge Trail. Turn left (west) onto West Ridge and retrace your steps to the parking area (3.4 miles).

MILES AND DIRECTIONS

0.0 From the parking lot, ascend steps and then switchbacks.

0.5 Intersection with South Ridge Trail (stay left on West Ridge). Follow orange blazes.

1.0 Intersection with Skyland Trail (stay straight on West Ridge). Cross small bridge over a stream.

1.1 Come to a Y with Ranger Cabin Trail (stay on the left fork, which is the West Ridge Trail).

1.5 Summit and tower. To return, descend 50 feet from summit and turn left onto Clark Trail (white blazes).

1.8 Turn right (southwest) onto the South Ridge Trail.

2.0 Intersection with Ranger Cabin Trail (stay left on South Ridge).

2.1 South Cardigan Peak.

2.5 Cross the Skyland Trail.

2.9 Intersection with West Ridge Trail. Take left (west) fork.

3.4 Arrive back at parking area.

16 BELKNAP MOUNTAIN VIA RED AND GREEN TRAILS

A steep but short loop hike through a locally conserved forest to a fire lookout resting upon a rocky perch.

General location: Gilford, New Hampshire
Highest point: 2,378 feet
Elevation gain: 695 feet
Distance: 1.8-mile loop
Difficulty: Easy
Hiking time: 1.5 hours
When to go: Year-round
Fees and permits: None
Trail contact: New Hampshire Forest Protection Bureau, Division of Forests and Lands, Department of Natural and Cultural Resources, 172 Pembroke Rd., Concord, NH; (603) 271-2214; dncr.nh.gov
Canine compatibility: Dog friendly
Trail surface: Dirt and rock

Land status: Public
Other trail users: Hikers, snowshoers
Water availability: None
Special considerations: None
Amenities: None
Maps: USGS West Alton Quad (Note that these trails are not displayed on the map.)
Maximum grade: 24 percent
Trail conditions: A local organization called Belknap Range Trail Tenders stewards these trails, which are part of a larger network. They are narrower than some of the better known and more well-traveled trails. They are well marked and well maintained.

FINDING THE TRAILHEAD

At the junction of NH 11A and Belknap Mountain Road near Gilford, New Hampshire, turn south on Belknap Mountain Road. Go 2.3 miles, then veer left (southeast) on Carriage Road. Pass a parking area (left side) and a gate, which opens daily from 9 a.m. until 6 p.m. from late spring until mid-fall. Carriage Road turns to gravel at 2.9 miles and becomes increasingly twisting, loose, and steep—although passable for most vehicles. The parking area and trailhead are at the end of the road at 3.5 miles. GPS: N43° 30' 58.86" / W71° 22' 42.563"

ABOUT THE LOOKOUT

Height: 44 feet
Cabin dimensions: 10 x 10 feet
Frame construction: Steel
Steps: Wood
Active lookout
Current tower: Constructed in 1915

Original tower: Ten feet were added to this tower in 1979.
What you'll see: Stunning views in all directions of mountains (including Washington, Shaw, and Gunstock) and Lake Winnipesaukee

THE HIKE

The Belknap Range isn't especially high, but it forms the western boundary of Lake Winnipesaukee, a lake that defines beauty whether you're swimming, boating, or looking down upon it from a neighboring mountaintop.

From the northern end of the parking lot, turn left onto the Carriage Road and proceed past the gate to a shed. The Green Trail (your return route) comes in just past the

The Belknap tower's cabin is locked when the firewatcher isn't on duty, but the views from the observation deck just below are stellar.

The Green Trail departs from Belknap tower's southern leg

gate; another twenty steps leads to the intersection with the Red and Blue Trails. The sign for the Red Trail must anticipate a heavy winter as it is placed 20 feet high on a tree.

The Red Trail (red blazes) enters a hardwood forest filled with oak, maple, and birch. It starts steep, and the first quarter of a mile ascends many granite steps placed courtesy of the local volunteer trail advocates, the Belknap Range Trail Tenders (BRATT). At 0.4 mile the ascent mellows briefly to cross a small stream as red spruce begins to take precedence. The going is mellower, but make no mistake: You're always ascending on the Red Trail.

At 0.9 the route passes under a phone line, which continues up through a very thick forest (this sheds light on one of the duties of a firewatcher: keeping the phone line clear). The trail comes to the summit clearing at 1.0 mile.

Without the tower, there is no view from the top of Belknap. There is a communications tower a short distance away through the trees to the south. The clearing can be muddy, but there are several concrete slabs too. The Belknap lookout is an active tower but, while structurally safe, appears a bit rickety. The cabin is locked unless the firewatcher is on duty, but the observation deck affords wonderful views. Lake Winnipesaukee dominates the eastern view, with Mount Shaw and the Ossipee Mountains guarding its northeastern shoreline. North is the peak of Gunstock Mountain and the top of Gunstock Mountain Resort's Panorama quad ski lift. On a clear day, Mount Washington is visible to the north.

There are plenty of trails leading off Belknap Mountain. Behind the tower to the north, the Blue Trail is a longer, more meandering route down to the parking area; it also connects with a trail to Gunstock Mountain. On the southern side, the White Trail leads

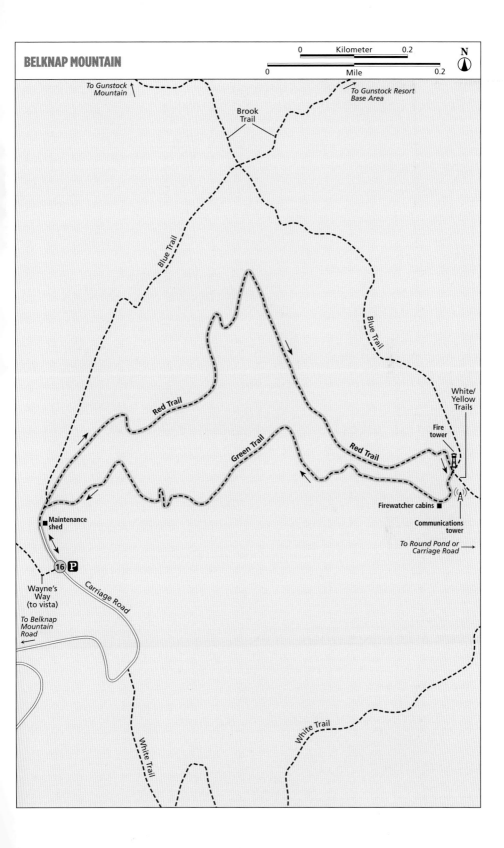

BELKNAP MOUNTAIN

Kilometer
0   0.2
0   0.2
Mile

N

To Gunstock
Mountain

Brook
Trail

To Gunstock Resort
Base Area

Blue Trail

Blue Trail

Red Trail

White/
Yellow
Trails

Fire
tower

Green Trail

Red Trail

Firewatcher cabins

Communications
tower

Maintenance
shed

To Round Pond or
Carriage Road

16 P

Wayne's
Way
(to vista)

Carriage Road

To Belknap
Mountain
Road

White Trail

White Trail

A FIREWATCHER'S TOOL

Whether it's 1910 or 2023, firewatchers across North America have relied on an ageless tool to accurately pinpoint the location of a plume of smoke: the Osborne Fire Finder. Invented by William Bushnell Osborne, a young US Forest Service forester in Oregon, in 1909, the tool is a type of alidade, a tool used to sight a distant object and determine a bearing on it. The Osborne model is a large circular map oriented (daily) to true north, with two vertical sights that can rotate around the map. The crosshairs on the sights are horsehair—that's how fine the readings of this device are.

The firewatcher lines up the fire or smoke through the sights to identify a line on the map where the fire is located—a bearing in degrees (known as an azimuth). Using geographic features and knowledge of the surrounding area, the firewatcher makes an estimate of the fire's location. If the plume is within sight of another tower, the two bearings will give an exact location.

Although technology—that is, aerial surveillance—has replaced many firewatchers and towers, the technology on the ground has remained mostly the same since Osborne spent two decades tinkering with his original models. On New England hikes, when you encounter an active firewatcher at work, most likely an Osborne Fire Finder will dominate the center of the tower's cabin. When you line up the sights and look through the tool, you will be doing the same thing firewatchers have been doing for over a hundred years.

The Osborne Fire Finder has been the tool of firewatchers since the early 1900s.

to other peaks in the Belknap range. This route, however, follows the Green Trail, which served as the original firewatcher's trail and which departs literally from the southern leg of the fire lookout.

Blazed with green markers, the trail starts through a tunnel of spruces and leads to a few cabins. The Green Trail zigs and zags steeply in and out of the woods as it crosses and recrosses under a power line. The going is pretty steep and in some places loose. Arrive back at the parking area at 1.8 miles.

MILES AND DIRECTIONS

0.0   From the parking lot, turn left (north) past a shed. Pass the junction with the Green Trail. Turn right (northeast) on the Red Trail (red blazes).

0.4   Stream crossing.

0.9   Cross under phone line.

1.0   Summit and tower. Follow Green Trail (green blazes) from southern leg of tower.

1.1   Pass cabins.

1.8   Arrive back at shed and parking area.

17 OAK HILL

A moderate hike through a town forest to a historic fire lookout.

General location: East Concord, New Hampshire
Highest point: 961 feet
Elevation gain: 536 feet
Distance: 4.1-mile figure 8
Difficulty: Moderate
Hiking time: 2.25 hours
When to go: Year-round
Fees and permits: None
Trail contact: New Hampshire Forest Protection Bureau, Division of Forests and Lands, Department of Natural and Cultural Resources, 172 Pembroke Rd., Concord, NH; (603) 271-2214; dncr.nh.gov
Canine compatibility: Dogs should be on leash.

Trail surface: Packed dirt with a few rocks
Land status: Public and private
Other trail users: Hikers, skiers, snowshoers
Water availability: None
Special considerations: None
Amenities: None
Maps: USGS Penacook, NH Quad (*Note*: This map doesn't show trails), Concord Trail System Map (can be found at concordnhchamber.com/UploadedFiles/Files/Concord_trail_system_guidebook__maps.pdf)
Maximum grade: 16 percent
Trail conditions: These well-maintained trails in a city forest are well signed and in good shape.

FINDING THE TRAILHEAD

From the intersection of exit 16 off I-93 and West Portsmouth Road, head east on West Portsmouth Road. Come to a traffic circle at 0.1 mile. Turn north onto NH 132 (the second exit off the traffic circle), also known as Mountain Road. At 0.5 mile turn slightly right onto Shaker Road. The parking area for the Oak Hill Hiking Area is on the right (southeast) side of Shaker Road at 2.9 miles. GPS: N43° 16′ 27.444″ / W71° 31′ 43.32″

ABOUT THE LOOKOUT

Height: 65 feet
Cabin dimensions: 8 x 8 feet
Frame construction: Steel
Steps: Wood
Active lookout

Original tower: 1928
Current tower: 1928
What you'll see: New Hampshire's state capitol, Gunstock and Belknap Mountains

THE HIKE

Here is the beauty of New England: Within 7 miles of a state's capital (Concord) and within 22 miles of its largest city (Manchester), you can hike in a peaceful forest like the Oak Hill Hiking Area. One of many recreation areas maintained by the Concord Conservation Commission, a municipal committee chartered in 1971, the Oak Hill trails are wide, moderate in difficulty, and traverse a beautiful forest area. While the fire lookout itself is a bit crowded by two neighboring communications towers, the hike itself is a quiet and well-marked trek through the woods.

The Tower Trail (yellow blazes) leaves the trailhead at the back of the parking area by a kiosk proclaimed to have been constructed by Eagle Scouts. Ledges Pass comes in from the right (south). If you are looking to add mileage either at the front or back end

Within view of New Hampshire's capital, Concord, the tower on Oak Hill stands as majestically as the state house.

An old service road leads to the summit clearing and at some point in history was most likely built or maintained by this grader.

of your journey, Ledges Pass leads 0.3 mile to an open lookout with views of Mount Kearsarge South.

Your ultimate route, however, goes straight through a hardwood forest on the Tower Trail. Pass by several trail intersections as you approach Oak Hill (remember, this is an urban forest). At 0.7 mile you'll come to a large clearing on the left of the trail, but you won't be tempted to explore as the landowner has enthusiastically signed the area with "Keep Out" and "Posted" notices. Veering right and away from the clearing, descend through a stand of hemlocks and across a small steel bridge over a trickling brook.

Pass another intersection at 0.8 mile—the Potter Ridge Trail goes to the right and the Dancing Bear Trail comes from the left. You'll return on Dancing Bear, but for now stay straight on the Tower Trail. In a third of a mile, go through another intersection; you will return to this spot again on your figure-eight descent down Krupa Loop and Dancing Bear. Past the intersection the Tower Trail passes some stagnant pools (prime mosquito-breeding grounds in a wet summer) before descending to a small bridge over a trickle that feeds the pools.

The Tower Trail turns sharply left at 1.6 miles (Ron's Way goes right; you'll follow it on your return). Step over a stone wall and begin the steepest ascent on the hike along a power line (courtesy of the aforementioned communications towers). The stone wall marks a town line between Concord and Loudon, New Hampshire. Reach the summit clearing at 1.9 miles, which is surrounded by trees (without the lookout, you'd have no

OAK HILL

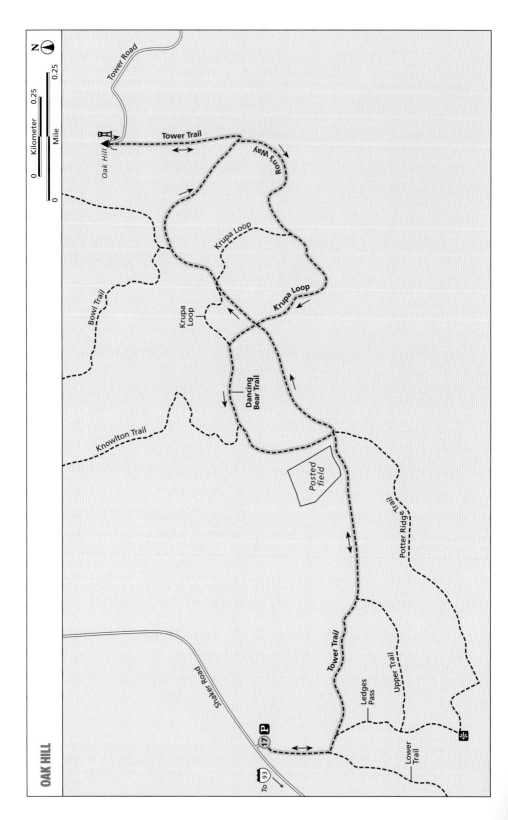

view). On your right as you enter the clearing is an auto road; hikers as well as maintenance vehicles for the comm towers use it to approach from Oak Hill Road on the western side of Oak Hill. On your left is a nearly century-old ancient piece of machinery that one can only assume was used at one time to grade the access road.

The wooden stairs on the tower are steep. To the southwest (and through some tree branches), you can see the golden dome of New Hampshire's capitol in downtown Concord. Northeast are Gunstock Mountain (home to Gunstock Mountain Resort ski area) and Belknap Mountain, which features a fire lookout.

For your descent, take advantage of the many different routes down. From the summit clearing, begin your descent the way you came—on the Tower Trail under the power line. At the stone wall (2.2 miles), leave the Tower Trail to descend on Ron's Way, which descends through another stand of hemlocks before returning to the maple and oak typical of most of the surrounding forest. Ron's Way terminates at Krupa's Loop (2.5 miles), forming a T. Turn left on Krupa's Loop, which crosses the Tower Trail at mile 2.8 and turns into the Dancing Bear Trail at 2.9 miles. The Dancing Bear returns to the Tower Trail at 3.3 miles, which returns you to the trailhead at 4.1 miles.

MILES AND DIRECTIONS

0.0 From the parking lot, follow the Tower Trail, ignoring the many side trails, marked and unmarked.

1.6 Come to a stone wall and intersection with Ron's Way. Stay on Tower Trail (the left fork), step over a stone wall, and follow the trail as it turns sharply left.

1.9 Arrive at summit clearing. To return, retrace your steps the way you came.

2.2 At the stone wall, leave the Tower Trail and instead follow Ron's Way.

2.5 Ron's Way ends at Krupa's Loop, forming a T. Turn left on Krupa's Loop.

2.8 Krupa's Loop crosses the Tower Trail.

2.9 Krupa's Loop turns into Dancing Bear Trail.

3.3 Dancing Bear Trail ends at the Tower Trail. Turn right onto the Tower Trail.

4.1 Arrive back at the trailhead and your vehicle.

18 PAWTUCKAWAY TOWER VIA MOUNTAIN AND SOUTH RIDGE TRAILS

A popular out-and-back hike in a state park with a little bit of every-thing: a moderate hike that includes exciting rocky scrambles to a unique tower with a beautiful view.

General location: Nottingham, New Hampshire
Highest point: 908 feet
Elevation gain: 646 feet
Distance: 5.8 miles
Difficulty: Moderate
Hiking time: 4 hours
When to go: Year-round
Fees and permits: There is a fee to enter Pawtuckaway State Park between mid-May and mid-October.
Trail contact: Pawtuckaway State Park, 7 Pawtuckaway Rd., Nottingham, NH; (603) 895-3031; nhstateparks.org, trailfinder.info/trails/trail/pawtuckaway-state-park
Canine compatibility: Dogs must be leashed. Note that pets are not allowed in the Pawtuckaway Lake beach area.
Trail surface: Dirt, mud, rocks, roots, slab
Land status: Public
Other trail users: Hikers, snowshoers
Water availability: Stream crossing and ponds
Special considerations: Pawtuckaway is a busy park with limited parking for day users. The busy summer months and autumn weekends may be good times to take advantage of the New Hampshire State Parks day-use reservation system at the website above.
Amenities: Restrooms at the parking lot. There's also a shop during Pawtuckaway State Park's open season (mid-May to mid-October).
Maps: USGS Quad Mount Pawtuckaway, NH
Maximum grade: 24 percent
Trail conditions: The first half of this trail is a smooth, packed-dirt forest floor. However, with ponds, vernal pools, and typical East Coast weather (which includes rain), the dirt does turn to mud in places, so it's a good idea to plan accordingly. When the path is wet, avoid stepping around muddy sections and going off the established path, as doing so causes the widening of trails and, therefore, erosion. Higher up, rocky scrambles add excitement but not difficulty.

FINDING THE TRAILHEAD

From the junction of NH 101 (exit 5) and NH 156, follow NH 156 north for 2.1 miles. Turn left onto Mountain Road. In 2.0 miles turn left into Pawtuckaway State Park. The visitor parking lot is immediately on the right. GPS: N43° 04' 42.708" / W71° 10' 20.388"

ABOUT THE LOOKOUT

Height: 35 feet
Cabin dimensions: 10 x 10 feet
Frame construction: Steel
Steps: Wood
Active lookout
Current tower: Built in 1914, raised 10 feet in 1971, and a new cab was installed in 1976.
Original tower: 1914
What you'll see: Pawtuckaway North Mountain, Belknap Mountain, the Boston skyline

Pawtuckaway lookout stands atop Pawtuckaway
South Mountain with views all the way to Boston.

THE HIKE

Pawtuckaway State Park is an absolute gem and a mecca for campers, anglers, boaters, swimmers, hikers, and rock climbers. It's also located in fairly close proximity to some of the urban centers of southern New Hampshire and Massachusetts, which makes it a deservedly well-loved and well-used park. With nearly 200 campsites and plenty more day users, follow this advice: Take advantage of the New Hampshire State Parks day-use reservation system if you plan to make this hike during peak seasons.

Pawtuckaway Tower is located on Pawtuckaway South Mountain, which can be accessed from the south or the west. This route details the longer, more scenic, and more action-packed route via the wide Mountain Trail (marked with intermittent white blazes) and the South Ridge Trail. In reality, the route starts at the state park visitor lot, as there is no parking allowed at the trailhead. Park at the northern end of the lot (by the pit toilets), take a right out of the lot exit, and follow the paved road for 0.4 mile to the trailhead. Have no fear: Even the road walk is scenic as you pass a pond on the left (west) side of the road.

The trailhead is immediately after the pond on the left (west) side of the road. The Woronoco Trail heads right (north), but you should take the Mountain Trail, which follows the pond shoreline. The trail is a wide, well-maintained dirt road here. At 0.9 mile come to an intersection with Round Pond Trail, which goes straight (and which interestingly doesn't lead to Round Pond). Stay on Mountain Trail, which veers to the right (northeast). The trail winds and rolls through hemlocks on a smooth dirt track, which gets muddy in places, particularly during wet seasons. After a stream crossing at 1.3 miles, the trail veers left (north) and uphill, and it becomes a bit rockier.

As you scale the top of a rise, you'll come to some large granite boulders on either side of the trail (if you're hiking with kids, they will definitely want to climb on the rocks) at 1.5 miles. After the boulders the trail crosses a stone wall, evidence of the area's agricultural history. Leaving the stone wall behind, pass a couple of vernal pools (in the summer and fall, you may never be aware that these seasonal wetland habitats even exist). At 1.9 miles there's another wetland worth stopping by as a snack or lunch spot—in this case a beautiful beaver pond through the trees on the left (west) side of the trail. There's no spur trail, and it could easily be missed. It's a peaceful and beautiful spot that's home to ducks and beavers.

From the pond, you gain elevation, and oak and beech begin to take over from the eastern hemlock that dominated the forest so far. At 2.3 miles the Mountain Trail ends at a T intersection. Tower Road goes left; you'll take South Ridge Trail to the right (east). Your turn onto South Ridge Trail (marked with white blazes and white diamonds) officially marks a shift from "peaceful walk in the woods" to "mountain adventure"—albeit a fairly safe and benign adventure. The trail twists, turns, and scales easy rocky ledges. At 2.5 miles pass more boulders and another stone wall. Here, the trail surface becomes slabby granite as the trees shift back to softwoods. The grade steepens as you gain the shoulder of Pawtuckaway South Mountain. At 2.9 miles the trees open in a clearing on a shelf of granite, and the summit is a few steps beyond.

The Pawtuckaway lookout was the first steel fire tower erected in New Hampshire. It isn't the tallest tower, and the topmost cab is padlocked unless a lookout is on duty. It's in wonderful condition, and there is an observation deck just below the enclosed cab. Directly to your north are the Pawtuckaway North and Middle Mountains. Beyond them in the distance is Belknap Mountain (home to another tower in this book). To the south is Pawtuckaway Lake with its islands and coves. On a very clear day (perhaps using your

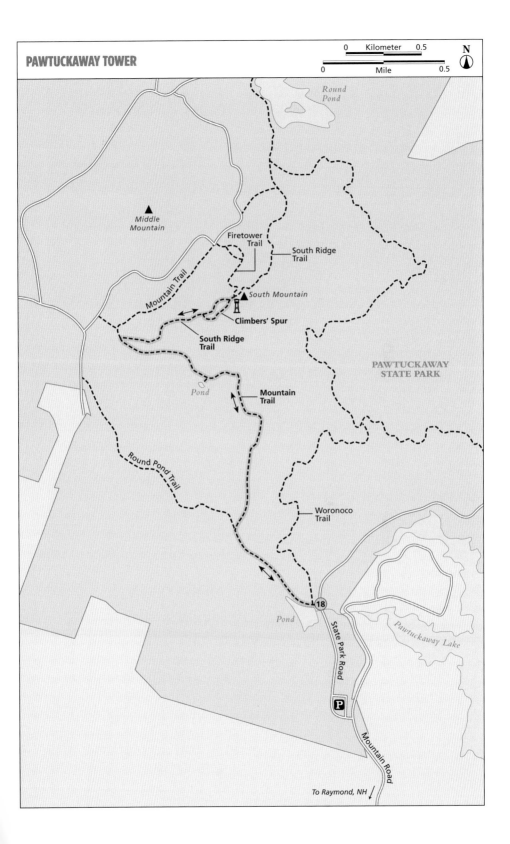

PAWTUCKAWAY TOWER

Kilometer
0   0.5
0   0.5
Mile

N

Round
Pond

Middle
Mountain

Firetower
Trail

South Ridge
Trail

South Mountain

Climbers' Spur

Mountain Trail

South Ridge
Trail

Pond

Mountain
Trail

PAWTUCKAWAY
STATE PARK

Round Pond Trail

Woronoco
Trail

Pond

18

State Park Road

Pond

Pawtuckaway Lake

P

Mountain Road

To Raymond, NH

Tree versus rock—who would win? After an easy bottom half, the final mile to the summit of Pawtuckaway South Mountain is rocky and rooty.

binoculars if your vision is anything less than razor sharp), the skyline of Boston is visible like the tips of tiny toothpicks, including the Hancock Tower and the Prudential Building.

Two trails depart from the northern end of the summit: the continuation of the South Ridge Trail (which leads to Round Pond) and the Firetower Trail (which leads to the end of Mountain Trail and could serve as an alternative—and much longer—route down). This route returns the way you came or, for variety, there is an unsigned spur trail that begins immediately from the southwest leg of the tower (red blazes). The spur, often used by rock climbers to access climbing crags, leads past beautiful clifftops that overlook Pawtuckaway Lake. It reconnects with the South Ridge Trail after a 0.2-mile meander. Turn left (west) on South Ridge Trail and return the way you came.

MILES AND DIRECTIONS

0.0 Exit the northern end of Pawtuckaway State Park visitor lot and turn right (north) onto the main road in the park.

0.3 Pond on left (west) side of road.

0.4 Immediately after the pond, the trailhead is on the left (west) side. Go straight (west) on the Mountain Trail (white blazes).

0.9 Intersection with Round Pond Trail. Follow Mountain Trail, which bends right (northeast).

1.5 Boulders around trail.

1.9 Hidden beaver pond on left (west) side through the trees.

2.3 Intersection with Tower Road and South Ridge Trail at a T intersection. Turn right (east) on South Ridge Trail (white blazes and white diamonds).

2.9 Summit and tower. To return, follow a short climbers' spur (red blazes) until it reunites with South Ridge Trail. Turn left (west) on South Ridge Trail and retrace your steps to return.

5.8 Arrive back at the parking area and your vehicle.

19 STRATHAM TOWER

An easy loop hike in a town park with views all the way to the Atlantic Ocean.

General location: Stratham, New Hampshire
Highest point: 292 feet
Elevation gain: 148 feet
Distance: 0.7 mile
Difficulty: Easy
Hiking time: 45 minutes
When to go: Year-round
Fees and permits: None
Trail contact: Town of Stratham, 10 Bunker Hill Ave., Stratham, NH; (603) 772-4741; strathamnh.gov/stratham-hill-park-shp
Canine compatibility: Pets are allowed but must be under voice or leash control on the trail. In the parking area and on the park lawns, they must be leashed.

Trail surface: Smooth, packed dirt and grass
Land status: Public
Other trail users: Bikers, snowshoers, skiers
Water availability: Available at the trailhead from May until October. Otherwise, none.
Special considerations: None
Amenities: Restrooms and a fountain are available at the Stratham Hill Park trailhead from May until October.
Maps: USGS Quad Newmarket, NH
Maximum grade: 11 percent
Trail conditions: This is a short, easy, very well-maintained trail.

FINDING THE TRAILHEAD

At the intersection of NH 101 and NH 108 in Stratham, follow NH 108 north. In 2.3 miles veer right onto NH 33. The trailhead is on the right side at Stratham Hill Park at 4 miles. GPS: N43° 2′ 29.4″ / W70° 53′ 34.295″

ABOUT THE LOOKOUT

Height: 53 feet
Cabin dimensions: 10-by-10-foot covered outdoor observation deck
Frame construction: Steel
Steps: Steel
No longer active

Current tower: 1931
Original tower: 1931
What you'll see: Great Bay, the Great Bay National Wildlife Refuge, the Atlantic coast, Long Hill

THE HIKE

You won't find adrenaline rushes, wilderness areas, and rocky scrambles on the hike to the fire lookout on Stratham Hill. You may encounter fitness buffs, joggers, and walkers out for a stroll. If you want an easy hike to a beautiful, clean, and well-maintained tower, this is it.

Stratham Hill Park is a town park with playing fields, facilities, a playground, and trails. During the summer months, there may be food trucks and a volunteer-run snack shop if your timing is right (don't count on this, however; these are not regular offerings). The point is that this is a "front country" (the opposite of backcountry) hike.

The Eagle Trail starts by the pavilion at the eastern end of Stratham Hill Park's parking area. At 0.1 mile pass a horseshoe pit. Along the trail are fitness stations, so fitness buffs should be sure to get their pushups and jumping jacks in as appropriate. You get your first glimpse of the tower through the trees to the southwest at 0.3 mile. Shortly thereafter,

Stratham Tower stands atop Stratham Hill.

Schoolkids do pay attention to the occupations of their parents, and President Lincoln's son Robert Lincoln was no exception.

the Lovell Road Trail comes in from the left; stay on the Eagle Trail, which turns right across a nicely mowed meadow.

Arrive at the tower a half mile into your hike. There are picnic tables but no restrooms.

Constructed in 1931 by the New Hampshire Department of Forests and Lands for fire detection, the Stratham Hill tower was used by the state for this purpose until 1976 when the town of Stratham took over responsibility for it with an understanding that the Department of Forests and Lands may use the tower as necessary during times of fire danger.

The tower steps are steep. There is a full observation deck one flight below the top for those who decide that "almost" to the top is high enough. Schoolchildren have decorated the railings of the top deck—a nice effect. The stunning view north is the Great Bay with its National Wildlife Refuge notably without dwellings or buildings along the shoreline. You'll notice that land simply stops when you look east: It's the edge of the North American continent and the beginning of the Atlantic Ocean. Long Hill, with its elevation of 288 feet (just 4 feet shorter than Stratham Hill), stands to the south.

After descending the tower, continue northwest across the meadow to the Lincoln Trail. The Tuck Trail goes right (north), TOWERrectly downhill to the parking area; the Lincoln Trail is more meandering and not quite as steep (it's more in line with the "easy stroll" theme of the route). Both routes are short. At 0.6 mile notice a plaque marking a place where Abraham Lincoln's son Robert—then a student at nearby Exeter Academy—read the Declaration of Independence on July 4, 1860, as the country stood on the brink of civil war. Parents: Your children do pay attention to your occupation.

The trail descends and bends right between two park pavilions and arrives back at the parking area at 0.7 mile.

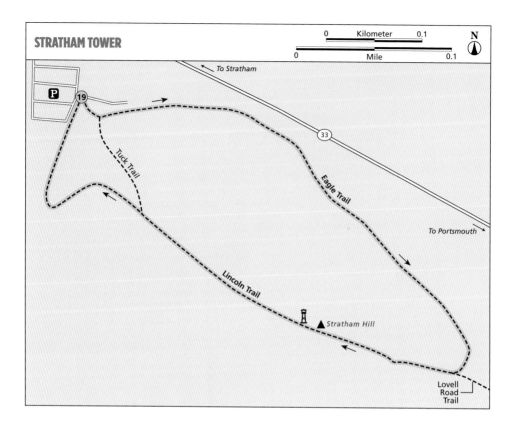

MILES AND DIRECTIONS

0.0 Follow Eagle Trail from eastern end of parking lot.

0.3 Intersection with Lovell Road Trail. Stay on Eagle Trail (right fork).

0.5 Summit and tower. Continue across the meadow beyond the tower (northwest) to Lincoln Trail.

0.6 Arrive at Lincoln plaque.

0.7 Arrive back at parking area.

20 PITCHER MOUNTAIN

An easy loop hike in a privately conserved forest to an active fire lookout.

General location: Stoddard, New Hampshire
Highest point: 2,163 feet
Elevation gain: 278 feet
Distance: 0.75 mile
Difficulty: Easy
Hiking time: 40 minutes
When to go: Year-round
Fees and permits: None
Trail contact: New Hampshire Forest Protection Bureau, Division of Forests and Lands, Department of Natural and Cultural Resources, 172 Pembroke Rd., Concord, NH; (603) 271-2214; dncr.nh.gov. Society for the Protection of New Hampshire Forests,

54 Portsmouth St., Concord, NH; (603) 224-0423; forestsociety.org.
Canine compatibility: Dog friendly
Trail surface: Dirt, rocks
Land status: Public
Other trail users: Hikers, snowshoers
Water availability: None
Special considerations: None
Amenities: None
Maps: USGS Marlow, NH Quad
Maximum grade: 20 percent (a brief, steep uphill section that climbs slabby rock)
Trail conditions: The trail is well marked and dirt, occasionally covered with noise-muffling pine duff.

FINDING THE TRAILHEAD

From the intersection of NH 123 and NH 10 between Marlow and Gilsum, New Hampshire, follow NH 123 east toward Stoddard. The trailhead parking area is on the left at 3 miles. GPS: N42° 5' 34.26" / W72° 8' 23.135"

ABOUT THE LOOKOUT

Height: 25 feet
Cabin dimensions: 10 x 10 feet
Frame construction: Steel
Steps: Wood
Active lookout
Current tower: 1941
Original tower: 1915

What you'll see: Andorra State Forest, the Presidentials (including Mount Lafayette), and Mount Monadnock along the New Hampshire–Vermont border, the Green Mountains

THE HIKE

Anyone who doesn't think the Northeast has a history of forest fires need only look at the Pitcher Mountain tower and its history. The first lookout at the site was established in 1915—a wooden tower with an open platform. A steel tower topped with a wooden cab (similar to towers on Mount Cardigan, Mount Belknap, and Red Hill) replaced the wooden tower in 1925. The tower miraculously survived the 1938 hurricane, but another disaster struck in 1941—a disaster somewhat related to the hurricane.

The timber downed in the northern forests as a result of the 1938 hurricane served as fuel just waiting for ignition. After one of the hottest and driest Aprils on record, a fire was accidentally ignited at a sawmill in Marlow, New Hampshire, that had been set up as trees downed by the hurricane were removed from the forests. The resulting Marlow-Stoddard fire raged for three days, threatening three towns. As the fire approached

The Pitcher Mountain tower on its rocky perch

Stoddard, New Hampshire, residents reportedly lined the town streets with water-filled rowboats as a means of transferring water to the fire.

Among the casualties was the Pitcher Mountain tower, where the firewatcher, Fred Jennings, observed and reported on the fire's movements until he was forced to flee as the tower caught fire. After three days the same thing that set up the fire ended it: weather. The wind died and a late-season snow and rain storm extinguished the blaze. The fire— the largest in New Hampshire history—destroyed many homes and ravaged 27,000 acres.

The current fire tower on Pitcher Mountain is the replacement for the tower that burned in the Marlow-Stoddard fire.

A logging road heads north from the northern side of the parking area; pick up the Blue Trail (blue blazes) before the logging road ducks into the trees. The trail surface is packed dirt with plenty of large rocks and has eroded into a ditch in places. Almost from the start, wild blueberry, black raspberry, and huckleberry bushes line the trail. Help yourself!

At 0.3 mile the trail ascends granite rocks and enters a large clearing. The Blue Trail comes to a T with the Monadnock-Sunapee Greenway; take the right fork of the T. The 49-mile Monadnock-Sunapee Greenway connects (you guessed it) Mount Monadnock and Lake Sunapee. Shortly after the intersection (at mile 0.4) is the summit and tower.

The summit of Mount Monadnock in the clouds

The state of New Hampshire owns a 5-acre plot of land at the summit and the fire tower. The surrounding 11,000 acres make up the Andorra Forest, one of the largest privately conserved forests in the country. The landowner placed the parcel under a conservation easement with the Society for the Protection of New Hampshire Forests in 1990.

The tower stands on a rocky perch and has a good deal of communications equipment and boxes attached to it. As an active fire tower, you may encounter a firewatcher (particularly if you visit on a summer weekend or time of high fire danger). Firewatchers are known to welcome polite visitors into the cabins, so by all means ask. Otherwise, the views from the landing below the cabin are good. Mount Monadnock dominates the southern view, and Mounts Lafayette and Lincoln and the Presidentials are visible to the northeast. Closer by, Island Pond is visible to the east, while Vermont's Green Mountains are west.

After chatting up the firewatcher and soaking in the view, continue southeast on the Monadnock-Sunapee Greenway trail passing the abandoned firewatcher's cabin. After an abrupt descent, the trail turns 90 degrees to the southwest before a large field. Following the edge of the field, pine and spruce needles cover the trail and muffle your footsteps until it veers northwest and away from the field at 0.5 mile. The trail becomes a doubletrack, and signs call it "Fire Wardens Road." At 0.6 mile the trail crosses a power line and returns you to the trailhead at 0.75 mile.

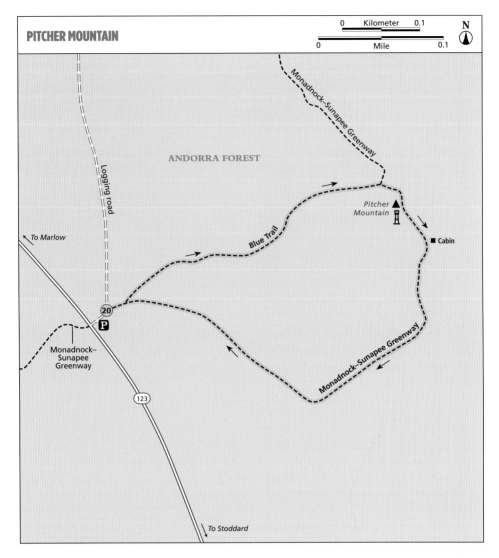

ANDORRA FOREST

Pitcher
Mountain

Cabin

Blue Trail

Monadnock–Sunapee Greenway

Monadnock–Sunapee Greenway

Monadnock–
Sunapee
Greenway

Logging road

To Marlow

20

P

123

To Stoddard

0   Kilometer   0.1

0   Mile   0.1

N

MILES AND DIRECTIONS

0.0 From the parking lot, ascend the Blue Trail (blue blazes).

0.3 Turn right at intersection with Monadnock-Sunapee Greenway trail.

0.4 Summit and tower.

0.5 Trail follows the edge of a field.

0.6 Cross power line.

0.75 Arrive back at parking area.

VERMONT

Of the thirty-eight towers that once stood in Vermont, sixteen remain. The state of Vermont and other organizations and groups have taken on the restoration and upkeep of these sentinels of the mountaintops and forests of the Green Mountain State. The result: some wonderful hikes to towers with views.

The most difficult tower in Vermont to hike to is Glastonbury. It's not included in this volume because most people decide to do it as an overnight backpack. All of the hikes included in this chapter are day hikes of no more than 6 miles. All of them traverse Green Mountain deciduous and coniferous forests. Many scale breathtaking mountaintops. All give you stunning views and scenery.

Hiking in Vermont (and everywhere) has taken off in popularity since men and women first took to the hills to watch for fires. Those hardy individuals would barely see a soul in an entire summer. Try to imagine their experience as you make these hikes and picture summering *alone* in the forests and hills of Vermont.

Looking across the northern Greens from the observation deck atop the Belvidere tower

Vermont's tallest peak, Mount Mansfield, from Camel's Hump, site of the state's first fire lookout

21 BALD MOUNTAIN VIA LONG POND TRAIL

An out-of-the-way Northeast Kingdom out-and-back hike to a tower with a commanding view of the northern Green Mountains and Quebec.

General location: Westmore, Vermont
Highest point: 3,315 feet
Elevation gain: 1,450 feet
Distance: 4.0 miles
Difficulty: Moderate
Hiking time: 3.5 hours
When to go: Year-round
Fees and permits: None
Trail contact: Vermont Department of Forests, Parks and Recreation, (802) 751-0136; fpr.vermont.gov. Westmore Association, westmoreassociation.org. Northwoods Stewardship Center, (802) 723-6551; northwoodscenter.org.
Canine compatibility: Dog friendly

Trail surface: Mostly packed dirt with some grass and a few rocks
Land status: The summit of Bald Mountain is on state-owned land. The rest of the hike is on private property. The owners live nearby and ask hikers to leave no trace and respect their land.
Other trail users: Hikers, snowshoers, skiers
Water availability: None
Special considerations: None
Amenities: None
Maps: USGS Island Pond Quad and USGS Westmore, Vermont Quad
Maximum grade: 34 percent
Trail conditions: This is a well-marked, well-maintained trail.

FINDING THE TRAILHEAD

From the intersection of VT 5A and Long Pond Road next to Lake Willoughby in Westmore, Vermont, turn east on Long Pond Road (dirt). In 2 miles pass the Long Pond boat launch on the right. The trailhead is a small parking area on the left (north) side of the road at 2.1 miles. GPS: N44° 45′ 25.729″ / W72° 1′ 5.322″

ABOUT THE LOOKOUT

Height: 55 feet
Cabin dimensions: 7 x 7 feet
Frame construction: Steel
Steps: Wood
No longer active
Current tower: 1940

Original tower: 1921
What you'll see: Burke Mountain, Mount Pisgah, Mount Hor, the end of Lake Willoughby, Wheeler Mountain, Quebec

THE HIKE

Bald Mountain perhaps flies under the radar of peaks with rocky summits above tree line (or that at least don't have two other peaks in Vermont with the same name). However, the Bald Mountain in Westmore is the only mountain in its immediate area that's over 3,000 feet, and even though its summit is tree covered (neither of the other two Bald Mountains in Vermont is bald either), the former fire lookout tower gives hikers one-of-a-kind views of Vermont's Northeast Kingdom.

Three trails access the summit of Bald Mountain. The Telegraph Trail (also known as the Lookout Trail) is unmaintained but passable. Mad Brook and Long Pond Trails pass

A hiker takes photos from the tower cab on Bald Mountain.

over private land with landowner permission. Parking can be tight at Mad Brook. Long Pond Trail, slightly shorter than Mad Brook, has ample parking and is easy to access from the Lake Willoughby area.

Long Pond Trail departs from the northern end of the parking area around a large gate. The trail starts as an overgrown logging road before forking right by a sign that says "Trail." Shortly thereafter (mile 0.2) the trail forks right again at the end of a clearing. The trail bends to the left and narrows to become more like a trail and less like a road. The trail follows blue blazes from here on. Cross a small stream at 1.0 mile. Several other streamlets follow, but none are reliable water sources.

After the stream crossings the ascent increases as the trail zigs and zags. Cross a small split-log bridge, and the ascent begins in earnest at 1.4 miles as the trail makes a few switchbacks before settling on a direct ascent. Look for a unique feature: a ledgy overhang on the trail, right at 1.7 miles, framed by two roots of a birch form a woodsy cave. Continue climbing after the cave to a hefty bridge that crosses a 1-foot-wide ditch. Reach the summit at 2.0 miles.

The tower and firewatcher's cabin stand in a clearing. Without the tower, there would be no view. And without local advocacy groups, there would be no climbing the tower: The state of Vermont acquired the summit land in 2000. Three nonprofits—the Green Mountain Club, the Westmore Association, and the Northwoods Stewardship Center— joined forces to replace the wooden steps and landings on the tower (which replaced a

The Bald Mountain tower gives hikers a view of Vermont's Northeast Kingdom.

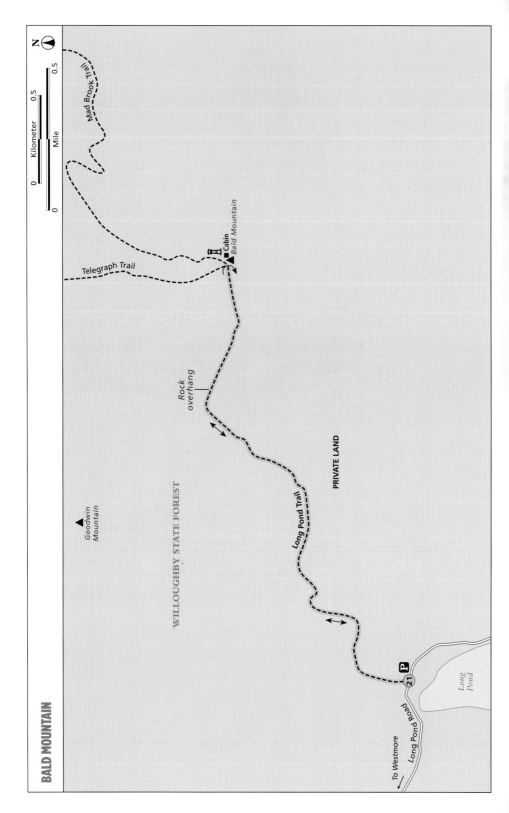

BALD MOUNTAIN

N

Kilometer   0.5   0.5

Mile

0   0

Mad Brook Trail

Telegraph Trail

Cabin
Bald Mountain

Rock
overhang

Goodwin
Mountain

WILLOUGHBY STATE FOREST

Long Pond Trail

PRIVATE LAND

P
21

Long Pond

Long Pond Road

To Westmore

Looking south from the Bald Mountain tower toward Bald Hill and Newark Ponds with Burke Mountain looming beyond

predecessor that was destroyed in the hurricane of 1938). Meanwhile, NSC tackled the cabin in 2016. In the effort to restore the cabin, NSC, a service and education program that employs 15-to-20-year-olds, reports that its crews carried 435 pieces of lumber in 240 trips up this trail as part of the cabin restoration. (So let's not complain about a heavy backpack!) They also got support from student volunteers from Burke Mountain Academy, a local private high school.

From the tower, the views are 360 degrees. Newark and Bald Mountain Ponds are south with the ski trails of Burke Mountain (site of Vermont's first fire tower) looking down on them. To the west is a sliver of Lake Willoughby, the alpine lake wedged between Mounts Pisgah and Hor, which are also visible. North is Quebec on the far shores of Lake Memphremagog, and the Presidentials tower to the east in New Hampshire.

The Mad Brook Trail comes in from the northern side of the clearing as does the Telegraph Trail. Retrace your steps to return to your car.

MILES AND DIRECTIONS

0.0 From the parking lot, walk around the gate and follow the grassy logging road.

1.0 Cross small streams.

1.7 Pass a cave formed by a rocky overhang and birch roots.

2.0 Summit and tower. Return by the same route.

4.0 Arrive back at the trailhead.

22 BELVIDERE MOUNTAIN VIA THE LONG TRAIL

Hike a moderate out-and-back through beautiful mixed Vermont forest to a tower with an open observation deck.

General location: Eden, Vermont
Highest point: 3,360 feet
Elevation gain: 2,087 feet
Distance: 5.4-mile round-trip
Difficulty: Strenuous
Hiking time: 4.5 hours
When to go: Year-round except during mud season
Fees and permits: None
Trail contact: Green Mountain Club, 4711 Waterbury-Stowe Rd., Waterbury Center, VT; (802) 244-7037; greenmountainclub.org
Canine compatibility: Dogs are allowed on the Long Trail under voice or leash control.

Trail surface: Varied. Dirt and rocks.
Land status: Public
Other trail users: Hikers, snowshoers
Water availability: Unreliable
Special considerations: None
Amenities: None
Maps: USGS Hazens Notch, VT Quad
Maximum grade: 27 percent
Trail conditions: This Long Trail section is well maintained but rugged. The trail is marked by white trail markers and can be uneven and even overgrown in places.

FINDING THE TRAILHEAD

From the junction of US 109 and US 118, follow US 109 north. At 0.6 mile Eden Pond appears on your left (north). The trailhead is on the left (north) at 1.7 miles. GPS: N44° 45' 48.384" / W72° 35' 17.556"

ABOUT THE LOOKOUT

Height: 50 feet
Open observation deck dimensions: 7 x 7 feet
Frame construction: Steel
Steps: Wood
No longer active

Current tower: 1940
Original tower: 1919
What you'll see: The Greens, the Cold Hollows, the largest asbestos mine in the United States, and, on a clear day, Mount Washington

THE HIKE

Belvidere is a northern Vermont classic, but just enough out of the way that it doesn't attract the crowds typical of other classics. Inside the region known as Vermont's Northeast Kingdom, there aren't many stores or other amenities on the way to Belvidere, so plan ahead for food, water, and fuel for your vehicle. While the hamlets of Waterville and Belvidere (from the south) do have general stores, you may be well-advised to fuel up and pick up any necessities in Cambridge, 20 miles south of the trailhead (or call ahead for store hours in the smaller towns). The nearest town to the north is Eden, 5 miles away.

The trail departs from the northern end of the parking area and gently ascends for 0.3 mile before crossing an unmarked logging road. After the road, it descends to cross a small streambed (which may or may not have running water). The trail follows the stream until 0.6 mile, where it widens and begins to climb again. At 1 mile it scales a

The lookout on Belvidere Mountain was built in
1940 after a hurricane ruined its predecessor.

A hiker takes in the view on the summit of Belvidere without having to climb the tower

steep ascent before leveling off in a forest of mixed hardwoods. At 1.4 miles the trail becomes a rocky slab, then climbs steeply before leveling again in a stand of hemlocks.

The fun really begins at 2 miles when the trail narrows before encountering some boulders and rocks that add variety to the hike. Cross a rockfall at 2.3 miles as you gain the shoulder of Belvidere, known as the Belvidere Saddle. The saddle spans the two summits of Belvidere. At 2.5 miles come to the intersection with the Forester's Trail—that is, the spur to the summit—on the right (southeast). The LT continues to the lower of these summits and on to Tillotson Camp, a shelter nearly a mile north. You, however, are heading to the main summit of Belvidere, so follow the Forester's Trail, which passes a fire ring and a tent site at 2.7 miles, and the summit is a few more steps from there.

The tower, an Aermotor design, has an open observation deck. Its predecessor comes with a pretty amazing story: According to Ron Kemnow's Eastern US Lookouts site (easternlookouts.weebly.com), the now defunct *Orleans County Monitor* reported that the original firewatcher on Belvidere, L. T. Kinsley, built the original wooden tower—and a firewatcher's cabin—in 1919. Did he have help? The writeup doesn't specify. Alone or not, firewatchers are special people to be sure. The wooden tower was struck by lightning and repaired in 1931, and it stood until 1938, when it likely fell prey to the hurricane of 1938.

The current tower was built in 1940. It is one of just three towers remaining on the Long Trail (the others are on Glastonbury and Stratton Mountains). The wooden stairs are steep, and the platform is airy. On a beautiful day, the view is difficult to beat. From the deck, Vermont's most remote region—its Northeast Kingdom—stretches in all directions. To the south, you can see the spine of the Greens and to the north the

BELVIDERE MOUNTAIN

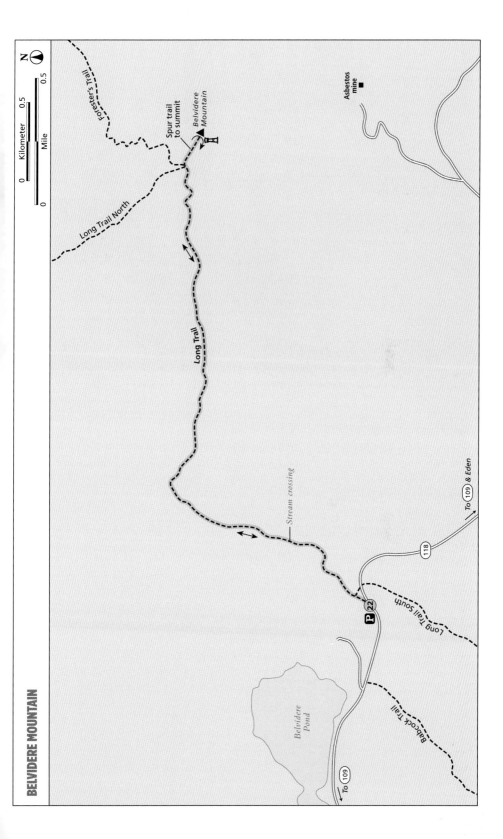

N

Foerster's Trail

Long Trail North

Spur trail to summit

Belvidere Mountain

Long Trail

Stream crossing

Asbestos mine

Long Trail South

P 22

118

To 109 & Eden

To 109

Belvidere Pond

Babcock Trail

Kilometer   0.5

0   0.5   Mile

Vermont's Cold Hollows from the observation deck on the Belvidere tower

Cold Hollow Mountains. Directly east, you can also see the remains of the largest former asbestos mine in the United States. On a clear day, Mount Washington is visible 70 miles to the east.

From the summit, the Forester's Trail continues toward the Frank Post Trail. You, however, will follow the same route on which you came in order to return to your car.

MILES AND DIRECTIONS

0.0 From the parking lot, follow Long Trail northeast.

0.3 Cross an unmarked logging road.

2.0 Ascend steep section over boulders and rocks.

2.3 Rockfall.

2.5 Turn right (southeast) onto spur trail to summit.

2.7 Summit and tower. Return by the same route.

5.4 Arrive back at your car and the trailhead.

23 MOUNT ELMORE LOOP

A popular family loop hike complete with rocky scrambles, a tower with awesome 360-degree views, and a giant balancing boulder that seemingly defies gravity.

General location: Lake Elmore, Vermont
Highest point: 2,608 feet
Elevation gain: 1,450 feet
Distance: 3.9 miles
Difficulty: Moderate
Hiking time: 3.5 hours
When to go: Year-round
Fees and permits: Elmore State Park charges a moderate entrance fee.
Trail contact: Elmore State Park, 856 Vermont Route 12, Lake Elmore, VT; (802) 888-2982; vtstateparks.com/elmore.html. Vermont Department of Forests, Parks and Recreation, Barre Office, 5 Perry St., Suite 20, Barre, VT; (802) 476-0182; fpr.vermont.gov. Green Mountain Club, 4711 Waterbury-Stowe Rd., Waterbury Center, VT; (802) 244-7037; greenmountainclub.org.
Canine compatibility: Dog friendly. Dogs must have proof of current rabies vaccination to enter Elmore State Park. Dogs are not allowed at the lake area. Leash must be under 10 feet long.
Trail surface: Dirt, gravel, and occasional rocky scrambles
Land status: Public
Other trail users: Hikers, snowshoers
Water availability: Unreliable
Special considerations: None
Amenities: The state park has restrooms and a public beach. (No dogs allowed at the beach.)
Maps: USGS Hyde Park Quad
Maximum grade: 35 percent
Trail conditions: This hike has everything from a wide service road to rocky scrambles. The scrambles are generally straightforward and tend not to be airy. It's a well-maintained trail, although the surface does get loose. The downhill route on Ridge Trail has particular issues with washouts and erosion, and maintenance of the trail is ongoing.

FINDING THE TRAILHEAD

From the junction of Routes 100 and 12 in Morrisville, take Route 12 south to Elmore State Park. The entrance to the park is on the west side of the road just before Lake Elmore. From the toll booth at the entrance to the state park, follow the road for a half mile to the trailhead. There is an old chimney stack where a cabin used to stand and picnic tables in the woods near the trailhead parking area. GPS: N44° 32′ 22.704″ / W72° 32′ 10.068″

ABOUT THE LOOKOUT

Height: 60 feet
Cabin dimensions: 7 x 7 feet
Frame construction: Steel
Steps: Wood
No longer active

Current tower: 1938
Original tower: 1938
What you'll see: Mount Mansfield, Jay Peak, Mount Washington, and many others

THE HIKE

The Worcester Range lies across the Stowe/Waterbury valley to the east of the towering Mount Mansfield ridge. Mount Elmore is the lowest peak in the Worcester Range, but also one of the more prominent and more hiked due to its position at the northern end of the range and its fire tower on top.

The Elmore Tower graces the top of the first peak of Vermont's Worcester Range.

From the parking area, follow the Fire Tower Trail (not the Nature Trail). The e starts uphill on a fire road dotted with blue Catamount Ski Trail markers. Walk around the gate, passing the stone chimney on the right in the woods and another chimney column on the left. A few minutes later, Ridge Trail exits to the right (0.2 mile). You'll close your loop here later.

At 0.5 mile, at the end of the fire road, the Catamount Ski Trail continues straight ahead. Take a sharp right (northwest) up stone steps and continue uphill on a singletrack. Look for blue blazes now instead of the plastic Catamount Trail markers.

The trail parallels a brook along a fairly steep but smooth grade. The incline eases somewhat as the trail swings sharply right and then continues climbing up stone steps. From here it winds up the hillside, gaining altitude in waves.

At 1.4 miles you reach a spur to a lookout on the left. The lookout is

Young hikers explore Mount Elmore.

the site of the old firewatcher's cabin, which was built by Civilian Conservation Corps (CCC) crews. All that remains is the stone chimney and rusty stove. The view, mainly to the east over Lake Elmore, stretches as far as Mount Washington in New Hampshire on a clear day. This is a nice destination in its own right, three-quarters of the way to the summit.

To continue to the fire tower, return to the main trail, climbing on more rugged, vertical terrain. After the short scramble, the trail levels off and arrives at a T intersection. Turn left (south) and go just a few steps to reach the fire tower at 1.7 miles. The Vermont Division of Forestry built the tower after the hurricane of 1938, using emergency funds. The view is phenomenal considering the short hike, with Mount Mansfield dominant to the west. Jay Peak and several peaks in southern Quebec fill the northern horizon. The Presidential Range, the Franconia Ridge, and Mount Moosilauke poke up along the eastern skyline. The rest of the Worcester Range and the main spine of the Green Mountains lie to the south.

The beauty of this hike is that you're not done just because you've reached the tower. After a rest and a pause to take in the views (for which you can thank the lookout, as the summit of Elmore is tree-covered and therefore wouldn't have the views without it), return to the T and head north, traversing the upper ridge of the mountain. You're now on Ridge Trail, which was rebuilt and extended by state trail crews in 2012. The trail is flat at first and then downhill, and the terrain is mossy, coniferous, and green—the stuff of elves, fairies, and trolls. It passes two outcrops—the first spies Mount Mansfield and

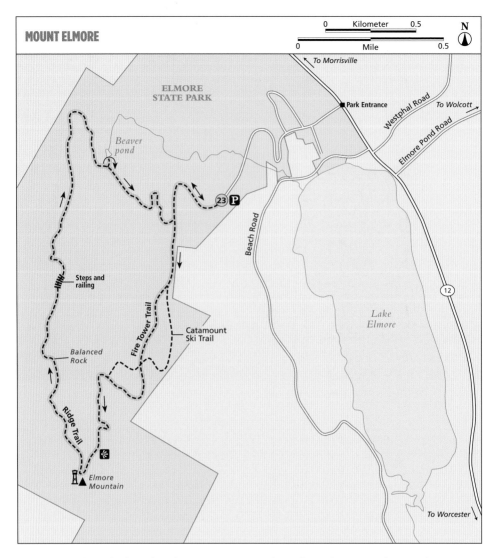

the second overlooks Lake Elmore. Arrive at Balanced Rock at 2.1 miles. As the name implies, Balanced Rock is a large boulder, about 20 feet long and 6 feet high, perched on a rock outcropping. It seems to defy gravity. Go ahead and push it with all your might—you can't move it.

After pondering Balanced Rock, continue along Ridge Trail, which descends gently. For all of the scrambling and rocks on the way up, the way down is mostly mellow, packed with soft dirt. At mile 3.0 descend over two wooden stairways (built over a pitch that pales in comparison to some of the rocky uphill scrambles before the fire tower, but for whatever reason didn't warrant human-made steps or railings). A short way later (mile 3.2), cross a bridge over a streambed. To the left, you'll notice the stream spills into a beaver pond. Just past the bridge, there's a faint spur that leads you past some of the beaver dams—wonders of natural engineering and determination. Back on the trail, you'll come to an example of human engineering as the trail switchbacks through a major washout of

Push on the Balanced Rock all you like—it won't move.

the old trail. State park crews plan to continue to adjust the route here in order to create a trail that sheds water more efficiently, so expect further changes in the coming years. After crossing another bridge over a streambed, Ridge Trail ends at the Catamount Trail at mile 3.6. Turn left and follow the Cat to the parking area at mile 3.9.

MILES AND DIRECTIONS

0.0   Start at the trailhead for the Fire Tower Trail, heading uphill on a fire road.

0.5   Turn sharply right at the end of the fire road.

1.4   Pass a short spur to the site of the former firewatcher's cabin.

1.7   Turn left to reach the summit and tower. After the tower, traverse the summit ridge north.

2.1   Balanced Rock!

3.2   Beaver pond.

3.6.   Turn left back onto Catamount Trail.

3.9   Arrive back at the parking area.

24 CAMEL'S HUMP

A beautiful lollipop hike past a World War II bomber plane crash site to one of Vermont's most iconic peaks—and its first fire lookout site.

General location: Duxbury, Vermont
Highest point: 4,083 feet
Elevation gain: 2,616 feet
Distance: 6.4 miles
Difficulty: Strenuous
Hiking time: 5.75 hours
When to go: Year-round except during mud season
Fees and permits: None
Trail contact: Camel's Hump State Park, vtstateparks.com/camelshump .html. Vermont Department of Forests, Parks, and Recreation, 111 West St., Essex Junction, VT; (802) 879-6565; fpr.vermont.gov. Green Mountain Club, 4711 Waterbury-Stowe Rd., Waterbury Center, VT; (802) 244-7037; greenmountainclub.org.
Canine compatibility: Dog friendly. Dogs must be on leash and on the trail in the alpine zone at the summit.
Trail surface: Dirt, rocks, rocky scrambles
Land status: Public
Other trail users: Hikers, snowshoers, skiers
Water availability: The trail crosses Hump Brook at mile 2.1.

Special considerations: Camel's Hump is one of Vermont's most popular hikes, and although this isn't the most commonly used trail (that distinction belongs to the Burrows Trail in Huntington), this parking area fills up on holiday weekends and during foliage season. There is an overflow lot 0.4 mile downhill from the main lot (with a cutoff trail back to the main trailhead), which will also fill. Don't park on the roadway as emergency vehicles need to be able to pass by. Cars that park on the road get towed.
Amenities: The ADA-accessible Camel's Hump View Trail is an 0.8-mile loop that features views of the summit. It leaves from the lower overflow parking lot.
Maps: USGS Huntington, Vermont Quad and USGS Waterbury, Vermont Quad
Maximum grade: 35 percent at a rocky scramble near the summit
Trail conditions: This is a rugged but well-traveled and well-marked trail.

FINDING THE TRAILHEAD

Approaching from the west, turn onto Cochran Road at the intersection of Cochran Road and US 2 in Jonesville and go over the Winooski River on the Jonesville Bridge. In 0.1 mile turn left (east) on Duxbury Road. Duxbury Road parallels the river and turns to dirt at 4.2 miles. At 6.0 miles turn right (south) on Camel's Hump Road. Stay on Camel's Hump Road past Marshall Road (which comes in from the right at 7.1 miles) and Scrabble Road (which comes in from the left at 8.2 miles). At 9.0 miles an overflow parking lot is on the left. This is also the parking lot in wintertime. The main parking area is at the end of the road at 9.4 miles.

Approaching from the east, at the traffic circle at the intersection of VT 100 and US 2, take the second exit onto VT 100 heading east. In 0.2 mile turn right (south) on Winooski Street, which crosses the Winooski River on a narrow bridge. Immediately after the bridge, turn right (west) onto River Road (dirt). At mile 3.9 turn left (south) on Camel's Hump Road. Follow directions above to the trailhead. GPS: N44° 18' 58.176" / W72° 51' 0.108"

The summit of Camel's Hump is completely unobstructed and did not require a tower. Background: Mount Mansfield.

ABOUT THE LOOKOUT

Height: This site never had a tower.
Cabin dimensions: N/A
Frame construction: N/A
Steps: N/A
Original lookout: 1911

What you'll see: Mount Mansfield, New Hampshire's Presidentials, Lake Champlain, New York's Adirondacks, Quebec

THE HIKE

What, no tower? Camel's Hump was the first lookout site established in Vermont for obvious reasons: The views are amazing, unobstructed, and 360 degrees. No tower was required—the Vermont Forestry Department merely constructed a concrete table at the summit on which a firewatcher could lay down maps of the surrounding areas in order to call in a plume of smoke that could be seen for miles in all directions.

Camel's Hump is Vermont's third-highest peak (a distinction it shares with Mount Ellen, visible to the south) and Vermont's highest undeveloped peak. It is also the state's most recognizable mountain, visible from high points all over Vermont, New Hampshire, and New York (and quite a few low points also). The hikes up the Hump are popular and beloved by locals and visitors alike, which is the only drawback of hiking trips here. A sunrise visit will almost always be solitary and peaceful; midday on a weekend will almost always be crowded.

Pick up the Monroe Trail (blue blazes) on the western end of the parking area by a kiosk and trail register. Named for early Green Mountain Club member Will Monroe, a University of Vermont professor who built original sections of Vermont's Long Trail and lived on a farm near the trailhead (and who is buried with his wife and dogs nearby),

Hikers examine the wreckage of a World War II bomber plane that has been patriotically decorated.

the Monroe Trail aggressively gains altitude from the beginning, bending south at 0.1 mile. Small bridges cross streamlets at 0.3 and 0.8 mile. The pitch lessens a bit and the trail comes to a junction with the Dean Trail at mile 1.3. The Dean Trail was built by the Vermont Youth Conservation Corps and makes a nice loop hike to the summit of Camel's Hump. It also leads to the Hump Brook tent site for those wishing to make Camel's Hump an overnight adventure.

This route, however, stays on the Monroe Trail. At 1.9 miles the trail surface becomes rockier as the Monroe bends 90 degrees to the southeast to traverse around a rocky crag, then crosses Hump Brook twice. The vegetation, which has been mostly mixed hardwood to this point, shifts to red spruce, balsam fir, and paper birch. At 2.2 miles the trail veers back toward the northwest and the trail surface turns to sheer rock.

At 2.5 miles the Alpine Trail crosses the Monroe. The Alpine Trail's main purpose is to serve as a cutoff for end-to-end hikers who choose to avoid the summit of Camel's Hump in bad weather. Turn left (west) on the Alpine Trail. (You'll return via the Monroe.) Ascend a few stone steps before you get your first taste of Camel's Hump views: At 2.7 miles at a break in the trees, you can look across Wind Gap, a valley between Camel's Hump and Mount Ethan Allen, named for the Revolutionary War hero and Vermont folk hero.

At 2.9 miles look for a short spur trail that leads to the fuselage of a World War II B–24 Liberator bomber that crashed into Camel's Hump in 1944, claiming nine lives including the pilot. Just one airman survived. Just uphill, another spur (at mile 3.0) leads to more plane wreckage.

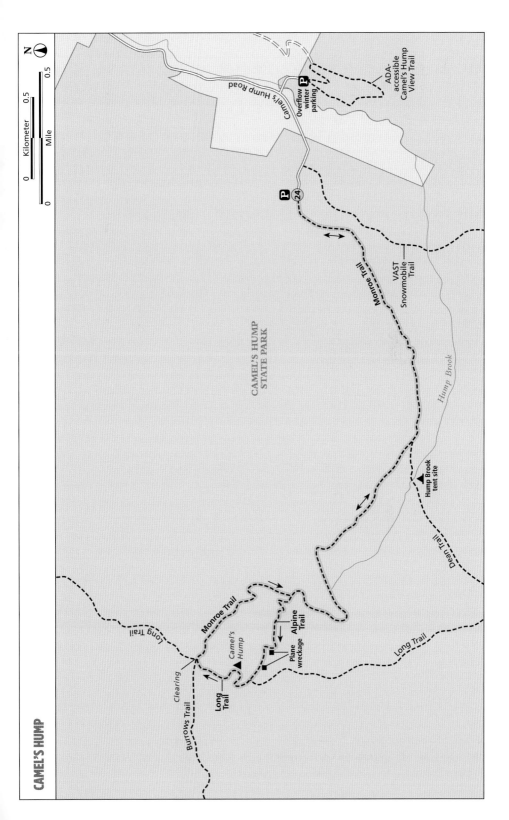

CAMEL'S HUMP

CAMEL'S HUMP
STATE PARK

Long Trail

Burrows Trail

Clearing

Monroe Trail

Camel's Hump

Long Trail

Plane
wreckage

Alpine
Trail

Long Trail

Dean Trail

Hump Brook
tent site

Hump Brook

Monroe Trail

VAST
Snowmobile
Trail

P
24

Camel's Hump Road

Overflow
winter
parking

P

ADA-
accessible
Camel's Hump
View Trail

N

0   0.5   Kilometer   0.5

0   Mile

Back on the Alpine Trail, the going gets steeper as the trail becomes a craggy scramble at mile 3.1. In the midst of this rocky pitch, the Alpine Trail ends at a T with the Long Trail. Turn right (north) on the Long Trail. Enter the alpine area, home to the hardiest of alpine grasses and plants—but they are also incredibly fragile when it comes to hikers walking on them. Walk only on rocks in this unique area so as not to damage the vegetation, some of which is endangered.

Arrive at the summit at 3.4 miles, taking in breathtaking 360-degree views. Lake Champlain dominates the western view with the Adirondacks, including Mount Marcy (New York's highest peak), Hurricane Mountain, and Whiteface Mountain, rising directly out of the lake. North is Mount Mansfield, and on a clear day, you can see all the way to Quebec. East is the Worcester Range with New Hampshire's Presidentials beyond. The tallest mountains to the south are Mounts Ellen and Abraham.

Camel's Hump has had several names. French explorer Samuel de Champlain called it the "Resting Lion" in 1609; Vermont politician Ira Allen called it "Camel's Rump" in the 1700s. The name "Hump" first appeared on maps around 1830. I prefer the Abenaki name Tawabotiiwajo, which means "place to sit in mountain" or "mountain seat." Often a solid approach is not to eat your sandwich right on the summit; rather, try to find a more out-of-the-way nook in the rocks nearby the Tawabotiiwajo summit area and then sit and reflect on the beauty all around.

Although there is no longer a firewatcher on Camel's Hump, the Green Mountain Club stations a caretaker at the summit to educate visitors about the fragile vegetation and to take pictures. To descend, continue north on the Long Trail, continuing to tread only on the rocks (and not on fragile vegetation) as the trail leads back into the stunted balsams. Come to a flat clearing at mile 3.6. Here, the Burrows Trail comes in from the Huntington (west) side of Camel's Hump. The Long Trail continues north. This route, however, descends to the southeast on the Monroe Trail. The trail proceeds without many turns or bends until coming to the junction with the Alpine Trail at 4.2 miles, which goes right (west). Continue straight on the Monroe Trail past the intersection with the Dean Trail (mile 5.4). Stay on Monroe, retracing your steps to the trailhead at 6.4 miles.

MILES AND DIRECTIONS

0.0 From the western end of the main trailhead parking lot, pick up Monroe Trail.

1.3 Junction with Dean Trail on left (west). Stay straight on Monroe Trail.

2.1 Cross and recross Hump Brook.

2.5 Junction with Alpine Trail. Turn left (northwest) onto Alpine Trail.

2.9 Spur trail to World War II plane wreckage.

3.0 Spur trail to more plane wreckage.

3.1 Alpine Trail ends in a T with Long Trail. Turn right (north) on Long Trail.

3.2 Enter the alpine zone, taking care not to tread on vegetation.

3.4 Summit! Continue north on the Long Trail.

3.6 Clearing where Burrows, Long, and Monroe Trails intersect. Turn right (southeast) to descend on Monroe Trail.

4.2 Junction with Alpine Trail. Stay straight on Monroe Trail.

5.4 Junction with Dean Trail. Stay straight on Monroe Trail.

6.4 Arrive back at your car and the parking area.

25 SPRUCE MOUNTAIN

Popular out-and-back climb over varied terrain through a mixed hardwood and softwood forest with impressive views from a classic fire lookout.

General location: Plainfield, Vermont
Highest point: 3,008 feet
Elevation gain: 1,132 feet
Distance: 4.4 miles out and back
Difficulty: Moderate
Hiking time: 3.25 hours
When to go: Year-round
Fees and permits: None
Trail contact: Vermont Department of Forests, Parks, and Recreation, Barre District, 5 Perry Rd., Barre, VT; (802) 476-0182; fpr.vermont.gov
Canine compatibility: Dog friendly. Dogs should be under control at all times and on leash around other hikers.
Trail surface: Varied. Packed dirt, rocky, and smooth, hard bedrock.
Land status: Public

Other trail users: Hikers, skiers, snowshoers
Water availability: Small stream crossing at mile 1.2, however, carrying water is recommended.
Special considerations: None
Amenities: None
Maps: USGS Barre East and Knox Mountain Quads, trailfinder.info/trails/trail/spruce-mountain
Maximum grade: 27 percent
Trail conditions: You could easily push a baby stroller along the mostly flat dirt doubletrack of the first 0.75 mile, but after the fork toward Seyon Lodge, the surface becomes more uneven and much rockier. Some of the smooth granite can be slippery when wet.

FINDING THE TRAILHEAD

From the junction of Route 2 and Main Street in the hamlet of Plainfield, turn southeast on Main Street. Cross the Winooski River (which parallels Route 2) and immediately turn right (south) on Mill Street. In less than a tenth of a mile, veer left (east) on Brook Road. At 1.1 miles Brook Road turns to dirt. At 1.6 miles turn left (southeast) up a hill on Fowler Road. When Fowler Road ends, turn right (south) on East Hill Road after 3 miles. Turn left (east) on Spruce Mountain Road at 3.6 miles. The trailhead—a spacious gravel parking area—is at the end of Spruce Mountain Road at 4.8 miles. Spruce Mountain Trail departs from the eastern end of the parking area. GPS: N44° 14' 3.876" / W72° 22' 32.735"

ABOUT THE LOOKOUT

Height: 55 feet
Cabin dimensions: 7 x 7 feet
Frame construction: Steel
Steps: Wood
No longer active

Current tower: 1943
Original tower: 1919
What you'll see: Camel's Hump, Mount Mansfield, the Presidentials, Noyes Pond, Signal Mountain

THE HIKE

Spruce Mountain is a local favorite. It's located in Vermont's first state forest (the L. R. Jones State Forest, established in 1909) and part of the larger Groton Management Unit (a parcel of over 27,000 acres that the state of Vermont manages both for conservation and recreational purposes). The area includes two state parks, two state forests, and two wildlife management areas. It is a hiking, paddling, camping, skiing, snowmobiling,

The lookout on Spruce Mountain is just one feature in the summit clearing.

rock climbing, and horse-riding paradise. The Spruce Mountain Trail starts mellow and gets steeper and rockier the farther along you go.

From the trailhead, pass a kiosk and metal gate and head east on a wide, smooth doubletrack. The trail is more road than path for the first mile, cutting through dense hardwoods. At mile 0.8 the forest, reflective of most of the Groton Management area, becomes a mix of evergreens and hardwoods.

The trail comes to a Y intersection at 0.9 mile. The right fork goes toward Seyon Lodge State Park through a hillside popular with local cross-country and backcountry skiers. Stay on the Spruce Mountain Trail (that is, the left fork). Shortly thereafter, the smooth trail turns rocky—if glaciers were construction workers, this would be the glacier version of a cobblestone street.

At 1.2 miles come to a beaver pond on the left and the first view of the round summit of Spruce Mountain.

You don't have to be young to explore the trailside rocks on upper Spruce Mountain Trail.

The rocks at pond's edge make a nice snack spot. At mile 1.3 cross Mskaskek (muh-SKAH-skeek)—the Abenaki word for red spruce—Brook. At 1.5 miles the trail bends sharply and steeply left as you begin to scale the flank of Spruce Mountain. Climb a small set of wooden steps as firs and red spruce trees overtake the hardwoods and the path, now singletrack, turns to smooth granite as you cut sidehill across the mountain. Young hikers will love exploring the cave-like crevices on the right side of the trail along this stretch (the spur trails heading right lead to fun scrambles). At 1.9 miles the trail turns straight up as you make your final summit push, pausing for a moment in a flat grassy area before pushing upward for the final climb.

The summit clearing is full of things to explore. The 55-foot-tall Aermotor-design tower and its 7-by-7-foot cab, which stands immediately at the top of the trail, was originally constructed in 1933 atop Bellevue Hill in St. Albans, Vermont, and moved to the current location in 1943. The first tower to stand on Spruce Mountain (constructed in 1919) had an open platform and stood at the north side of the clearing directly above the firewatcher's cabin—the stone cellar hole of which invites curious hikers to explore. A second tower of spruce logs replaced the first in 1931.

A perfect multi-level picnic ledge on the eastern side of the clearing behind the cabin cellar hole affords the only view from the ground looking at Noyes Pond and Signal Mountain. From the tower, however, you can see it all: the Presidentials in New Hampshire to the northeast, and Camel's Hump and the Worcester Range with Mount Mansfield peeking from behind to the west.

After exploring the many features on the summit, return by the same route.

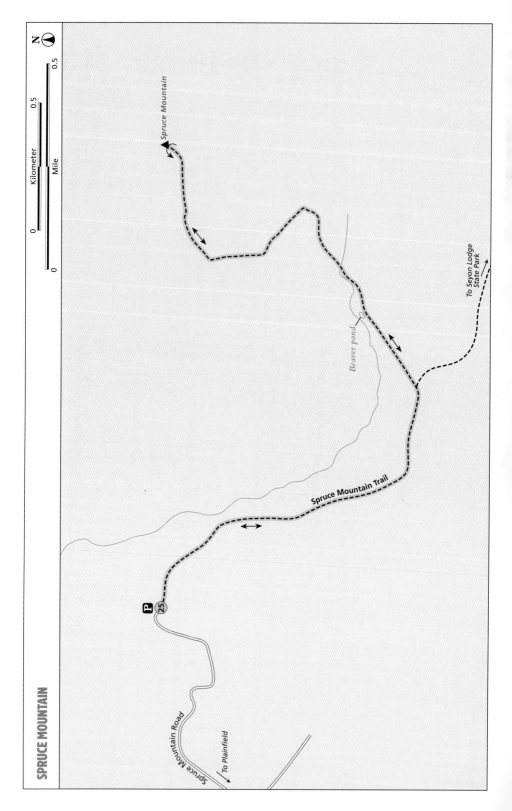

SPRUCE MOUNTAIN

N

Kilometer
0   0.5

Mile
0   0.5

Spruce Mountain

Beaver pond

Spruce Mountain Trail

To Seyon Lodge
State Park

Spruce Mountain Road

To Plainfield

P
25

Near the tower on the summit, the cellar hole from the original firewatcher's cabin

MILES AND DIRECTIONS

0.0   Start at the trailhead at the eastern end of the parking area.

0.9   Come to a Y. The trail to Seyon Lodge State Park goes right. This route stays left on Spruce Mountain Trail.

1.2   Beaver pond on left side of trail and stream crossing shortly after.

1.5   Trail bends left and steepens briefly.

1.9   Grade gets much steeper.

2.2   Summit. Return by same route.

4.4   Arrive back at trailhead.

26 BEAR HILL

A drive-up fire lookout with a pretty nature hike attached.

General location: Randolph, Vermont	**Canine compatibility:** Dog friendly
Highest point: 2,024 feet	**Trail surface:** Dirt, rocks
Elevation gain: 342 feet	**Land status:** Public
Distance: 1.4 miles	**Other trail users:** Hikers, snowshoers, skiers
Difficulty: Easy	**Water availability:** None
Hiking time: 1 hour	**Special considerations:** Be aware that this is a drive-up tower. The trail starts and ends at the tower.
When to go: Year-round	
Fees and permits: Entry into Allis State Park is free (unless you are camping there).	**Amenities:** None
	Maps: USGS Roxbury, Vermont Quad
Trail contact: Allis State Park, 284 Allis State Park Rd., Randolph, VT; (802) 276-3175; vtstateparks.com/allis.html	**Maximum grade:** 29 percent on a set of steps
	Trail conditions: Well-marked, well-maintained trail

FINDING THE TRAILHEAD

To approach from the north, take exit 5 off I-89. Turn east onto VT 64. At 0.6 mile turn right (south) onto Stone Road (dirt). Stone Road parallels the interstate. At 3.9 miles turn right (west) on Norwich Road, which passes under the interstate. After the underpass, turn left onto West Street at mile 4.1. In half a mile VT 65 joins West Street from the left; turn right onto VT 65 at mile 4.7. At 6.5 miles Bear Hill Road veers left, but you should stay right on VT 65. At 6.9 miles turn left on Allis State Park Road. *To approach from the south*, take exit 4 off I-89. Turn west on VT 66 and follow it toward Randolph. At 1.4 miles turn right (northwest) on Windover Fork Road. Veer right onto VT 12 at mile 1.9. At 5.3 miles turn right (northeast) on West Street (dirt). At 5.6 miles veer left onto Bear Hill Road. At 9.2 miles Bear Hill Road ends at VT 65. Follow VT 65 north. At 9.6 miles turn left onto Allis State Park Road.

The state park entrance is 0.7 mile up Allis State Park Road. Follow it to the end to drive to the fire lookout and nature trail. GPS: N44° 2' 35.304" / W72° 38' 1.752"

ABOUT THE LOOKOUT

Height: 58 feet	**Current tower:** 1956 (relocated from Gilson Mountain)
Cabin dimensions: 7 x 7 feet	
Frame construction: Steel	**Original tower:** 1932
Steps: Steel	**What you'll see:** Killington Peak, Camel's Hump, Mount Mansfield, the Monroe Skyline
No longer active	

THE HIKE

Bear Hill is the only fire lookout in this volume to which you don't have to hike. It is included because it is a wonderful tower with 360-degree views and because the 1.4-mile nature trail that departs and returns from the tower clearing is great for kids, birdwatchers, and anyone who loves the woods.

The trail loop can be hiked in either direction, as the trail starts and ends at the tower. This description starts at the northeastern corner of the parking lot. It is best described

The Bear Hill tower with its relatively short nature hike makes it a favorite of families and future firewatchers.

as a "down and up"; it loses elevation at the beginning and then makes it up at the end. That said, the trail starts on a gradual descent to an abandoned chimney at 0.1 mile. It continues its descent through maple, beech, and other hardwoods until red spruce takes over at 0.6 mile. At 0.7 mile the trail traverses next to a rock wall. Halfway up the wall is a hole known as the "Bear Den," for which Bear Hill got its name.

At 1.1 miles the trail begins to regain the altitude it lost as it ascends a thirty-seven-step wooden staircase. Shortly thereafter, a stone wall crosses the trail, a reminder of the area's agricultural history: Indeed, the Allis family, which donated the land for Allis State Park, farmed the land, which was completely open and deforested, for generations. Finally, the trail returns to the southern end of the clearing at 1.4 miles with the fire lookout in full view.

The tower, put together by the Vermont Forest Service (now the Department of Forests, Parks, and Recreation) in 1956, formerly stood on Gilson Mountain in Fletcher, Vermont, where it was built in 1936 and then decommissioned in lieu of aircraft surveillance. The original tower on Bear Hill, built by the state in 1932, was a wooden tower with a glass-enclosed octagonal cabin and a hard-luck history: In the hurricane of 1938, it was nearly blown over (state records indicate that winds blew the tower so that it was leaning on two legs and held up only by its guy wires; also, the telephone line was damaged). After it was repaired, it was struck by lightning and burned. The state repaired, then replaced this tower with a steel base and wooden cab only to have the replacement fall into disrepair, leading to the relocation of the current tower.

Views from the top are stupendous: Mansfield and Camel's Hump dominate the north; Mounts Ellen and Abraham form the Monroe Skyline to the west; Killington, Pico, and Ascutney stand in the south. New Hampshire's White Mountains are visible to the east.

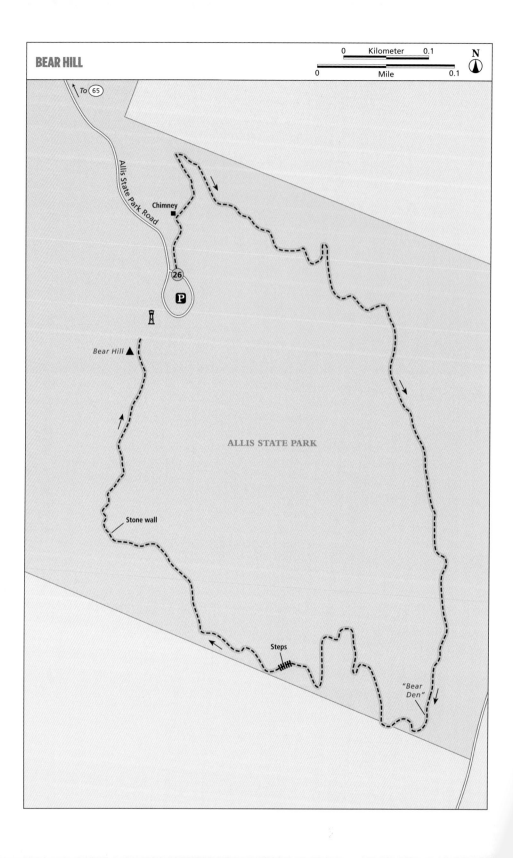

BEAR HILL

0   Kilometer   0.1

0   Mile   0.1

N

To (65)

Allis State Park Road

Chimney

26

P

Bear Hill ▲

ALLIS STATE PARK

Stone wall

Steps

"Bear Den"

The Bear Hill tower was erected in 1956.

The only drawback to Bear Mountain is that, from the car, the tower comes first and then the hike. Otherwise, the site makes for a quiet and pleasant outing.

MILES AND DIRECTIONS
0.0 Pick up the trail in the northeastern corner of the parking lot, near tower.

0.1 Abandoned chimney.

0.7 "Bear Den."

1.1 Ascend wooden steps.

1.2 Cross stone wall.

1.4 Tower, near parking lot.

27 GILE MOUNTAIN

This out-and-back hike brings a major reward for not much investment. A short hike in Vermont and the 360-degree views on a clear day from this tower are mind-blowing.

General location: Norwich, Vermont
Highest point: 1,850 feet
Elevation gain: 385 feet
Distance: 1.4 miles
Difficulty: Easy
Hiking time: 1 hour
When to go: Year-round
Fees and permits: None
Trail contact: Town of Norwich Trails Committee, 300 Main St., Norwich, VT; (802) 649-1419; norwich.vt.us/trails-committee
Canine compatibility: Dogs allowed on leash.

Trail surface: Dirt, stone steps
Land status: Public
Other trail users: The trail crosses a mountain-biking trail at several points.
Water availability: None
Special considerations: None
Amenities: None
Maps: USGS South Strafford, VT
Maximum grade: 18 percent
Trail conditions: This is a popular and well-maintained trail. Volunteers of the Upper Valley Trails Alliance constructed hundreds of stone steps.

FINDING THE TRAILHEAD

From the intersection of I-91 and VT 5 in Norwich, head north on VT 5. In a tenth of a mile, VT 5 veers right (east); stay straight on Main Street. At 1.2 miles turn left (west) on Turnpike Road, which passes a park on the left and turns to dirt at 2.6 miles. The trailhead is on the left (west) at 6.3 miles. GPS: N43° 47' 21.984" / W72° 20' 34.691"

ABOUT THE LOOKOUT

Height: 67 feet
Cabin dimensions: 7 x 7 feet
Frame construction: Steel
Steps: Wood
No longer active
Current tower: 1940
Original tower: 1940

What you'll see: "What won't you see?" would be a more apt question. Ascutney and Killington stand southwest and west. Mounts Lafayette and Moosilauke dominate the eastern view, while on a clear day, you'll see Mount Mansfield and Camel's Hump to the north.

THE HIKE

Stone steps—and lots of them. That's what you will experience on the trail to the Gile Mountain fire lookout. The trail is steep, and runoff can cause erosion. This prompted the Norwich, Vermont, Trails Committee in 2010 to recommend a project to make the trail more enduring. Using state grant money procured by the Trails Committee and the nonprofit Upper Valley Trails Alliance, crews installed steps over a period of five years. The result is the Gile Mountain trail. The point? Trails in the woods don't just "happen"—they often take organizations, municipalities, volunteers, and, in this case, money to protect and maintain them.

From the western side of the parking area, pick up the wide, smooth-surfaced dirt track. At 0.2 mile the trail crosses two small streams on bridges—one made of wood and

The tower at Gile Mountain has an open observation deck.

Killington Peak from the Gile Mountain tower

one of stones. Continue on a moderate pitch to a power line at 0.3 mile. The power line carries power from Wilder Dam on the Connecticut River. On the far side of the power line, cross a mountain bike trail (the Blue Ribbon Trail). Here, the stone steps start . . . and they don't really ever stop.

At 0.6 mile the Blue Ribbon Trail recrosses and then you come to the former fire-watcher's cabin on the right. A short distance beyond the cabin is the summit of Gile Mountain and its tower. The summit is not above the tree line, so you have to climb the tower in order to admire the view (there is chain-link fencing at the landings to give a sense of security). And what a view it is!

Directly west is Killington Peak, Vermont's second-highest peak and also home to a fire tower (although not open for climbing by the public). To the northwest, Mounts Ellen (Vermont's third-highest peak) and Abraham bookend the Monroe Skyline. Mount Mansfield and Camel's Hump, Vermont's highest mountain and tied for third highest, respectively, are north. Mount Ascutney dominates the southern horizon, and New Hampshire's White Mountains are east.

State records indicate the tower was constructed in 1940 and is the original tower on-site, although members of the Norwich Historical Society believe the tower went up earlier. During World War II the tower was used as a lookout for enemy aircraft, whereby volunteers would sit in the tower for several hour-long shifts with an aircraft identification booklet.

It is best to save Gile for a clear day because the view of the Vermont surroundings is impressive. Return by the same route.

GILE MOUNTAIN

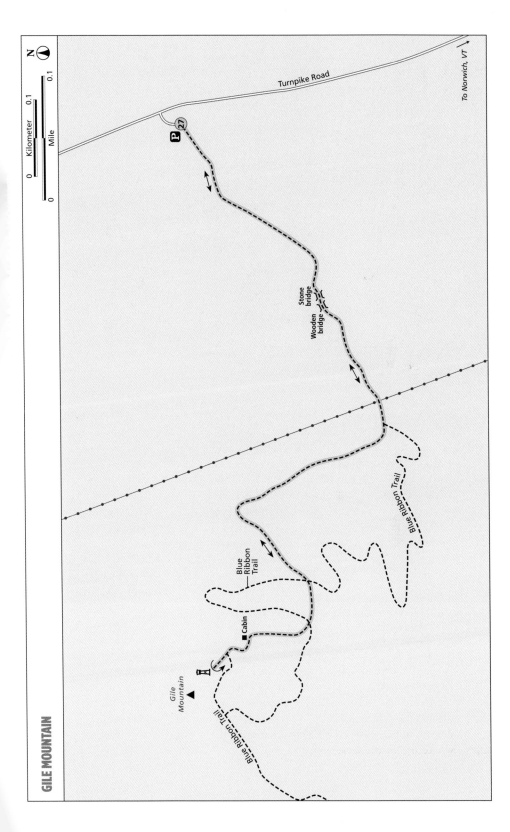

Turnpike Road

To Norwich, VT

P 27

Stone bridge

Wooden bridge

Blue Ribbon Trail

Blue Ribbon Trail

Cabin

Gile Mountain

Blue Ribbon Trail

N

0   Kilometer   0.1

0.1

0   Mile   0.1

The stone steps on the Gile Mountain trail were installed from 2011 to 2016.

MILES AND DIRECTIONS

0.0 From the parking lot, follow dirt track.

0.2 Cross bridges.

0.3 Cross power line and a bike trail.

0.6 Cross another bike path, then come to cabin on your right.

0.7 Summit and tower. Return by same route.

1.4 Trailhead.

28 MOUNT ASCUTNEY TOWER VIA WEATHERSFIELD TRAIL

An exciting hike past cliffs, canyons, waterfalls, and lookouts to a tower with 360-degree views of mountains in all corners of Vermont—and in surrounding states.

General location: Ascutney village in Weathersfield, Vermont
Highest point: 3,144 feet
Elevation gain: 1,990 feet
Distance: 5.8 miles
Difficulty: Strenuous due to elevation gain
Hiking time: 5 hours
When to go: Year-round
Fees and permits: None
Trail contact: Mount Ascutney State Park, 1826 Back Mountain Rd., Windsor, VT; (802) 674-2060; vtstateparks.com/ascutney.html
Canine compatibility: Dogs should be on leash at the trailhead and the summit.

Trail surface: Rugged. The dirt trail is rocky and rooty.
Land status: Public
Other trail users: Hikers, snowshoers
Water availability: Unreliable
Special considerations: The trail leads to the tops of waterfalls and cliffy lookouts, which make for great explorations and viewpoints. However, respect the cliff edges.
Amenities: None
Maps: USGS Windsor, VT NH Quad
Maximum grade: 32 percent
Trail conditions: This is a heavily used and well-maintained trail. It's steep and rocky, but many of the steepest places have helpful stone steps.

FINDING THE TRAILHEAD

From exit 8 on I-91, follow VT 131 west for 3.1 miles. Turn right on the dirt Cascade Falls Road and follow it for 450 feet. Turn left on High Meadow Road and follow it to the trailhead parking area at the end (0.4 mile). GPS: N43° 25′ 36.732″ / W72° 27′ 58.032″

ABOUT THE LOOKOUT

Height: 23.5 feet
Cabin dimensions: 10 x 10 feet
Frame construction: Steel
Steps: Wood
No longer active
Current tower: The tower was relocated to the current spot and

lowered, although the exact date is not known.
Original tower: 1921
What you'll see: The short answer: everything. Ascutney has views of New Hampshire's White Mountains, the Berkshires in Massachusetts, and Vermont's Green Mountains.

THE HIKE

If you have ever driven in Vermont on I-91 between the Massachusetts border and I-89, then you have seen the 3,144-foot monadnock Mount Ascutney, which dominates the landscape of the I-91 corridor along the Connecticut River. The name Ascutney derives from an Abenaki word meaning "wide mountain."

On every side of Mount Ascutney is a small town or village. Mount Ascutney State Park, located on the eastern side of the mountain, was built by Civilian Conservation

The Mount Ascutney Tower is the same height as the surrounding trees . . . for now.

Corps (CCC) crews in the 1930s and includes campsites, four hiking trails, and an auto road. (Even those who drive up the mountain have to earn it—the upper parking lot brings them a mile from the top.) Mount Ascutney is well loved and well used by campers, hikers, bikers, and hang gliders.

From the highway, the mountain appears forested and round. But the forest hides a volcanic history, and the Weathersfield Trail is rugged and exciting (as are the other routes), with ledges, cliffs, lookouts, and waterfalls. Although challenging, Ascutney is a wonderful climb and will hold the interest of any hiker regardless of age. The Weathersfield passes through state park land and the Windsor Town Forest.

The Weathersfield Trail (white blazes) begins at a set of wooden stairs at the northeast corner of the parking area—a sign that, although the trail is rough in places, trail stewards have put in plenty of stone steps, switchbacks, and other features to aid your ascent. At 0.4 mile the trail crosses a streambed, which dries up in the summer. To your right (south), the water plummets 30 feet down over a drop-off known as Little Cascade Falls. The trail goes through hemlocks as it follows an impressive cliff band and finally finds a break in the cliffs in front of a narrow canyon (0.6 mile)—it's definitely worth pausing to explore the canyon before continuing. The ascent through the cliff band would certainly be a scramble were it not for several stone steps and convenient wooden stairs. At the top of the stairs, the trail surface is slabby and it reenters a hardwood forest filled with oak, maple, and ash trees.

At 1.1 miles the trail splits. The right, blue-blazed track bypasses Crystal Cascade Falls. Why you'd want to miss this amazing geographical feature is a mystery (and staying on the main trail only adds 0.2 mile to the route), so stay straight on the

Weathersfield Trail. The forest changes again as you reenter a stand of hemlocks, and the trail descends toward Crystal Cascade. Like Little Cascade, you're standing at the top of the falls—this time, a drop of approximately 100 feet. The rocky streambed formations are fun to explore—taking care, of course, to respect the edge (Parents should clearly express this to young mountaineers!).

After cooling off in the pools of the stream (which slows to a trickle in some years), follow the trail, which parallels the stream before veering sharply right (northeast). Gain back the altitude you lost and reconnect with the bypass trail at 1.3 miles. The trail continues to ascend before dropping back into the stream's gully and ascending the opposite bank. At 1.8 miles the trail bends left (northwest) at "Halfway Brooks," a confluence of several mountain streambeds. (If you are tired, you'll be glad to know the streams are ill-named; you are well over halfway there!)

The trail twists and turns uphill as hardwoods reappear before giving way to widely spaced red spruce. There are actually ropes to help hikers stay on course over the roots and rocks (2 miles). At 2.3 miles the steady ascent relents and you pass Harry's Lookout, a perch named for avid hiker and volunteer trail worker Harry Edward Temple. Much of the maintenance of the trail falls on the Ascutney Trails Association, a volunteer group who build and maintain multiuse trails locally. Harry's is a south-facing perch that is mostly obscured by spruce. A bit farther along, however, at 2.5 miles, you come to Gus's Lookout, named for Augustus Aldrich, another ATA volunteer. This rocky outcrop gives you south-facing views of New Hampshire's Mount Monadnock and, to the southwest, Stratton and Globe Mountains.

More great views can be had a little farther still at the West Peak of Ascutney (mile 2.6). A short spur trail leads left (west) to the perch, which looks straight southwest at Hawks Mountain, with Globe and Stratton looming beyond. Moving right along the horizon are the ski trails of Okemo on Ludlow Mountain (west) and Killington Peak and Breadloaf Mountains to the northwest.

Returning to the trail, you come to yet another lookout point where the Hang Glider Trail crosses at 2.7 miles. If you turned right, it would lead a mile to the upper parking lot of the auto road. Left on the Hang Glider Trail leads a few steps to a wooden platform from which hang gliders launch. Unless you brought your glider, use the platform to admire the view northwest to Killington Peak and the town of Brownsville at the foot of Mount Ascutney.

Back on the Weathersfield Trail, pass through a small patch of ferns and another intersection (the 1976 Trail comes in from the left/north). At 2.9 miles come to a Y. The right fork leads just a few steps to the summit (and the original footings of the fire tower, which was moved to the current site and lowered). The left fork leads to the fire tower, also just a few steps away.

The steel lookout stands 24.5 feet high and has chain link along the railings and landings for added safety and security. Be advised that there is a gate at the top of the stairs with a latch. The latch works but may require a bit of jiggling.

It's always a bummer when radio equipment obstructs or impedes on views, and the three radio towers near the Mount Ascutney lookout are the only drawback of this hike. The southern tower is so obnoxious it actually has a blinking light—even during the day. The 360-degree views are awesome despite the communications eyesores. North, you can see as far as Burke Mountain. Northwest are Mansfield and Camel's Hump. East is the town of Claremont, New Hampshire, and Mount Sunapee, and southeast are Mount

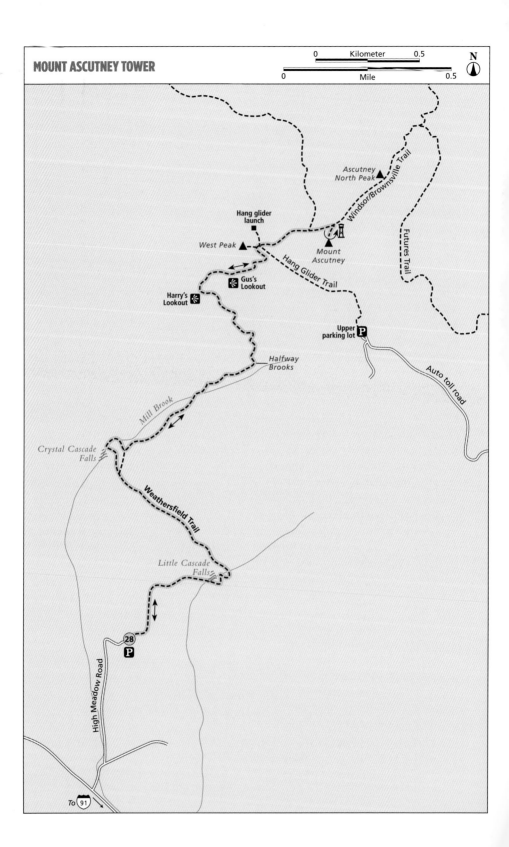

Kilometer

Mile

N

Ascutney
North Peak

Windsor/Brownsville Trail

Futures Trail

Hang glider
launch

West Peak

Mount
Ascutney

Gus's
Lookout

Hang Glider Trail

Harry's
Lookout

Upper
parking lot

P

Halfway
Brooks

Mill Brook

Auto toll road

Crystal Cascade
Falls

Weathersfield Trail

Little Cascade
Falls

28

P

High Meadow Road

To 91

The author studies the view from Gus's Lookout.

Monadnock in New Hampshire and Wachusett Mountain in Massachusetts. Southeast are the Connecticut River and the town of Bellows Falls, Vermont.

There's a lot to look at so take your time. When you're ready, descend the tower and return to the trailhead by the same route.

MILES AND DIRECTIONS

0.0 The Weathersfield Trail (white blazes) leaves from the northeastern corner of the parking area at some wooden steps.

0.4 Cross above Little Cascade Falls.

1.1 Trail splits at a Y. Take the left fork.

1.2 Crystal Cascade Falls.

1.3 Another Y. Take the left fork.

1.8 Trail comes to Halfway Brooks, a confluence of several sometimes-dried-up streams.

2.3 Harry's Lookout on left (south) side of trail.

2.5 Gus's Lookout on right (south) side of trail.

2.6 West Peak spur on left (west) side of trail.

2.7 Hang Glider Trail crosses Weathersfield Trail. Spur to left leads to northwest-facing perch.

2.9 Trail comes to Y. Right fork leads short distance to summit and original tower footings. Left fork leads to tower. Return by same route.

5.8 Arrive back at the trailhead.

29 OKEMO MOUNTAIN (AKA LUDLOW MOUNTAIN) VIA HEALDVILLE TRAIL

An out-and-back hike through a wonderful hardwood forest along an often-cascading brook to a fire lookout with beautiful Green Mountain views.

General location: Mount Holly, Vermont
Highest point: 3,343 feet
Elevation gain: 1,943 feet
Distance: 6.0 miles
Difficulty: Strenuous (due to total elevation gain)
Hiking time: 4 hours
When to go: Year-round
Fees and permits: None
Trail contact: Okemo State Forest, Vermont Department of Forests, Parks and Recreation, (802) 289-0603; fpr.vermont.gov/okemo-state-forest
Canine compatibility: Dogs allowed.

Trail surface: Dirt, packed dirt, rocks
Land status: Public
Other trail users: Hikers, skiers, snowshoers
Water availability: There are many brook crossings.
Special considerations: None
Amenities: None
Maps: USGS Mount Holly Quad and USGS Ludlow Quad
Maximum grade: 29 percent (for a brief moment; otherwise this is a pretty reasonable pitch)
Trail conditions: This is a popular, well-packed trail. The bridges on the trail are well maintained.

FINDING THE TRAILHEAD

From the intersection of VT 100 and VT 103 in Ludlow, head northwest on VT 103. At 2.7 miles turn left (south) on Station Road, which bends southwest. Cross railroad tracks at 3.4 miles. The trailhead parking area is on the left (east). GPS: N43° 25′ 56.784″ / W72° 45′ 42.3″

ABOUT THE LOOKOUT

Height: 60 feet
Cabin dimensions: 7 x 7 feet
Frame construction: Steel
Steps: Wood
No longer active

Current tower: 1934
Original tower: 1923
What you'll see: Mount Washington, Mount Monadnock, Mount Ascutney, many Green Mountains

THE HIKE

This beautiful hike (blue blazes) on the backside of the same mountain that plays home to Okemo Mountain Resort departs the parking area on its eastern side and immediately crosses over a new bridge. The name Okemo comes from the Chippewa meaning "chieftain." Okemo Mountain is also known as Ludlow Mountain, named for a wealthy eighteenth-century English lord.

The Healdville Trail enters a hardwood forest and zigs and zags with the Catamount Trail for the first mile as the ski trail crosses and recrosses the trail. At 0.6 mile come to a small waterfall. Here the trail gets rockier and steeper.

Autumn hiking on the Healdville Trail

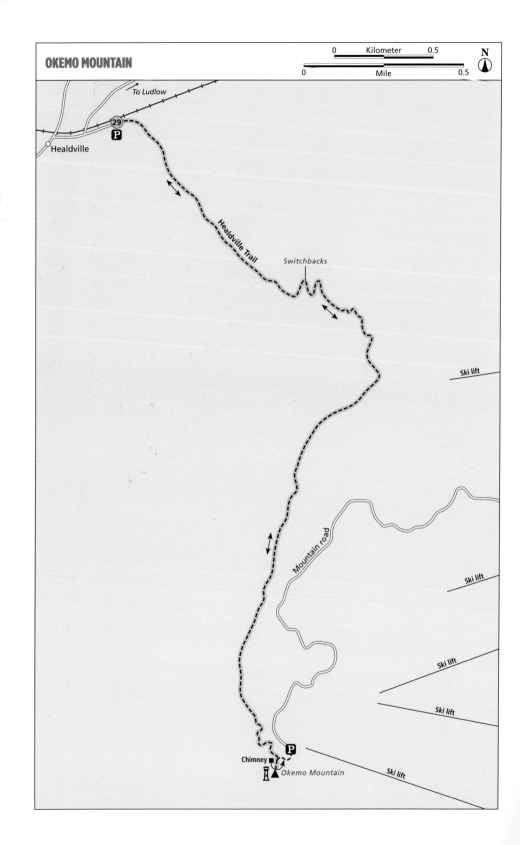

0   Kilometer   0.5

0   Mile   0.5

N

To Ludlow

29

P

Healdville

Healdville Trail

Switchbacks

Ski lift

Mountain road

Ski lift

Ski lift

Ski lift

Ski lift

Chimney

P

Okemo Mountain

At 1.0 mile the trail ascends a few switchbacks and shortly after some stone steps. The Catamount Trail again joins it, then bends away for the last time.

At 1.6 miles the trail bends right as it follows a contour through a wide-open forest of beech and maple for about a third of a mile. At 2.2 miles cross a cascading brook and begin to once again gain altitude. At 2.5 miles the forest around you begins to shift as red spruce begins to dominate and the trail starts to weave around mossy rocks. At 2.9 miles the overhanging spruces feel like a tunnel, at the end of which you come upon a stone chimney and a fork in the trail. The left fork goes to a parking lot (yes, it's possible to drive here). The right fork goes less than 0.1 mile and ends at a viewless summit, unless you came on a clear day and dare to climb the tower.

Atop the tower you'll find no cabin, and you'll look down upon Okemo Mountain Resort and its ski lifts, which operate in both winter and summer. There's also an auto road, with the parking lot nearby. There may be a good number of people on the summit, and if you made a winter ascent, many of them may be sliding around on skis. Northeast is Mount Washington and the White Mountains. Closer to home, Mount Ascutney dominates to the south. Meanwhile, Mount Monadnock rises in the distance beyond the top of the chairlift, while the Green Mountains sprawl to the west.

The 60-foot-tall Okemo fire lookout was added to the National Historic Lookout Register in 1998.

After your summit exploration, return by the same route.

MILES AND DIRECTIONS

0.0   Pick up the Healdville Trail (blue blazes) from the east side of the parking lot.

0.6   Small waterfall.

1.0   Switchbacks.

1.6   Traverse a flat saddle.

2.2   Cross a brook.

2.9   Come to a Y by an old chimney. Take the right fork.

3.0   Summit and tower. Return by the same route.

6.0   Arrive back at the trailhead.

30 STRATTON MOUNTAIN VIA THE LT/AT

A beautiful mountain out-and-back through a national forest to an iconic tower with amazing views.

General location: Stratton
Highest point: 3,936 feet
Elevation gain: 1,662 feet
Distance: 7.6 miles
Difficulty: Strenuous
Hiking time: 5 hours
When to go: Year-round
Fees and permits: None
Trail contact: Green Mountain Club, (802) 244-7037; greenmountainclub. org. Green Mountain National Forest, Manchester District, (802) 362-2307; fs.usda.gov/gmfl.
Canine compatibility: Dogs are allowed on the Long Trail under leash or voice control.

Trail surface: Dirt, rocks, roots
Land status: Public
Other trail users: Hikers, snowshoers, skiers
Water availability: Spring at 3.1 miles
Special considerations: Much of Kelly Strand Road and some of Stratton-Arlington Road are not plowed in the winter.
Amenities: None
Maps: USGS Stratton Mountain, Vermont Quad
Maximum grade: 22 percent
Trail conditions: The Long Trail/ Appalachian Trail is a rugged but well-used trail.

FINDING THE TRAILHEAD

Approaching from the east, take the Stratton-Arlington Road west from its intersection with VT 100 by a triangular field in Wardsboro, Vermont. Follow Stratton-Arlington Road (dirt) for 3.4 miles to the town of Stratton (not the ski resort) and continue past the small village. Pass the Stratton snowmobile-trail parking area on the right at mile 6.1. (Note that the road is not plowed beyond this point from November 1 to June 1.) Continue to the trailhead on the right (north) side of the road at mile 6.8. *Approaching from the west*, from exit 3 on US 7 in Sunderland, Vermont, take VT 313 west off the exit (*Note:* You are 0.1 mile from the Orvis flyfishing outfitter's world headquarters). In 0.2 mile turn right (north) on S Road. At 0.9 mile turn right (east) on Kansas Road, which goes under US 7. At 1.5 miles turn right (south) onto Kelly Strand Road (dirt), which eventually heads east. At 4.8 miles Kelly Strand Road becomes Stratton-Arlington Road. Follow Stratton-Arlington Road past dispersed camping sites and trailheads until mile 6.6. The LT/AT trailhead to Stratton Mountain is on the left (north) side. Note that Kelly Strand Road is not plowed or maintained from November 1 to June 1. GPS: N43° 3' 40.176" / W72° 58' 3.899"

ABOUT THE LOOKOUT

Height: 55 feet
Cabin dimensions: 7 x 7 feet
Frame construction: Steel
Steps: Wood
No longer active
Current tower: 1934

Original tower: 1914
What you'll see: Stratton Pond, Mount Ascutney, Mount Equinox, the Berkshires in Massachusetts, Grand Monadnock in New Hampshire

Stratton Mountain has an elevation of almost 4,000 feet, and the Stratton tower lifts hikers over the 4,000-foot threshold.

THE HIKE

Stratton Mountain holds a firmly entrenched place in the annals of hiking in the eastern United States. Vermont's Green Mountain Club founder James Taylor was on the summit of Stratton when he conceived the idea for the Long Trail. The Long Trail (LT), which stretches from the Massachusetts border 272 miles across the Green Mountains to the Canadian border, was the first of its kind in the United States. Later, Benton MacKaye, founder of the Appalachian Mountain Club, published an article proposing the Appalachian Trail (AT)—the 2,190-mile route along the spine of the Appalachians from Georgia to Maine. Like Taylor, MacKaye said his idea was sparked near the summit of Stratton. MacKaye's vision—carried on to this day by both the GMC and AMC—wasn't just about building footpaths: He hoped that communities along the trails would become both beneficiaries and stewards of the trail.

Long before these trails climbed the mountain, Stratton was known as Manicknung, from the Mahican "place where the mountain heaps up."

In southern Vermont the LT and AT follow the same corridor. This route to the summit of Stratton Mountain, where the ideas for both of these iconic trails germinated, follows the LT/AT.

The parking area is a cleared space on the shoulder of the road, and the LT/AT (white blazes) departs from the northeastern corner of the lot. The first 0.75 mile is a gentle ascent through a mixed hardwood forest, crossing some puncheon logs, a number of small streams, and plenty of wet ground. At 0.8 mile red spruce takes over and the trail crosses a larger stream that is fed from a marsh on the left (north) side of the trail.

Water from this spring a half mile from the summit of Stratton should be treated before drinking.

At 1 mile the trail hits a plateau surrounded by a stand of gray beech trees and paper birches and makes for smooth walking until it bends easterly, narrows, and climbs more steeply. At 1.4 miles cross Forest Service Road 341 (also known as the IP Road for the International Paper company, which originally built the road for logging purposes), a popular biking route and snowmobile trail in the winter. (Note: Neither bicycles nor snowmobiles are allowed on the LT/AT.) Here, the trail bends northeast and begins a more assertive ascent diagonally across the mountain.

At 1.75 miles the trail zigs and zags before cutting a traverse across the mountainside and eventually changing to a bouldery and rocky walking surface. At 2 miles the going continues over the rocky surface with occasional stone steps before a saddle covered in old maples, spruces, and young beeches. The trail heads north and flattens before ascending a few stone steps to an area with flat rocks and tall cedars (2.3 miles)—a nice snack spot. This stretch of a smoother trail surface follows the path of the phone line that used to run from the fire tower. From here the trail traverses the flank of Little Stratton Mountain to mile 2.7, where it gains the saddle between Little Stratton and the larger Stratton Mountain.

This ridgeline continues to ascend Stratton Mountain through a tunnel of spruce before the trees open up in a stand of taller spruce and balsam fir as you make your summit push. At 3.1 miles a spring provides a water source (except on the driest summer days); the GMC advises that hikers treat the water. The trail continues to climb as the balsams become more and more covered with lichen. At 3.7 miles the trail passes the firewatcher's cabin, now used by GMC caretakers who are stationed at the summit most summer days. The summit and tower are just ahead at 3.8 miles.

FIREWATCHERS AND CARETAKERS

Hugh and Jeanne Joudry have been fixtures at the top of Stratton Mountain for decades. They served two stints on the mountaintop in two different capacities: Hugh and Jeanne were fire lookouts employed by the state of Vermont from 1968 until 1979, and later they served as Green Mountain Club caretakers from 1996 until 2021. In both roles they lived in the one-room firewatcher's cabin for half the year.

Their dual careers atop Stratton were completely different experiences. They would see more people in a day as caretakers than they saw during their entire tenure as fire lookouts. "We were hermits," says Hugh, who leaped at the opportunity to disappear into the forest after race riots broke out in 1968 in Buffalo, New York, where he lived. "You had a deep communion with nature," he says. "I was a writer and there were things in my life I wanted to clarify."

Turning back time to when Hugh and Jeanne Joudry served as the firewatchers on Stratton Mountain
GREEN MOUNTAIN CLUB ARCHIVE

On top of getting away from the rat race, Hugh and Jeanne took their roles as protectors of the forest seriously. They maintained the trails and kept the phone line free of branches. During dry summers, they'd have to hike their water up the mountain every few days. Challenges included keeping up with the many daily chores (like splitting wood and collecting rainwater from a gutter) and reporting the exact geographical information when they did see smoke. "And black flies . . . ," Hugh added.

As caretakers, Hugh and Jeanne didn't live alone on the mountaintop. "We brought our cats," says Jeanne. But a caretaker cat's life isn't easy either: "They had to walk themselves up the mountain," she says. Hugh and Jeanne would hike the trail, and the cats would turn up a few hours later. When one of their beloved cats passed away, they piled his ashes at the foot of the tallest balsam fir.

Hugh and Jeanne retired as caretakers in 2021, fifty-four years after their first season as firewatchers. "It's amazing how we went from being solitary firewatchers to interacting with 8,000 people in a single summer," says Hugh, who says his years as a firewatcher shaped and saved his life. And as caretakers, they feel fortunate to have witnessed AT and LT end-to-enders having their own life-changing and lifesaving experiences.

"We have had more magic in our lives than we can even imagine," says Hugh.

Hugh and Jeanne before they retired as GMC caretakers in 2021
GREEN MOUNTAIN CLUB ARCHIVE

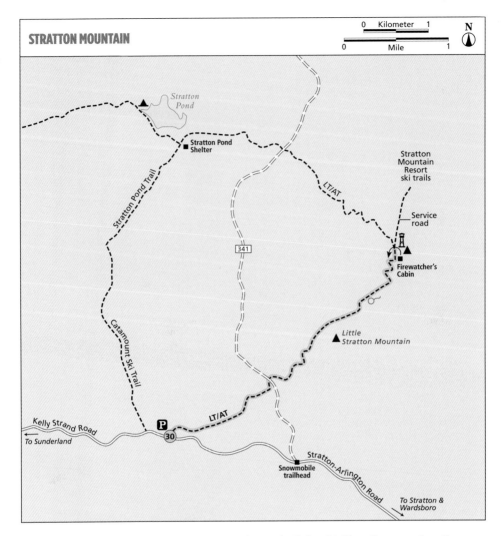

Stratton Pond

Stratton Pond Shelter

Stratton Mountain Resort ski trails

Service road

LT/AT

Firewatcher's Cabin

341

Little Stratton Mountain

Catamount Ski Trail

Stratton Pond Trail

Kelly Strand Road

To Sunderland

P

30

LT/AT

Snowmobile trailhead

Stratton-Arlington Road

To Stratton & Wardsboro

N

0   Kilometer   1
0   Mile   1

The tower is a classic steel Aermotor design, built by Civilian Conservation Corps crews in 1934 and renovated in 1988. It was added to the National Historic Lookout Register in 1989. Ascending to the top of the tower, you get wonderful 360-degree views. Northeast, at the foot of Stratton Mountain, is Stratton Pond, the largest tackcountry pond in Vermont. The LT/AT continues to Stratton Pond, which makes a rewarding but long loop hike: The Stratton Pond Trail, whirh reconnectstwith Stratton-Arlington Road 0.9 mile froilhead, makes for an 11.5-mile day. The loop is a popular backpack. For those enthusiastic about an overnight adventure, there are first-come, first-served campsites on the western shore of the pond for hikers, and Stratton Pond Shelter is not far from the pond. Farther west is Mount Equinox, the largest mountain of the Taconic Range, which stretches into New York State. South is Mount Snow. Mount Ascutney, another peak with a fire lookout, is northeast, and New Hampshire's Mount Monadnock is southeast. On clear days, Mounts Wachusett and Greylock (southeast and southwest) are visible in Massachusetts, and Killington Peak is visible to the north.

The LT/AT is a rugged but well-traveled trail on Stratton Mountain.

Back on the ground, a service road heads north to the top of the ski trails at Stratton Mountain Resort and its gondola. In the summer months the gondola is the reason behind the crowd of people with whom you are likely to share the tower. The LT/AT continues northwest beyond the tower. Unless you prepared for the longer loop hike, retrace your steps to return to your car.

MILES AND DIRECTIONS

0.0 From the parking lot, follow the LT/AT (white blazes) along a gentle ascent for 0.75 mile.

0.8 Stream crossing.

1.4 Cross Forest Road 341 (also known as the IP Road).

1.8 Pitch increases and footing becomes rocky.

2.7 Trail gains saddle of Stratton and Little Stratton Mountains.

3.1 Water source.

3.7 Firewatcher's cabin.

3.8 Summit and tower. Retrace your steps to return to your car.

7.6 Arrive back at the trailhead.

An easy loop in a state park through a mixed forest past old farm equipment and stone walls to a tower with Green Mountain views.

General location: Wilmington, Vermont	**Trail surface:** Varied. Packed dirt and rocks.
Highest point: 2,415 feet	**Land status:** Public
Elevation gain: 495 feet	**Other trail users:** Hikers, skiers, snowshoers
Distance: 1.8-mile loop with a spur to summit and tower	**Water availability:** None on the trail. Molly Stark State Park has a fountain at the parking area.
Difficulty: Easy	
Hiking time: 1.5 hours	**Special considerations:** None
When to go: Year-round	**Amenities:** At the trailhead, none. There are free restrooms with running water and picnic tables at the summit when the state park is open (Memorial Day to Columbus Day).
Fees and permits: There is an admission fee to enter Molly Stark State Park.	
Trail contact: Molly Stark State Park, 705 Route 9 East, Wilmington, VT; (802) 464-5460; vtstateparks.com/mollystark.html	**Maps:** USGS Jacksonville, VT Quad
	Maximum grade: 22 percent
Canine compatibility: Dogs are permitted on leash.	**Trail conditions:** Well-maintained packed-dirt trail

FINDING THE TRAILHEAD

From exit 2 on I-91, follow VT 9 west for 15.1 miles. The entrance to Molly Stark State Park is on the left (south) side. GPS: N42° 51′ 7.92″ / W72° 48′ 53.28″

ABOUT THE LOOKOUT

Height: 60 feet
Cabin dimensions: 7 x 7 feet
Frame construction: Steel
Steps: Wood
No longer active
Original tower: 1930

Current tower: 1949
What you'll see: New Hampshire's Mount Monadnock, Mount Snow, Massachusetts's Berkshires, and a local wind farm

THE HIKE

General John Stark of New Hampshire, a hero of Revolutionary War battles at Bunker Hill and Trenton, led New Hampshire and Vermont militia groups to victory over an army of Hessians allied with the British at the Battle of Bennington (which was actually fought at nearby Walloomsac, New York) in 1777. On the eve of the battle, Stark famously told his men: "Yonder are the Hessians! Tonight, the American flag flies over yonder hill or Molly Stark sleeps a widow!" The battle, in which the British and Hessians suffered heavy losses (200 dead and 700 injured, compared to 14 and 50 for the American side), served as a precursor to the American victory at Saratoga—a turning point in the war and a stretch that caused Native American allies to the British to lose faith and interest.

Stark's wife, Elizabeth "Molly" Stark, was neither widowed that day, nor did she sit idly at home. In addition to mothering eleven children in her husband's absence, she recruited

Green mountain view from the cabin of the Mount Olga lookout

men to fight in her husband's New Hampshire militia prior to Bennington and opened her home as a hospital for injured and ill soldiers.

The thirty-four-campsite Molly Stark State Park sits on 150 acres and includes Mount Olga, named for Olga Haslund, who donated a third of the park's land to the state of Vermont in 1939.

The hike to the lookout on Mount Olga is a loop and can therefore be hiked in either direction. This outline is the counterclockwise route, which starts by walking south from the main state park building toward the main campground and past the restrooms. After campsite number ten (the numbering of which could, of course, change), the Mount Olga Trail (blue blazes) ducks south into the woods and crosses a small wooden bridge before bending east. The trail parallels a stone wall, evidence of the area's agricultural history.

At 0.4 mile the stone wall ends and you come to an intersection with the Shearer Hill Trail of the Wilmington town trail network. Continue on the left fork (east) on the Mount Olga Trail as the pitch increases.

Cross a small stream at 0.7 mile and pass a collection of large boulders.

At 1 mile come to a Y intersection. The right (east) fork is the short spur trail that leads to the tower and firewatcher's cabin. There is cell communications equipment around the tower; otherwise it's a beautiful spot with incredible views into two neighboring states. From the tower, Vermont's Mount Snow is northwest, New Hampshire's Mount Monadnock is east, and the Berkshires of Massachusetts are visible to the south. To the west is the Searsburg wind farm.

In the spirit of reusing, the current steel tower formerly stood on Bald Mountain in Townshend, Vermont. The original wooden tower was interesting because it had an

The Mount Olga lookout formerly stood on Bald Mountain in Townshend, Vermont.

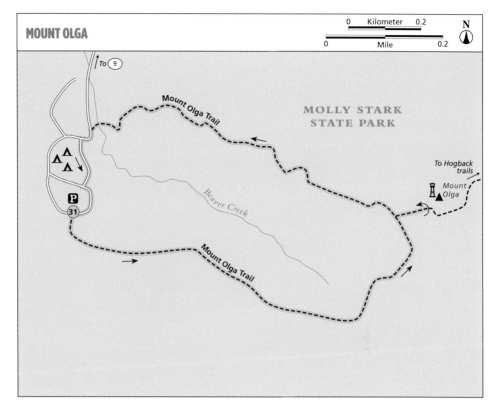

octagonal cabin at its top—a design that, according to the National Historic Lookout Register (on which the current tower is listed), was unique to towers in Vermont.

Across the clearing the Tower Trail comes in from Hogback Mountain, the site of a former ski area. The area is conserved by a nonprofit (Hogback Mountain Conservation Association) for recreational, educational, and environmental uses. To return, however, turn back on the spur trail and turn right (northwest) at the intersection with the Mount Olga Trail. At 1.5 miles the trail turns steeply downhill briefly as it passes through a stand of quiet hemlocks. It levels out at 1.7 miles and finds another (or is it the same as at the beginning?) stone wall. The trail ends at a metal bridge over Beaver Creek, which leaves you across the parking lot from the main state park building (1.8 miles).

MILES AND DIRECTIONS

0.0 Leave trailhead.

0.4 Intersection with Shearer Hill Trail. Continue left (east) on the Mount Olga Trail.

0.7 Cross stream and pass boulders.

1.0 Intersection with spur trail on right (east). Follow spur to tower. Return on spur.

1.1 Turn right (north) on Mount Olga Trail.

1.8 Arrive back at parking lot.

The view north toward New Hampshire's Mount Monadnock
from Warwick Tower on Mount Grace

MASSATHUSETTS, CONNECTICUT, AND RHODE ISLAND

The southern New England states—Massachusetts, Connecticut, and Rhode Island—have beautiful forestlands and mountains and a history of fire watching. Because these states are more heavily populated, many of the towers are located by roadsides, next to fire departments, or in the midst of towns and villages.

For this reason, included in this book are two towers—Heublein Tower in Simsbury, Connecticut, and Laura's Tower in Stockbridge, Massachusetts—that were never used as fire lookouts. These hikes and towers won't disappoint (Heublein is the largest structure in this book and Laura's has a one-of-a-kind straight staircase).

The other hikes in the book showcase the southern New England fire history and the fact that these states too have rural and beautiful landscapes. Many of the fire towers in southern New England are still active, with men and women who continue to scan the horizon ready with a radio to call in a plume of smoke.

The Works Progress Administration constructed the Stone Tower in Lynn Woods in 1936.

32 WARWICK TOWER ON MOUNT GRACE

An out-and-back hike in a state forest to an active tower featuring beautiful views into three states.

General location: Warwick, Massachusetts
Highest point: 1,621 feet
Elevation gain: 733 feet
Distance: 3.0 miles
Difficulty: Easy
Hiking time: 2.5 hours
When to go: Year-round
Fees and permits: None
Trail contact: Mount Grace State Forest, 78 Winchester Rd., Warwick, MA; (978) 544-3939; mass.gov/locations/mount-grace-state-forest
Canine compatibility: Dog friendly

Trail surface: Packed dirt, rocks, tree roots
Land status: Public
Other trail users: Hikers, skiers, snowshoers
Water availability: None
Special considerations: None
Amenities: There is a pavilion and picnic area at the trailhead but no restrooms.
Maps: USGS Mount Grace Quad
Maximum grade: 17 percent
Trail conditions: Well-maintained and well-marked trail

FINDING THE TRAILHEAD

From the intersection of MA 10/MA 63 and Warwick Road in Northfield, Massachusetts, turn east on Warwick Road. Warwick Road becomes Northfield Road. Regardless of the road's name, follow it for 7.1 miles, where it comes to a Y with Wendall Road. Stay left on Northfield Road until it ends at MA 78 (also known as Winchester Road) at 7.7 miles. The gravel parking lot for Mount Grace State Forest (it's also a parking area for Ohlson Field) is on the left (west) side at 8.1 miles. GPS: N42° 41' 20.76" / W72° 20' 28.176"

ABOUT THE LOOKOUT

Height: 68 feet
Cabin dimensions: 10 x 10 feet
Frame construction: Steel
Steps: Wood
Active lookout

Current tower: Built in 1939 (cabin rebuilt in 1968)
Original tower: 40-foot iron tower built in 1911
What you'll see: Mount Monadnock, Mount Wachusett, the Berkshires

THE HIKE

A monadnock is an Abenaki word meaning an isolated hill or lone mountain in the middle of a surrounding area. The definition applies to Mount Grace.

The hike up Mount Grace to Warwick Tower begins at Ohlson Field, a public space in Warwick with a picnic area and pavilion. There are forks of the trail at both the front and rear corners of the southern end of Ohlson Field; this description assumes you use the trailhead closest to the parking area. Ducking into the hemlocks and white pines, the path begins as a wide dirt and needle-covered walkway.

At 0.3 mile come to a Y. The left fork leads back to MA 78. Take the right (west) fork, which leads to another Y. Ignore the muddy ATV track to the left; again, follow the right

Warwick Tower atop Mount Grace

WARWICK TOWER ON MOUNT GRACE

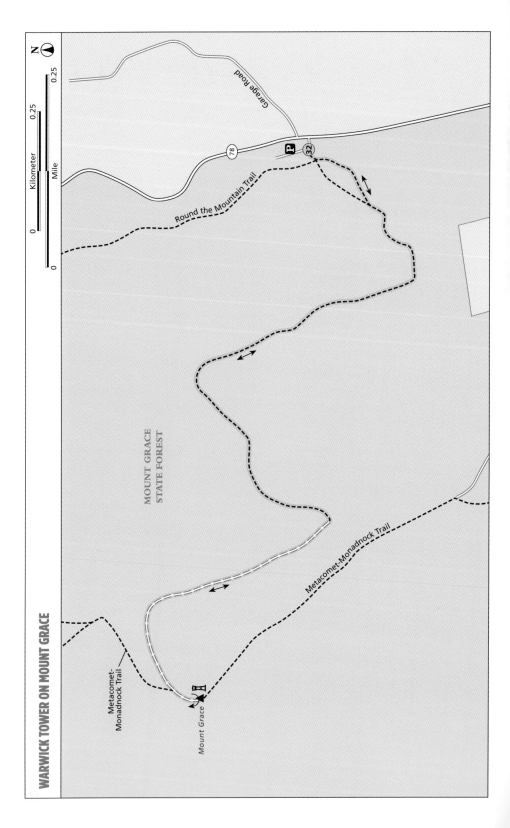

MOUNT GRACE
STATE FOREST

Round the Mountain Trail

Garage Road

Metacomet-Monadnock Trail

Metacomet-Monadnock Trail

Mount Grace

N

Kilometer
0   0.25

Mile
0   0.25

The view from Warwick Tower includes giant boulders in the summit clearing and picnickers.

fork. The route steepens as you begin to cut north across the shoulder of Mount Grace. The path remains smooth, and conifers give way to smooth, gray-bark beeches.

At 0.9 mile the trail dead-ends on a gravel road. Go right (north) on the road. At 1.4 miles a side road peels off to the left (south) toward a radio tower. Such radio and cell communications towers that crowd fire lookouts are always disappointments, so it is nice that this one is positioned a good distance from Warwick Tower. Stay straight on the gravel road. Arrive at the lookout and summit clearing at 1.5 miles.

Along with several giant boulders, there is a picnic table in the clearing. A search through the tall grass at the periphery of the clearing will uncover the footings (and pieces) from the original lookout on this site—a 40-foot structure constructed in 1911. On either end of the clearing, the Metacomet-Monadnock Trail, a 114-mile scenic trail that runs the width of Massachusetts into southern New Hampshire, enters and exits.

It's a viewless summit because of the surrounding trees, which makes it a good thing there is a fire tower! From the top of Warwick Tower, New Hampshire's Mount Monadnock dominates the northeastern view. Mount Wachusett stands in the distance to the east, while the Berkshires are south.

Enjoy the view and a snack and then return by the same route.

MILES AND DIRECTIONS
0.0 From the parking lot, pick up the trail at the southern end of Ohlson Field.

0.3 Take the right fork at the Y. Then take another right at another Y.

0.9 Trail dead-ends at gravel road. Go right.

1.5 Summit clearing and tower. Retrace your steps to return.

3.0 Arrive back at the parking area.

33 SHELBURNE TOWER ON MASSAEMETT MOUNTAIN

One of Massachusetts's best, this is a hike through a diverse forest to a unique stone tower with views of three states.

General location: Shelburne Falls, MassachusT MOUNTAINetts
Highest point: 1,569 feet
Elevation gain: 1,001 feet
Distance: 2.9-mile lollipop
Difficulty: Easy
Hiking time: 2.5 hours
When to go: Year-round
Fees and permits: None
Trail contact: Town of Shelburne, 51 Bridge St., Shelburne, MA; (413) 625-0300; townofshelburne.com
Canine compatibility: Dogs must be on a leash.
Trail surface: Dirt forest floor, some tree roots and rocks

Land status: Public
Other trail users: Snowshoers
Water availability: None
Special considerations: Parking is limited; please respect the neighbors on Halligan Avenue.
Amenities: None
Maps: USGS Shelburne Falls Quad (the USGS Quad doesn't show trails); Townofshelburne.com/files/Shelburne_Trails_brochure.pdf
Maximum grade: 21 percent
Trail conditions: These are well-maintained, well-signed trails.

FINDING THE TRAILHEAD

From exit 43 and the intersection of I-91 and MA 2, drive west on MA 2 for 8.9 miles. Turn right on Halligan Avenue. The trailhead and trail parking are immediately on the uphill (left) side of Halligan Avenue. Note that there are only four or five parking spaces here, but there is additional parking at a trailhead 0.5 mile beyond on MA 2 (also known as the Mohawk Trail). Also note that there are signs posted on Halligan Avenue about respecting neighbors and directing hikers to turn around right at the parking spaces rather than in neighbors' driveways. GPS: N42° 36' 10.944" / W72° 43' 49.871"

ABOUT THE LOOKOUT

Height: 63 feet
Cabin dimensions: 10 x 10 feet, but the cab is closed to the public.
Frame construction: Stone
Steps: Concrete

Active lookout
Current tower: 1911
Original tower: 1911
What you'll see: Mount Monadnock, Mount Toby, New York's Taconics

THE HIKE

The hike to the Shelburne fire lookout at the summit of Massaemett Mountain (also known as Bald Mountain) is special for several reasons. The lookout is one of just two stone towers in New England. Built in 1911, it's one of the oldest (if not the oldest, according to the National Historic Lookout Register) continually active towers in the United States. And it's one of the very few fire lookouts in the state of Massachusetts to which people can hike and that's open for people to climb and admire the view. All of this and it's also a really nice hike in the woods.

The Shelburne Tower is one of two active stone fire lookouts in New England.

Appropriately, big trees line
the Big Trees Trail.

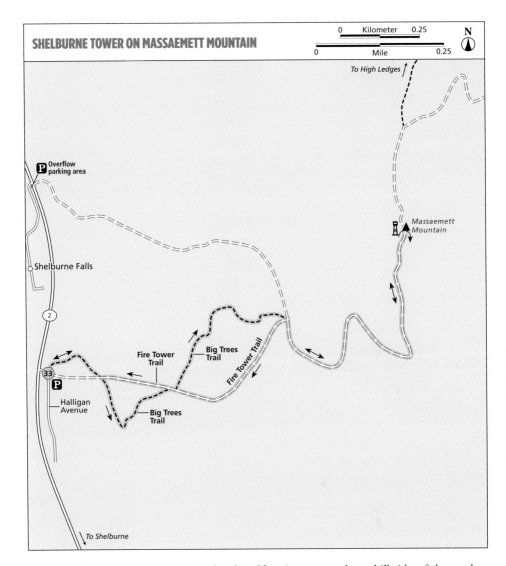

0   Kilometer   0.25

N

0   Mile   0.25

To High Ledges

Overflow
parking area

Massaemett
Mountain

Shelburne Falls

2

Fire Tower
Trail

Big Trees
Trail

Fire Tower Trail

33

Halligan
Avenue

Big Trees
Trail

To Shelburne

The Shelburne Fire Tower Trail (white blazes) starts on the uphill side of the road (parking is on both sides of the road). The first quarter mile is a smooth and wide single-track with interpretive signage educating hikers about plant and tree species (there's a diversity of old-growth hardwoods and evergreens throughout the hike), invasive species (there's plenty of garlic mustard along the route), and forest management.

At 0.25 mile the Fire Tower Trail encounters the Big Trees Trail (yellow blazes), a second route established in 2020 by the private landowner, which crisscrosses the Fire Tower Trail. The Fire Tower Trail goes left; this will be the return route. Follow the Big Trees Trail (which isn't as steep), the right fork. The trail climbs gradually before doubling back to cross the main trail again at 0.5 mile. Cross a power line and then come to a stone wall at 0.75 mile. The wall parallels the trail as you begin to notice evidence supporting the Big Trees Trail's name: gigantic hemlocks, beeches, and oak trees with trunk circumferences way too large to even come close to reaching your arms around.

The Big Trees Trail rejoins the Fire Tower Trail at 0.9 mile as the pitch steepens and traverses through mountain laurel bushes and a stand of hemlocks. At 1 mile the pitch levels as you pass more mountain laurel, other undergrowth, and new-growth trees. The path gets rockier but is still quite walkable. The trail rolls until you reach the summit at 1.5 miles.

The summit area is grassy with a couple of picnic tables. On the northern side is the fire tower—a stone monolith jutting into the sky with a 10-by-10-foot wooden cabin on top. The cabin, unfortunately, is closed, but the public can still climb the tower and get great views. The climb itself is dark and creepy, up spiraling concrete steps. Every time you think it's getting dark, sunlight appears through the next barred window around the corner. At the top of the tower, look out the northern window to see New Hampshire's Mount Monadnock dominating the northeastern skyline with Mount Olga directly north. Due east, you'll see Mount Greylock and New York's Taconic range beyond it. To the southeast is Mount Toby.

Behind the tower the Ridge Trail heads north toward the High Ledges Wildlife Sanctuary, a property owned by the nonprofit Mass Audubon. Your route down is to depart the way you came on the Fire Tower Trail. Follow the Fire Tower Trail all the way, crossing the Big Trees Trail twice (once at 2.1 miles and again at 2.6). Follow the trail to the trailhead.

MILES AND DIRECTIONS

0.0   From the parking lot, follow the Fire Tower Trail (white blazes).

0.25 Intersection with the Big Trees Trail. Follow the right fork to take the Big Trees Trail.

0.5   Big Trees trail crosses Fire Tower Trail (stay on Big Trees).

0.6   Cross a power line.

0.9   Big Trees and Fire Tower Trails come back together.

1.5   Tower and summit. Return by following the Fire Tower Trail.

2.1   Big Trees Trail goes right; stay straight on Fire Tower Trail.

2.6   Intersection with Big Trees Trail (stay straight on Fire Tower Trail).

2.9   Arrive back at the parking area.

34 LYNN TOWER

An urban hike to a unique stone tower in a green space outside of Boston, with views of the seacoast and the city skyline.

General location: Lynn, Massachusetts
Highest point: 284 feet
Elevation gain: 196 feet
Distance: 1.2 miles
Difficulty: Easy
Hiking time: 40 minutes
When to go: Year-round
Fees and permits: None
Trail contact: City of Lynn, Massachusetts, 3 City Hall Sq., Lynn, MA; (781) 477-7123; lynnwoodsranger@aol.com; lynnma.gov
Canine compatibility: Dogs should be on leash. Owners are responsible for removing waste. Dogs are not allowed to swim in reservoirs.
Trail surface: Dirt, gravel

Land status: Public
Other trail users: Walkers, hikers, bikers, skiers, snowshoers
Water availability: None
Special considerations: Lynn Woods are open from dawn to dusk. The stone tower is open when the park ranger is on duty, generally Tuesday through Saturday until 2:30 p.m. He encourages visitors to call or email to confirm the tower will be open and unlocked.
Amenities: None
Maps: USGS Lynn, Massachusetts Quad (The USGS quadrangle doesn't include trails.)
Maximum grade: 15 percent
Trail conditions: Gravel and dirt road

FINDING THE TRAILHEAD

From exit 63B off I-95, drive east on MA 129 toward Lynn. At 0.2 mile take the second exit at the traffic circle, staying on MA 129. At 2.1 miles turn right on Great Woods Road. At 2.4 miles you'll see a ballfield on the right and the road ends at a reservoir. The parking area is on the left. GPS: N42° 29' 34.872" / W70° 58' 40.799"

ABOUT THE LOOKOUT

Height: 48 feet
Cabin dimensions: The tower is 12 feet in diameter at the top landing.
Frame construction: Steel
Steps: Concrete and iron
No longer active

Current tower: 1936
Original tower: 1926
What you'll see: The skyline of Boston, the Lynn waterfront, and, 62 miles away, Mount Monadnock

THE HIKE

As the most urban hike in this book, the Stone Tower in Lynn Woods gives you a view of the Boston skyline. The 2,200-acre Lynn Woods reservation was established as a green space in 1881, and it still serves as a popular destination for walkers, runners, hikers, and mountain bikers. Although you won't find large cliffs, you will find rock climbers. The many large granite boulders scattered throughout Lynn Woods make it a very popular bouldering destination, and it is quite common to find climbers clawing their way up the boulders above foam pads that they lay on the ground to protect from falls. The best-known boulder, located on the opposite side of the park from the Stone Tower, is

The Stone Tower was built in 1936 to complement an existing steel tower for fire detection.

The skyline of Boston from the top of the Stone Tower

Dungeon Rock, a huge boulder with an iron door and a cave believed to house pirates' treasure. (Be advised that the treasure is as yet undiscovered.)

The Works Progress Administration built the Stone Tower in 1936 to complement an already-operating steel fire lookout. The original steel tower, built ten years ahead of the Stone Tower, still stands on Mount Gilead, minutes from the stone tower on Burrill Hill, a dilapidated tower whose stairs have been removed due to its state of disrepair. There is some debate as to whether the Stone Tower was ever actually put to use as a fire lookout, but the intention was there. The Stone Tower is definitely the feature of this hike, however, with its impressive views (although one can visit both by hiking another 15 minutes to get to the original).

From the western side of the parking area, walk around a green gate onto Great Woods Road, a wide dirt doubletrack. At the Y intersection at mile 0.3, go left onto Cooke Road, which begins your uphill climb. The tower clearing and the Stone Tower itself are at the top of the hill at mile 0.5. The Stone Tower is a beautiful piece of architecture, constructed of stone and concrete. Concrete steps on the outside bring you to the first floor. An iron spiral staircase accesses landings two, three, and four. Unlike other stone towers, this one isn't claustrophobic, thanks to large windows at every landing. At the top, be sure to check out the view through all the windows. Fifty miles to the northwest, Mount Monadnock dominates. To the southeast is the waterfront in Lynn; and south is Cape Cod and the Atlantic. The featured view, however, is the Boston skyline, southwest of the tower.

From the tower clearing, Richardson Pathway crosses both east and west and Cooke Road continues south. If you wanted to check out the steel tower, you would continue

LYNN TOWER

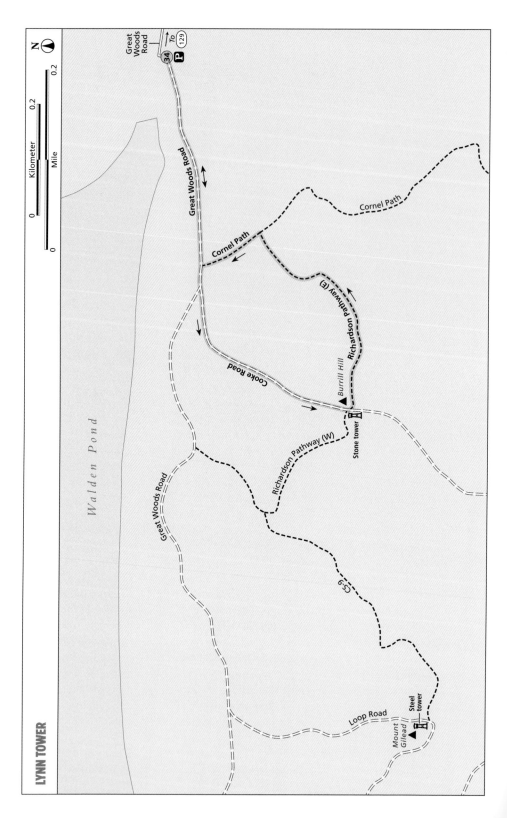

Walden Pond

Great Woods Road

To 129

34 P

Great Woods Road

Cornel Path

Cornel Path

Richardson Pathway (E)

Burrill Hill

Cooke Road

Stone tower

Richardson Pathway (W)

Great Woods Road

CS.9

Loop Road

Mount Gilead

Steel tower

N

Kilometer

0   0.2

0   0.2

Mile

The spiral stairs access the second, third, and top landings in the Stone Tower.

west on Richardson's Pathway, which leads to trail CS-9 and a connector to the original. You could return on Loop Road and Great Woods Road, which would make your total mileage about 2 miles.

To return directly from the Stone Tower, take the Richardson Pathway east. On the descent, pass several huge granite boulders among the eastern white pines—and very likely climbers bouldering on them. At 0.8 mile turn left on Cornel Path, which returns you to Great Woods Road at 0.9 mile. Turn right on Great Woods Road and return to your car at 1.2 miles.

MILES AND DIRECTIONS

0.0 From western end of parking area, follow Great Woods Road.

0.3 Take left at Y onto Cooke Road, which climbs a hill.

0.5 Tower! To return, head east on Richardson Pathway.

0.7 Granite boulders on left.

0.8 Turn left on Cornel Path.

0.9 Turn right on Great Woods Road.

1.2 Arrive back at parking area.

35 LAURA'S TOWER AND ICE GLEN

An easy hike to a gem of a tower in the Berkshires with a bonus side hike to a unique and amazing geological feature.

General location: Stockbridge, Massachusetts
Highest point: 1,488 feet
Elevation gain: 649 feet
Distance: 3.0 miles
Difficulty: Easy
Hiking time: 1.75 hours
When to go: Year-round
Fees and permits: None
Trail contact: Laurel Hill Association, PO Box 24, Stockbridge, MA 01262; (413) 298-2888; laurelhillassociation.org

Canine compatibility: Dogs must be leashed.
Trail surface: Packed-dirt forest floor with some roots and rocks
Land status: Public
Other trail users: Hikers, snowshoers
Water availability: None
Special considerations: None
Amenities: There is a town park near the trailhead.
Maps: USGS Quad Stockbridge, MA
Maximum grade: 20 percent
Trail conditions: This is a smooth and well-maintained trail.

FINDING THE TRAILHEAD

Follow US 7 south from the junction of US 7 and MA 102 in Stockbridge, Massachusetts. In 0.2 mile turn left onto Park Street. Stockbridge Town Park is on the right side of the road. The trailhead parking area is at the end of Park Street (0.5 mile). GPS: N42° 16' 41.736" / W73° 18' 27.18"

ABOUT THE LOOKOUT

Height: 30 feet
Cabin dimensions: 6-by-6-foot observation deck
Frame construction: Steel
Steps: Steel
Not an active fire lookout

Current tower: 1931
Original tower: 1931
What you'll see: Mount Greylock, the Berkshires, the Catskills, the Green Mountains

THE HIKE

In 1853 Mary Hopkins of Stockbridge overheard an out-of-town visitor remark about the town of Stockbridge's poor sanitation and general lack of decor. Hopkins founded the Laurel Hill Association, an organization dedicated to the improvement and beautification of Stockbridge, which in the twenty-first century remains a quaint and historic New England town. The Laurel Hill Association is still in existence—the oldest "village improvement society" in the United States.

Among the association's prize projects is the stewardship of Laurel Hill, a rugged, natural forest area adjoining Stockbridge. Here, you will find Laurel Hill Park, Laura's Tower Trail, and the Ice Glen Trail. Laura's Tower Trail goes to an observation tower that was never used for fire detection but affords wonderful views for hikers. The Ice Glen is a short, must-see side trail.

Never used for fire detection, Laura's Tower is the product of the Laurel Hill Association, the oldest "village improvement society" in the United States.

Laura's Tower Trail crosses the Housatonic River on the Goodrich Memorial Bridge.

Laura's Tower Trail starts at the southern corner of the parking lot at the Mary Hopkins Goodrich Memorial Bridge. Across the bridge on the far side of the Housatonic River, the wheelchair-accessible Mary Flynn Trail goes east along an old trolley railbed. (Just upriver, you'll notice abutments of the old trolley bridge, which the association purposely routed just out of downtown. The square building at the beginning of Park Street was the old trolley ticket office.) Stay straight on Laura's Tower Trail and cross another set of railroad tracks. On the other side of the tracks, the trail enters a forest of giant white pines and eastern hemlocks, and the pine needle duff muffles all footsteps. From the right, the bottom of the Ice Glen Trail comes in; ignore this and follow Laura's Tower Trail straight into the woods.

At 0.3 mile come to the main intersection with the Ice Glen Trail. If you decide to take the side trip into Ice Glen on your return trip (and you absolutely should—more on this later), you will turn here. For now, however, continue along Laura's Tower Trail, the left (southeast) fork. In 0.1 mile the trail passes large moss-covered boulders as it switchbacks and gains altitude. As maple, beech, dogwood, and ash trees begin to take over from the softwoods, you'll arrive at the summit of Laurel Hill at 1.0 mile.

Laura Belden Field donated the tower in memory of her father, David Dudley Field of the prominent Field family (one of Field's brothers was a Supreme Court justice; another laid the first transatlantic cable). Civilian Conservation Corps crews delivered the tower to the site in pieces. The steel tower, designed and built by Joseph Franz, a local engineer, is unique in that the stairs ascend directly to the cab.

Trees make the summit of Laurel's Hill viewless unless you ascend the tower. From there, you can see Stockbridge Mountain to the west, with New York's Catskills looming

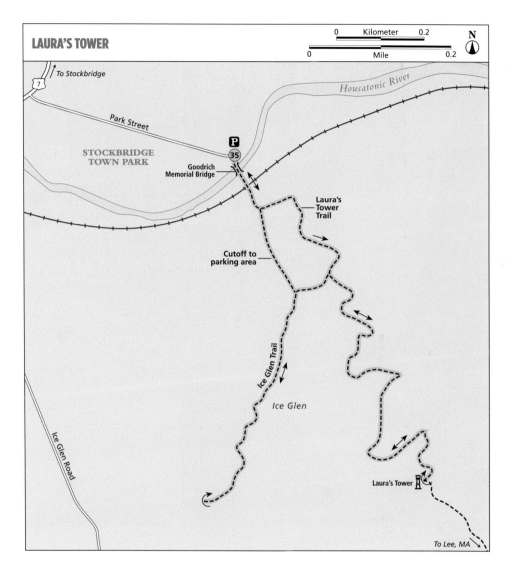

70 miles beyond. Mount Greylock stands directly north, with Vermont's Green Mountains standing in the distance. Obstructed by trees, the 1,710-foot Monument Mountain is due south. From the tower, Laura's Tower Trail continues east to Beartown Mountain Road in Lee, Massachusetts.

Head down the way you came until you reach the left turn (west) for Ice Glen Trail at 1.7 miles. The round-trip to Laura's Tower is 2 miles, but you really shouldn't miss the side hike to Ice Glen. If your hiking partners are children, they will definitely find the side trip to be the highlight of the outing, and you will too. The half-mile-long Ice Glen Trail traverses a rugged, rocky, and moss-covered canyon. The Laurel Hill Association has seen to having rock steps installed so the going is easy. Even on muggy and humid July days, the air escaping the cavernous holes at the base of the glen hits you as a cool breeze. The trail ends in a half mile just shy of Ice Glen Road. Turn and return the way you came, taking

The observation deck on Laura's Tower

a cutoff trail back to Goodrich Memorial Bridge (also designed by Joseph Franz) and the parking lot. The Ice Glen Trail side hike adds a total of 1 mile to your hike.

MILES AND DIRECTIONS

0.0 From the parking lot, cross Goodrich Memorial Bridge.

0.3 Intersection with Ice Glen Trail. Take the left (southeast) fork.

1.0 Summit and tower. Return the way you came.

1.7 Turn left (west) to take Ice Glen side hike. Canyon!

2.2 Trail ends just shy of Ice Glen Road. Return the way you came.

2.7 Cutoff back to Goodrich Memorial Bridge.

3.0 Arrive back at the parking area.

36 SHARON TOWER

A loop hike in a protected forest to an active lookout tower.

General location: Sharon, Massachusetts
Highest point: 534 feet
Elevation gain: 163 feet
Distance: 1.2 miles
Difficulty: Easy
Hiking time: 45 minutes
When to go: Year-round
Fees and permits: None
Trail contact: Mass Audubon Moose Hill Wildlife Sanctuary, 293 Moose Hill Pkwy., Sharon, MA; (781) 784-5691; massaudubon.org/moosehill
Canine compatibility: Dogs are not allowed.
Trail surface: Dirt
Land status: Public
Other trail users: Hikers, snowshoers, skiers

Water availability: None
Special considerations: There is a fee, which can be paid at a self-serve cannister in the parking area, for non-Massachusetts residents to hike on Mass Audubon trails.
Amenities: There are restrooms, a nature center, and a shop at the trailhead (check website for hours). There are also electric car–charging stations.
Maps: USGS Mansfield, Massachusetts Quad
Maximum grade: 18 percent on a brief steep uphill section
Trail conditions: Well maintained and well marked

FINDING THE TRAILHEAD

From the north, take exit 21 off I-95 and turn left (south) on Coney Street. At 0.4 mile turn right (west) on MA 27. At 1.0 mile turn left (south) on Moose Hill Street. At 2.3 miles you will see the Mass Audubon Moose Hill Wildlife Sanctuary headquarters on the left (east). Go past these buildings and turn left onto Moose Hill Parkway. The parking area is immediately on the left side of the road. *From the south*, take exit 17 off I-95 and turn right (north) onto South Main Street toward Sharon, Massachusetts. At 1.3 miles turn left (north) onto Moose Hill Street. At 2.4 miles turn right (east) onto Moose Hill Parkway. The parking area is immediately on the left side of the road. GPS: N42° 7' 23.376" / W71° 12' 29.879"

ABOUT THE LOOKOUT

Height: 68 feet
Cabin dimensions: 10 x 10 feet
Frame construction: Steel
Steps: Wood
Active lookout
Current tower: 1966

Original tower: Built in 1912 on neighboring Bluff Hill and moved to Moose Hill in 1917
What you'll see: The tower is unfortunately not open to the public (it has a locked chain-link fence around it), and it is located on a viewless summit.

THE HIKE

Mass Audubon is New England's largest nature-based conservation organization—the support of which is reason alone for hiking to the Sharon Tower. To be clear, the hike to Sharon Tower has no view, and the tower is closed to the public. Moose Hill Wildlife Sanctuary is the oldest of Mass Audubon's sixty sanctuaries; the organization owns

Only firewatchers get to enjoy the view from the active Sharon fire lookout, which is closed to the public.

SHARON FIRE TOWER
MOOSE HILL
ELEVATION 534 FT.

New England forests are lined with miles of forgotten stone walls that speak to the area's agricultural history.

40,000 acres of protected lands in Massachusetts and offers trails, educational programming, and summer camps.

The trail starts on the opposite side of Moose Hill Street from the parking area at a small kiosk. One hundred feet from the trailhead is a junction. Billings Farm Trail goes straight; this will be the return route. Take a right (west) on Summit Trail. At 0.2 mile the Moose Hill trail crosses; Summit Trail continues straight. After this intersection the trail climbs a fairly steep section with wooden water bars. The summit clearing with the Sharon Tower is at 0.4 mile.

Sharon Tower is an active fire lookout. The Massachusetts Department of Conservation and Recreation's Bureau of Forest Fire Protection generally staffs it in times of high fire danger. It is unfortunately surrounded by a locked chain-link fence, and the dense forest obscures any views. The Summit Trail continues right (north), but our route cuts behind the tower on the Bay Circuit Trail (left, southwest). The Bay Circuit Trail rolls pleasantly through a forest of eastern white pine, white oak, and hickory trees and over bedrock showing the striations of glacier-dragged rocks from thousands of years ago.

At 0.7 mile turn left (east) on the Old Pasture Trail. Several stone walls come and go, remnants of the area's agricultural heritage. These cultural relics are causes for reflection on the backbreaking labor that must have accompanied the clearing of fields of thousands of large stones. At 0.9 mile the Old Pasture Trail passes a couple of connector trails on the right side before coming to a four-way intersection with a connector to Billings Farm Loop trail. Turn right on the connector, which ends in a T at Billings Farm Loop. Take a left on Billings Farm Loop trail, which returns to the trailhead at mile 1.2.

SHARON TOWER

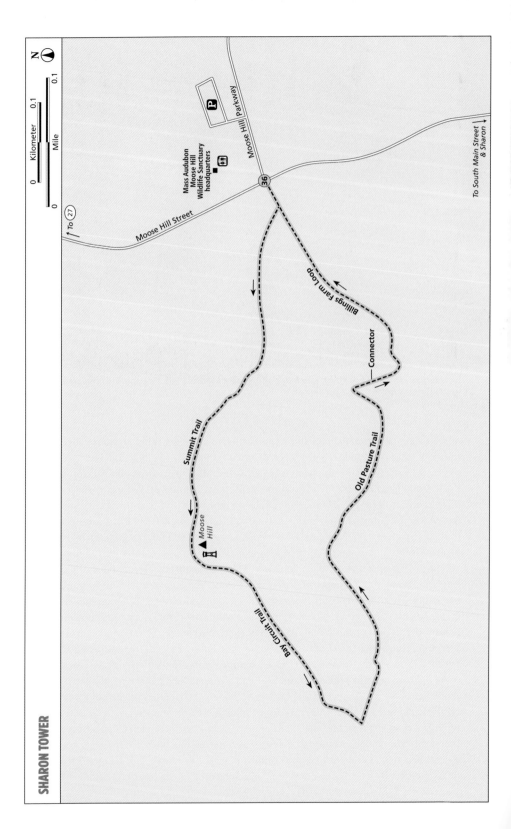

N

Kilometer
0   0.1   0.1

Mile
0   0.1

To 27

Moose Hill Street

Mass Audubon
Moose Hill
Wildlife Sanctuary
headquarters

P

36

Moose Hill Parkway

To South Main Street
& Sharon

Billings Farm Loop

Connector

Summit Trail

Old Pasture Trail

▲ Moose Hill

Bay Circuit Trail

The original Moose Hill tower originally stood on nearby Bluff Hill.

MILES AND DIRECTIONS

0.0 From the parking lot, cross Moose Hill Street to the trailhead. One hundred feet after the trailhead, turn right (west) on Summit Trail.

0.2 Moose Hill Trail crosses. Stay straight on Summit Trail.

0.4 Summit and tower. Continue across clearing to Bay Circuit Trail.

0.7 Turn left (east) on Old Pasture Trail.

0.9 Turn right on a connector trail to Billings Farm Loop. Take a left on Billings Farm Loop.

1.2 Arrive back at the trailhead.

37 HEUBLEIN TOWER

A family friendly out-and-back hike to an impressive tower and building in a popular Connecticut state park.

General location: Simsbury, Connecticut
Highest point: 1,035 feet
Elevation gain: 402 feet
Distance: 2.6 miles
Difficulty: Easy
Hiking time: 1.75 hours
When to go: Year-round
Fees and permits: Connecticut state parks charge an entry fee for non-resident vehicles.
Trail contact: Talcott Mountain State Park (c/o Penwood State Park), Connecticut Department of Energy and Environmental Protection, 57 Gun Mill Rd., Bloomfield, CT; (860) 424-3200; deep.stateparks@ct.gov
Canine compatibility: Pets must be on a leash and owners must pick up their waste.

Trail surface: Gravel, packed dirt
Land status: Public
Other trail users: Hikers, snowshoers
Water availability: Fountain at the summit
Special considerations: This is a popular destination, and the parking area does fill up.
Amenities: Restrooms (at trailhead and summit), museum, and gift shop in the tower from Memorial Day until Columbus Day
Maps: USGS Avon, CT Quad, Talcott Mountain State Park map (portal.ct.gov/DEEP/State-Parks/Parks/Talcott-Mountain-State-Park/Maps)
Maximum grade: 19 percent
Trail conditions: Smooth, packed, well-maintained trail

FINDING THE TRAILHEAD

Follow CT 189 south from the intersection of US 44 and CT 189 in West Hartford. In 0.8 mile turn slightly left on CT 185 by a golf course. At 5.6 miles turn left (west) on Summit Ridge Drive. Parking is on the right side of Summit Ridge Drive. The trailhead is on the left. GPS: N41° 50' 22.38" / W72° 47' 33.288"

ABOUT THE LOOKOUT

Height: 165 feet
Cabin dimensions: 22.6 x 22.6 feet
Frame construction: Concrete
Steps: Steel and concrete

Current tower: 1914
Original tower: 1810
What you'll see: Farmington River valley, downtown Hartford skyline

THE HIKE

In an area without many fire towers to hike to, Heublein Tower isn't a fire tower. But it is a very impressive tower nonetheless. Although located in Talcott Mountain State Park, Heublein Tower dominates the Metacomet ridgeline from Talcott Mountain to King Phillip Mountain, an abrupt landform overlooking Connecticut's Farmington River valley. The tower was built by wealthy German immigrant Gilbert Heublein, who promised his then-fiancée he would build her a "castle on the hill."

Heublein Tower (pronounced HOY-bline, as the family came from Germany) wasn't the first tower in this location. Three towers graced the top of the ridgeline prior,

Heublein Tower has no fire detection history, but it has a rich history ranging from land wars to steak sauce. STEPHANY DAUZAT

Be sure to explore the grounds around Heublein Tower, including this outdoor fireplace.

beginning with a 55-foot-tall wooden observation deck built in 1810. Gilbert Heublein, who built his structure a few hundred feet from the site of the original towers, inherited a restaurant business from his father that introduced the world to A1 Steak Sauce and that his descendants eventually sold to RJ Reynolds for $1.4 billion in 1982.

Steak sauce aside, this is a nice family hike on which you are likely to encounter many other hikers. There is a wooden kiosk at the trailhead that is filled with purple violets in springtime. The trail is wide and paved with smooth gravel, and you gain quite a bit of elevation at first. At 0.4 mile the trail bends sharply to the left. There are two parallel trails: Take the more westerly trail for multiple lookouts and a view of the river valley far below. There are plenty of downed logs and benches on which to rest or take a snack break as you look out across the expanse. At 1.1 miles a terraced cliff towers over the left side of the trail—young hikers will certainly choose to climb on this impressive feature. Shortly thereafter, the Metacomet Trail goes left. The Tower Trail stays straight, briefly marked with the Metacomet Trail's blue blazes until the Metacomet Trail leaves to the right. Stay straight on Tower Trail.

At 1.25 miles the trail arrives at Heublein Tower, an impressive structure with surrounding picnic areas complete with a pavilion, barbecues, pit toilets, and—inside the

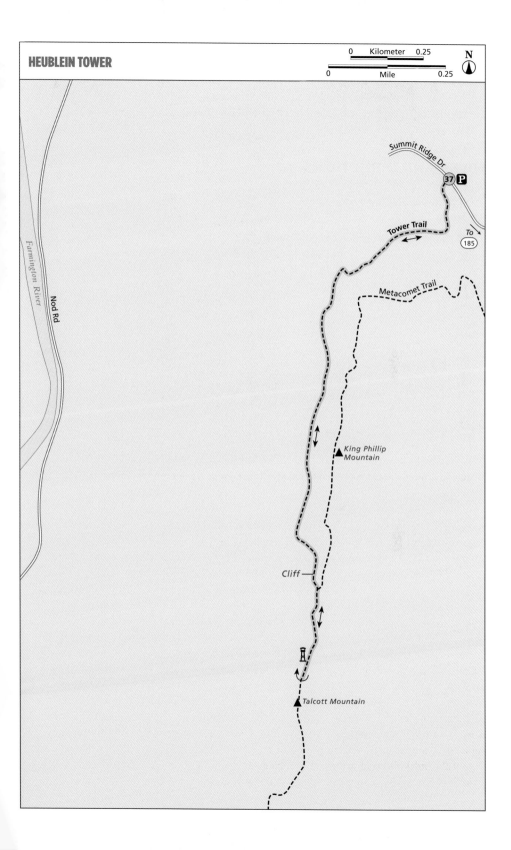

0   Kilometer   0.25

0   Mile   0.25

N

Summit Ridge Dr

37 P

To 185

Tower Trail

Metacomet Trail

Farmington River

Nod Rd

King Phillip Mountain

Cliff

Talcott Mountain

tower—a gift shop and museum. From the top of the tower (which is thought to have housed Connecticut's first residential elevator), the views to the west are of the Farmington River valley, and to the east you can see the Hartford skyline.

The grounds around the Heublein structure, which was built into the bedrock in 1914, are fascinating to explore and examine. Heublein Tower really is an engineering feat.

Return by the same route.

MILES AND DIRECTIONS

0.0   From the parking lot, pick up the wide Tower Trail.

0.4   Lookout. Trail bends left (south).

1.1   Large cliff on left (east) side of trail. Metacomet Trail crosses.

1.25 Summit and tower. Return by the same route.

2.5   Arrive back at the parking area.

38 MOHAWK MOUNTAIN VIA CUNNINGHAM TOWER

An off-the-beaten-path out-and-back hike to a fire lookout site that passes a stone tower along the way.

General location: Cornwall, Connecticut
Highest point: 1,683 feet
Elevation gain: 210 feet
Distance: 2.4 miles
Difficulty: Easy
Hiking time: 1.5 hours
When to go: Year-round
Fees and permits: None
Trail contact: Mohawk State Forest, Mohawk Mountain State Park, Connecticut Department of Energy and Environmental Protection, 79 Elm St., Hartford, CT; (860) 424-3200; deep.stateparks@ct.gov

Canine compatibility: Pets must be leashed.
Trail surface: Packed dirt, rocks
Land status: Public
Other trail users: Hikers, snowshoers
Water availability: None
Special considerations: None
Amenities: None
Maps: USGS Quad Cornwall, CT
Maximum grade: 15
Trail conditions: Although well marked and signed, the trail is narrow with a tendency to get overgrown.

FINDING THE TRAILHEAD

From the intersection of CT 4 and CT 63 at the rotary in Goshen, Connecticut, follow CT 4 west. In 4.1 miles enter the Mohawk State Forest on the left (east), on Toomey Road. Two roads enter the forest: The left fork is a dirt road; Toomey Road is the paved right fork. Toomey Road bends sharply right at 1.4 miles at an intersection with Mohawk Mountain Road. Two-tenths of a mile farther, Toomey Road bends sharply again—this time to the left (there is a small circular parking area on the right side of the road here). Toomey Road continues to the fire lookout site on the summit of Mohawk Mountain. However, the parking area for this hike is on the left side of the road at 1.8 miles. There is space for just a few cars; overflow parking is back two-tenths of a mile at the circular parking area. GPS: N41° 49' 43.248" / W73° 18' 22.247"

ABOUT THE LOOKOUT

The original lookout on Mohawk Mountain no longer stands, but you can see the footings of two prior towers.

Height: 37 feet
Cabin dimensions: 7 x 7 feet
Active lookout
Current tower: 1953
Original tower: 1883

What you'll see: Connecticut's Bear Mountain, the Berkshires in Massachusetts (including Mount Greylock), the Taconic Mountains in New York, miles of Connecticut forestlands

THE HIKE

Mohawk Mountain is located within a state park and a state forest. There is a tower at the summit, but it is not open to the public. When AT&T built a relay station on the summit, the communications company cut a deal with the state of Connecticut: In order

There have been several towers on Mohawk Mountain. These footings are for a tower that the CCC built in 1937. It was taken down in 1953.

The antenna-laden tower atop Mohawk Mountain is a multipurpose structure. It houses communications equipment and is still an active fire lookout.

to construct the tower on state land, it agreed to build an observation deck at the top for fire detection purposes. The cab is still used today for fire detection, but there is a locked wire fence around the entire tower that denies entry to the public. There are, however, still nice views to be had from the ground, and the tower footings from the original tower are front and center at the summit.

There have been a number of towers on the site dating back to 1883, when landowners, including Cynthia J. "Nina" White, constructed a 40-foot tower for sightseers. This tower fell into disrepair and fell down in 1898. In 1912 another neighboring landowner, Seymour Cunningham, built a stone circular tower with a 30-foot diameter on the northwestern slopes of Mohawk. Cunningham Tower still stands, albeit in some disrepair, and is the stopping point on this hike. Another neighbor, Andrew Clark, donated 5 acres of land to the state of Connecticut, which marked the birth of the state forest (originally named Mohawk Mountain Park). White's estate acquired and donated nearly 3,000 acres (including the tract where Cunningham Tower was built), and this was combined with the original donated property.

Several other towers went up and came down on Mohawk Mountain, including a wooden tower that was eventually taken down by the Civilian Conservation Corps (CCC) and replaced with a steel firewatcher's tower in 1937. That tower was used for fire detection until AT&T replaced it with the current tower in 1953.

From the parking area, cross the street and pick up the trail by a large metal gate. In a tenth of a mile, arrive at a clearing, in the center of which is the circular, stone Cunningham Tower. The tower is not maintained but has weathered the passage of time in spite

Constructed by Seymour Cunningham, Cunningham Tower is 30 feet high and 30 feet wide.

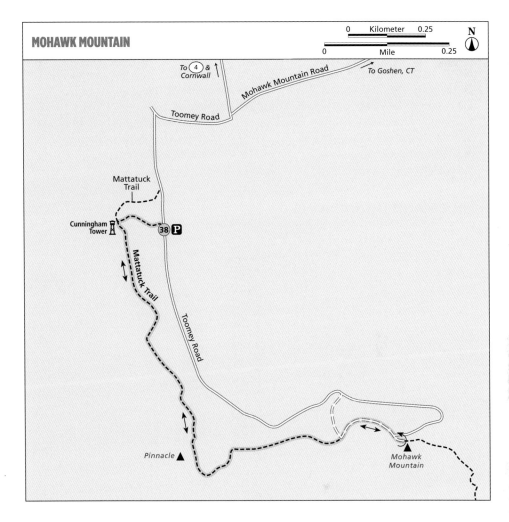

of this. There are no stairs or roof. Some hikers find the tower "creepy" and speculate that it's haunted. It's hard to totally dispel these sentiments.

The Mattatuck Trail (blue blazes) crosses the clearing in front of the tower. Follow the trail south through beech trees and birches. At 0.3 mile pass a rusty old water pump and cross several bridges over muddy patches. The trail is mostly flat with wild geraniums blooming in the spring on both sides of the trail. At 0.5 mile it crosses a stone wall, veers slightly east, and begins to climb. Here, the trail crosses a grassy doubletrack, and you can see Toomey Road to the left (east). Continue a short distance before passing through some natural rocky pillars. The uphill terminates at a height of land called the Pinnacle, which is viewless and tree covered, at 0.7 mile.

The trail descends the eastern side of the Pinnacle, crosses another stone wall, then follows the wall for 0.1 mile before climbing to regain the lost altitude. At 1.0 mile the trail spills onto a dirt road; this is your trail now. Turn right (east) onto the road and walk the remaining 0.2 mile to the summit.

The summit is fairly busy. Toomey Road comes in from the east, and the Mattatuck Trail continues in that direction. There are a few picnic tables and a charcoal grill. Otherwise the summit is laden with communications equipment—there is a radio antenna and the observation tower, both fenced off. In the 1960s locals constructed another tower for the public, but this wooden tower was taken down in 2008. Have no fear: There are still beautiful views from the ground. For anyone unaware of the beauty of Connecticut, look south across miles of forestlands all the way to Long Island Sound. Northwest are Bear Mountain and Mount Frissell, the two high points of Connecticut (although the peak of Frissell is in Massachusetts), and Mount Everett in Massachusetts.

Return the way you came.

MILES AND DIRECTIONS

0.0   From the parking area, cross the street, walk around a gate, and pick up a grassy trail.

0.1   Cunningham Tower. Turn left (south) on Mattatuck Trail.

0.5   Cross a stone wall and gain altitude.

0.7   The Pinnacle.

1.0   Trail joins dirt road. Turn right (east).

1.2   Summit. Admire antenna-laden tower from a distance. Return the way you came.

2.4   Arrive back at your car and the parking area.

39 MOUNT TOM

An easy loop hike to a climbable stone tower with views of Connecticut, Massachusetts, New York, and the Atlantic at a state park with a swimming area.

General location: Litchfield, Connecticut
Highest point: 1,284 feet
Elevation gain: 343 feet
Distance: 1.3-mile loop
Difficulty: Easy
Hiking time: 1 hour
When to go: Year-round
Fees and permits: Mount Tom State Park charges a fee on weekends and holidays for out-of-state vehicles from mid-May through September.
Trail contact: Mount Tom State Park, Connecticut Department of Energy and Environmental Protection; (860) 567-8870 from Memorial Day until Labor Day, (860) 868-2592 all other dates; portal.ct.gov/DEEP/State-Parks/Parks/Mount-Tom-State-Park
Canine compatibility: Pets should be on a leash. Note: Pets are not allowed at the Mount Tom State Park swimming area.
Trail surface: Packed dirt, scattered rocks
Land status: Public
Other trail users: None
Water availability: None
Special considerations: None
Amenities: There are no amenities at the trailhead, but during the summer there are restrooms a short distance away at the swimming area.
Maps: USGS Quad New Preston, CT
Maximum grade: The going is fairly easy, with 17 percent at one spot during the ascent.
Trail conditions: These are well-used trails. The trail blazes and markings are a bit haphazard at times.

FINDING THE TRAILHEAD

From the intersection of CT 202 and CT 209 near Litchfield, Connecticut, follow CT 202 west through the hamlet of Bantam, Connecticut. After 3 miles the beautiful Mount Tom Pond appears on the left side of the road. At 3.1 miles turn left onto Old CT 25, which is really just a pullout on the side of the new Route 25. Turn onto Mount Tom Road. After the park entrance, there are multiple parking areas within walking distance of the trailhead. The trailhead parking is the first right after the entrance. GPS: N41° 41′ 43.296″ / W73° 16′ 48.431″

ABOUT THE LOOKOUT

Height: 34 feet
Tower dimensions: 15 feet diameter on the roof
Frame construction: Stone
Steps: Wood
No longer active

Current tower: 1921
Original tower: 1888 (wooden structure)
What you'll see: Mount Tom Pond, Mount Everett, New York's Catskills, Long Island Sound

THE HIKE

There are two parking areas at Mount Tom State Park, which has a wonderful beach and swimming area at the edge of Mount Tom Pond. Just because the swimming area gets the larger of the parking areas (just a few hundred feet from the trailhead) doesn't make the hike less worthwhile.

The stone tower on Mount Tom replaced a
wooden tower that stood until 1921.

The Mount Tom tower is a tiny nub from across Mount Tom Pond.

The trail to the Mount Tom tower departs from the southern end of the dirt trailhead parking lot. You'll come to a gate after a few steps; simply walk around the gate. The trail starts as a road that gains elevation before bending east and leveling out. It's blazed with pink trail markers initially, which then change to yellow. At 0.3 mile the trail becomes a trail instead of a road.

At 0.4 mile go left at a T intersection. At 0.5 mile, at another intersection with lots of side trails, stay right following the yellow blazes. Now the trail climbs through an impressive rockfall of gneiss and schist; the footing is uneven but quite navigable. At 0.7 mile a side trail leads to a rocky outcrop with views of forestlands to the west. Just beyond, the trail brings you to the summit and the impressive stone tower.

Although not Connecticut's first state park, Mount Tom State Park was the first to actually get its paperwork in order to actually open to the public (which happened in 1917). Charles H. Senff donated the land that comprises Mount Tom State Park in 1911 with a caveat: He stipulated that an observation tower be maintained at the summit of Mount Tom. If he could see it today, he would not be disappointed. The stone tower, built in 1921 of hard black gneiss rock collected on-site, continues to be in great shape, and it is immaculately devoid of litter or graffiti. The tower supported other active fire towers in the area.

The current stone structure replaced a wooden tower. It is 34 feet tall and 15 feet in diameter, and its roof makes a perfect viewing platform from which you can see Mount Tom Pond at the foot of the mountain, with Massachusetts's Mount Everett in the far distance, the Catskills of New York to the west, and Long Island Sound to the south. If

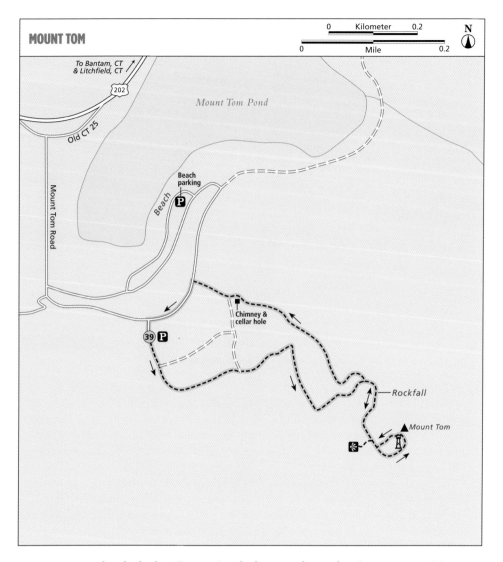

0 Kilometer 0.2

N

0 Mile 0.2

To Bantam, CT
& Litchfield, CT

202

Old CT 25

Mount Tom Pond

Mount Tom Road

Beach

Beach
parking

P

39 P

Chimney &
cellar hole

Rockfall

▲ Mount Tom

you ever wondered whether Connecticut had any rural areas, here's your answer: Mount Tom is surrounded by miles of forestland.

For your descent, follow the trail down behind the tower (the southeast side). It circumnavigates the summit before rejoining the main trail after a few hundred feet. Retrace your steps through the rockfall area. At 0.9 mile find the intersection with many side trails. Choose a side trail (they all seem to connect two main trails), and go right—a different route than you used ascending. Pick your way through a steep descent, and then come to a cellar hole and chimney at 1.1 miles. Shortly thereafter, pass a grassy connector road on the left (you'll stay straight), and follow the trail to the state park road. Follow the road 0.1 mile to the parking area.

After your adventure, by all means visit the swimming area (keeping in mind that pets are not allowed on the beach).

MILES AND DIRECTIONS

0.0 From the parking lot, go around the gate and follow the road (pink blazes turn to yellow blazes).

0.3 Road narrows to become a trail.

0.4 Stay left (northeast) at a T.

0.5 Go right at another intersection with lots of side trails.

0.7 Ascend through a rockfall.

0.8 Summit and tower. Descend on the trail behind the tower (the southeast side), rejoining the original trail shortly.

0.9 At the intersection with many side trails, stay right and descend through a tricky downhill.

1.1 Cellar hole and chimney.

1.2 Pass a grassy connector trail on the left and follow the trail to the park road. Turn left on the road and follow it to the parking area.

1.3 Arrive back at the parking area.

40 WICKABOXET HILL (AND NOOSENECK HILL TOWER)

A two-stop loop and a sleuthing project that brings you to the former site of a tower (and a search for its footings) and a visit to its present drive-up location.

General location: West Greenwich, Rhode Island
Highest point: 519 feet
Elevation gain: 117 feet
Distance: 2.0 miles
Difficulty: Easy
Hiking time: 1.25 hours
When to go: Year-round
Fees and permits: None
Trail contact: Rhode Island Department of Environmental Protection, 235 Promenade St., Providence, RI; (401) 222-4700; dem.ri.gov
Canine compatibility: Dogs are allowed.
Trail surface: Loose dirt, gravel
Land status: Public

Other trail users: Hikers, snowshoers, bikers, hunters
Water availability: None
Special considerations: None
Amenities: None
Maps: USGS Coventry Center, RI, Quad. Also check out the Nature Conservancy's map at their site for the neighboring Tillinghast Pond Management Area (nature.org/en-us/get-involved/how-to-help/places-we-protect/tillinghast-pond-management-area).
Maximum grade: 10 percent
Trail conditions: Although public land, this trail is not heavily trafficked. It may be somewhat overgrown.

FINDING THE TRAILHEAD

From the West Greenwich Fire Department on RI 3, cross RI 3 and follow Robin Hollow Road west for 2.5 miles. Turn right (north) on RI 102 and follow it for another 1.5 miles. Turn left (west) on Plain Meeting House Road. Follow Plain Meeting House Road for 2.9 miles. The small parking area (with a sign that says Wickaboxet Management Area) is on the right. GPS: N41° 38' 11.688" / W71° 44' 8.879"

ABOUT THE LOOKOUT

Height: 60 feet
Cabin dimensions: 7 x 7 feet
Frame construction: Steel
Steps: Wood
No longer active
Current tower: 1933 (relocated in 1950 to West Greenwich Fire Department)

Original tower: 1933
What you'll see: At the Nooseneck Road site: the West Greenwich Fire Department. At Wickaboxet Management Area: a beautiful conserved forest but no real view.

THE HIKE

Of the eleven standing fire lookouts remaining in the state of Rhode Island, none are open to be scaled by the public. None of them are on hiking trails; they are either located next to roadways, on private property, or—in the case of Chop Mist Tower in Scituate—on property that is restricted from the public.

Just in the trees behind a slabby rock, you'll find the footings of the tower that used to stand guard over the Wickaboxet Management Area.

However, one fire lookout, Nooseneck Tower, located behind the West Greenwich Fire Station on Nooseneck Road (also known as Rhode Island State Route 3), didn't always reside on this spot. In fact, its former home was a rocky ledge in what is now the Wickaboxet Management Area, a tract of conserved land now managed by the state of Rhode Island. Wickaboxet is in the midst of a larger conservation effort: It's surrounded by Tillinghast Pond Management Area, a Nature Conservancy–managed tract and popular paddling destination (many of the indigenous groups in Rhode Island spoke Algonquin dialects, and Wickaboxet translates to "by the edge of a small pond"). On the eastern side of Wickaboxet is the Pratt Conservation Area, another state-managed parcel. Between these three, there are nearly 3,000 acres of wild forests and ponds in western-central Rhode Island.

Somewhere in this space are the footings to the former Wickaboxet Tower (now Nooseneck). It bears mentioning that modern maps of the area don't include all of the trails or place names; for example, on no modern map will you find the name "Wickaboxet Hill," where the tower is purported to have stood. Even the above-mentioned USGS Coventry Center Quad accurately renders the physical land characteristics but does not detail the trails in this hike (which do, in fact, exist!). Likewise, the Nature Conservancy map doesn't include a complete rendering of the trails. Using private investigator skills, one can fill in the blanks by searching unofficial blog postings and maps put out by hikers. Or try to find an out-of-date USGS Coventry, Rhode Island, Quad from the year 1950 at a library. This map shows the fire tower on a ridge due north of a

The Wickaboxet Tower no longer resides in the Wickaboxet Management Area; it lives behind the West Greenwich Fire Station and is known as the Nooseneck Tower.

The Wickaboxet Management Area sign indicates the trailhead.

protuberance known as Rattlesnake Ledge and some of the trails. Why modern maps no longer show the trails is not clear.

To be clear, the route to the Wickaboxet site is on public land, and the trails described here do exist even if they are omitted from modern maps. They are legitimate (the Wickaboxet Trail is even blazed), and they are unlikely to be crowded.

From the parking area, the trail starts at a red gate and heads north. Just a few steps from the gate is a Y. Follow the left branch of the Y; the other branch will be your return route. The trail is clear but not overly traveled, so there is a tendency for it to get grassy. Eastern white pines crowd both sides.

At 0.7 mile the trail ends at a dirt road. The left fork goes toward the Tillinghast property. For this route, take a right on the road and head east. At 1.0 mile come to a spur on the left (north) side of the doubletrack. At the end of the 0.1 mile spur is a fire ring and

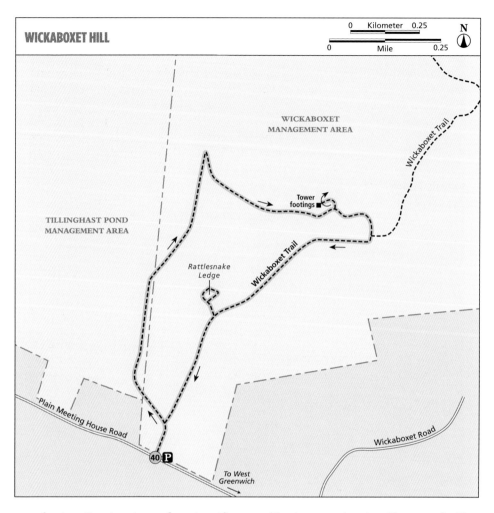

WICKABOXET
MANAGEMENT AREA

Wickaboxet Trail

Tower
footings

TILLINGHAST POND
MANAGEMENT AREA

Rattlesnake
Ledge

Wickaboxet Trail

Plain Meeting House Road

Wickaboxet Road

40 P

To West
Greenwich

a clearing. One imagines a fine view, if one could gain some elevation. For example, if one could stand at the top of a 60-foot steel tower. At the edge of the trees behind the fire ring is a large rocky slab on the ground. Investigate closely: The footings that once held Wickaboxet fire tower in its place are still here, in the trees just behind the rock. Civilian Conservation Corps crew members constructed these footings and the tower at this site in 1933. The FFLA claims it was moved to Nooseneck Road in 1950; members of the West Greenwich Fire Department say it was moved in the 1970s. These footings serve as a testament to the crews who did so much Depression-era work—and to the fire-detection history of Rhode Island.

After adequately pondering state fire history, retrace your steps along the spur back to the trail. Continue left (east) along the trail as it bends south and then dead-ends at the blue-blazed Wickaboxet Trail (1.3 miles). HTurn right (south) on the Wickaboxet Trail. At 1.6 miles there's another spur on the right worth checking out. Rattlesnake Ledge, a 60-foot hunk of granite, juts suddenly out of the ground. A trail leads around the crag. Trees obscure the view here too, although it's an impressive landform. The rock (and other egg-shaped boulders in the area) would certainly be a legitimate climbing and bouldering challenge (in fact, a search will turn up Rattlesnake Ledge in various climbing databases and list-serves). However, there is little sign of much recent climbing activity.

Back at the trail, head south (that is, take a right from the spur trail). A stone wall appears alongside the trail until the original intersection at 1.9 miles. Stay straight and arrive at the gate and your car.

It is worthwhile to visit Nooseneck Tower at the West Greenwich Fire Station, taking care not to park in front of any of the garage bays that house fire trucks. Nooseneck is one of the few towers in the state that is not fenced off. Don't, however, try to climb it—the wooden steps and landings are rotten, and the tower is generally in disrepair. Bees sometimes inhabit the cab. Although it is not safe to climb, it is quite safe to knock on the station door and ask questions about the tower. Members of the squad are justifiably proud of their tower: In their yard is a piece of Rhode Island history.

MILES AND DIRECTIONS

0.0 From the parking lot, go around a red gate and follow the trail north. In less than a tenth of a mile, turn left at an intersection.

0.7 Trail comes to a T. Turn right (east) on a doubletrack.

1.0 Spur trail on left (north) side of trail. Follow spur for 0.1 mile. Find a fire ring and a large granite slab by the trees. The footings for the Wickaboxet Tower are in the trees just behind the slab. Return to the main trail and turn left, continuing in the same direction you were traveling.

1.3 Trail comes to a T at Wickaboxet Trail (blue blazes). Turn right (south) on Wickaboxet Trail.

1.6 Spur to Rattlesnake Ledge.

1.9 Original intersection (continue straight ahead).

2.0 Arrive back at the parking area.

Climbing the observation tower on Ricker Peak

APPENDIX A: OTHER HIKES

- Glastonbury Tower, Vermont. *22 miles out and back on the Long Trail.*

- Ricker Mountain, Vermont. *3 miles out and back to a wooden observation deck at a ski area.*

- Burke Mountain, Vermont,. *6-mile loop to tower. There is also an auto road with an ADA-accessible trail to the summit.*

- Ossipee Tower, Maine. *1.9 miles round-trip to an active tower.*

- Coburn Mountain, Maine. *3.5 miles out and back to a remote tower.*

- Oquossoc Bald, Maine. *2.3 miles out and back to an observation deck.*

- Pack Monadnock, New Hampshire. *3.1 miles out and back in a state park.*

- Kearsarge South, New Hampshire. *2.9-mile loop in a state park.*

- Buck Hill Management Area, Rhode Island. *Several hike options to a former tower site . . . and the tower, now a roadside tower, is located nearby.*

APPENDIX B:
FOR MORE INFORMATION

Trail Maintenance Organizations

- Green Mountain Club, greenmountainclub.org
- Appalachian Mountain Club, outdoors.org
- Vermont Youth Conservation Corps, vycc.org
- Dartmouth Outdoors, outdoors.dartmouth.edu
- NorthWoods Stewardship Center, northwoodscenter.org
- Belknap Range Trail Tenders, belknaprangetrailtenders.org

Government Agencies

- Maine State Parks, Bureau of Parks and Lands, maine.gov/dacf/parks
- Acadia National Park, nps.gov/acad
- New Hampshire Department of Forest Protection, dncr.nh.gov
- New Hampshire State Parks, nhstateparks.org
- City of Concord Conservation Commission, concordnh.gov/trails
- White Mountain National Forest, fs.usda.gov/whitemountain
- Green Mountain National Forest, fs.usda.gov/gmfl
- Vermont Department of Forests, Parks, and Recreation, fpr.vermont.gov
- Town of Norwich Trails Committee, norwich.vt.us/trails-committee
- Massachusetts Department of Conservation and Recreation, mass.gov/locations/mount-grace-state-forest
- Connecticut Department of Energy and Environmental Protection, deep.stateparks@ct.gov
- Rhode Island Department of Environmental Protection, dem.ri.gov

The US Forest Service and Dartmouth Outdoors steward the Lambert Ridge Trail on Smarts Mountain.

Other Organizations

- Appalachian Trail Conservancy, appalachiantrail.org
- Society for the Protection of New Hampshire Forests, 54 Portsmouth St., Concord, NH 03301; (603) 224-0423; forestsociety.org
- The Nature Conservancy, naturemaine@tnc.org
- Forest Fire Lookout Association, https://firelookout.org
- Mass Audubon, massaudubon.org
- Kennebec Land Trust, tklt.org
- Lakes Region Conservation Trust, lrct.org
- Westmore Association, westmoreassociation.org

APPENDIX C: FURTHER READING

Books

- *Hiking the Green Mountains* by Lisa Ballard and Mark Aiken (Globe Pequot Press, 2022)

- *Hiking the White Mountains* by Lisa Ballard and James Buchanan (Globe Pequot Press, 2020)

- *From York to the Allagash: Forest Fire Lookouts of Maine* by David N. Hilton (Moosehead Communications, 1997)

- *A Field Guide to New Hampshire Firetowers, 2nd Ed.* by Iris W. Baird and Chris Haartz (2005)

- *360 Degrees: A Field Guide to Vermont's Fire and Observation Towers* (Green Mountain Club, 2005)

- *Day Hiker's Guide to Vermont* (Green Mountain Club, 2011)

Websites

- Firelookout.org

- NHLR.org

- HikeSafe.org

- Trailfinder.info

- topozone.com

Stratham Tower stands atop Stratham Hill

THE TEN ESSENTIALS OF HIKING

American
Hiking
Society

American Hiking Society recommends you pack the "Ten Essentials" every time you head out for a hike. Whether you plan to be gone for a couple of hours or several months, make sure to pack these items. Become familiar with these items and know how to use them.

1. Appropriate Footwear
Happy feet make for pleasant hiking. Think about traction, support, and protection when selecting well-fitting shoes or boots.

2. Navigation
While phones and GPS units are handy, they aren't always reliable in the backcountry; consider carrying a paper map and compass as a backup and know how to use them.

3. Water (and a way to purify it)
As a guideline, plan for half a liter of water per hour in moderate temperatures/terrain. Carry enough water for your trip and know where and how to treat water while you're out on the trail.

4. Food
Pack calorie-dense foods to help fuel your hike, and carry an extra portion in case you are out longer than expected.

5. Rain Gear & Dry-Fast Layers
The weatherman is not always right. Dress in layers to adjust to changing weather and activity levels. Wear moisture-wicking clothes and carry a warm hat.

6. Safety Items (light, fire, and a whistle)
Have means to start an emergency fire, signal for help, and see the trail and your map in the dark.

7. First Aid Kit
Supplies to treat illness or injury are only as helpful as your knowledge of how to use them. Take a class to gain the skills needed to administer first aid and CPR.

8. Knife or Multi-Tool
With countless uses, a multi-tool can help with gear repair and first aid.

9. Sun Protection
Sunscreen, sunglasses, and sun-protective clothing should be used in every season regardless of temperature or cloud cover.

10. Shelter
Protection from the elements in the event you are injured or stranded is necessary. A lightweight, inexpensive space blanket is a great option.

Find other helpful resources at AmericanHiking.org/hiking-resources

PROTECT THE PLACES YOU LOVE TO HIKE.
Become a member today and take $5 off an annual membership using the code **Falcon5**.

AmericanHiking.org/join

American Hiking Society is the only national nonprofit organization dedicated to empowering all to enjoy, share, and preserve the hiking experience.

American Hiking Society

HIKING FIRE LOOKOUTS NEW ENGLAND

HELP US KEEP THIS GUIDE UP TO DATE

Every effort has been made by the author and editors to make this guide as accurate and useful as possible. However, many things can change after a guide is published—trails are rerouted, regulations change, techniques evolve, facilities come under new management, etc.

We appreciate hearing from you concerning your experiences with this guide and how you feel it could be improved and kept up to date. While we may not be able to respond to all comments and suggestions, we'll take them to heart and we'll also make certain to share them with the author. Please send your comments and suggestions to the following email address:

Falcon Guides
Reader Response/Editorial Department
Falconeditorial@rowman.com

Thanks for your input, and happy trails!